PHILOSOPHY AND SOCIAL ISSUES

Philosophy
and Social Issues
FIVE STUDIES

Richard A. Wasserstrom

UNIVERSITY OF NOTRE DAME PRESS

NOTRE DAME   LONDON

Copyright © 1980 by
University of Notre Dame Press
Notre Dame, Indiana 46556

Library of Congress Cataloging in Publication Data

Wasserstrom, Richard A
  Philosophy and social issues.

  Includes bibliographical references and index.
  1. Social problems—Moral and religious aspects.
I. Title.
HN18.W37   362'.042   79-9486
ISBN 0-268-01535-X
ISBN 0-268-01536-8 pbk.

Manufactured in the United States of America

To my mother,
  Gertrude Kopp Wasserstrom

and my father,
  Alfred Howard Wasserstrom

Contents

Acknowledgments

The five studies that comprise this book are, in part, rewritten and expanded versions of pieces that have previously been published. "Racism and Sexism" is an expanded version of Parts I-A and II of "Racism, Sexism and Preferential Treatment," first published in 24 *UCLA Law Review* 581, copyright 1977. Most of "Preferential Treatment" is new; however, some portions of it appeared in Part III of "Racism, Sexism and Preferential Treatment," and some in "The University and the Case for Preferential Treatment," 13 *American Philosophical Quarterly* 165 (1976). Very little has been altered in "The Obligation to Obey the Law," which first appeared as an article bearing the same title in 10 *UCLA Law Review* 780, copyright 1963 by the Regents of the University of California.

A small amount of material in "Punishment" was published in my essay "Some Problems with Theories of Punishment" in a volume edited by J. B. Cederblom and William L. Blizek; it is reprinted with permission from *Justice and Punishment*, copyright 1977, Ballinger Publishing Company. "Conduct and Responsibility in War" is drawn largely from two earlier pieces: "The Laws of War," 56 *The Monist* 1 (1972) and "The Responsibility of the Individual for War Crimes" in Virginia Held et al. (eds.), *Philosophy, Morality and International Affairs*, copyright 1974 by Oxford University Press. I wish to express my thanks to each of the publishers for permission to reproduce this material.

The previously published pieces were themselves preceded by papers that were read in various versions and stages of completion at philosophy colloquia and meetings. In every such case I was the beneficiary of comments and criticisms that revealed respects in which my ideas were inadequate, insufficiently developed, and not clearly stated. I am indebted to the large number of persons who, as members of the philosophical community, assisted me through their discussions with me of my attempts to think about the topics of these essays. I was especially assisted in bringing three of these studies to fruition by the invitation extended by the Notre Dame Department of Philosophy to spend a week in residence at Notre Dame during the 1977–78 academic year to give a series of three lectures on issues of social justice. And I owe special thanks, which I am pleased to be able to acknowledge, to three persons with whom I talked a great deal and from whom I learned even more: the late Arnold Kaufman, who was first a teacher of mine at the University of Michigan and a colleague both at Tuskegee Institute and UCLA; and Professors Herbert Morris and Leon Letwin of UCLA, both of whom have been valued colleagues and even more valued friends for many years.

Introduction

These studies have as their subjects five social issues that have been of concern in contemporary American life: racism and sexism, preferential treatment, the obligation to obey the law, punishment, and conduct and responsibility in war. The focus of the essays is a normative one, upon questions of what morally is defensible and not defensible, justifiable and not justifiable, in respect to these issues, and for what reasons. The examination is a philosophical one conducted within the tradition of Anglo-American analytic philosophy.

While the essays are a part of that philosophical tradition, they are not wholly characteristic of it. They are quite unlike the articles published in the philosophy journals of twenty-five years ago, and they are different, although substantially less so, from much of the philosophical writing that appears in journals today. Much philosophical inquiry has been and is concerned with issues having nothing to do with moral and social issues, but the differences are of still another sort, distinguishing these essays from many inquiries within the general area of moral and social philosophy.

Twenty-five years ago, one general motif within analytic philosophy emphasized the limited, if not nonexistent, domain of all of philosophy. The traditional philosophical problems and concerns were all to be viewed as potentially pseudoproblems, capable of being dissolved through careful attention to the misleading language that described what they were supposed to be about. Philosophical analysis, if correctly done, might lead, therefore, to the conclusion that philosophy simply had no subject matter that was properly its own. To the degree to which there were any topics of genuine philosophical interest within the area of moral and social philosophy, the problems were of a very restricted and special sort.

Within moral philosophy, attention was focused very largely upon metaethical analysis of the nature of moral language and the meaning of certain moral terms such as "good," "ought," and "right." One primary concern was that of whether moral discourse

1

was essentially emotive in character — a disguised and confusing way of saying what the speaker desired or felt — or whether it was in some way or another about the world rather than the speaker's feelings. Social and political philosophy was much more neglected; it was a central concern of comparatively few academic analytic philosophers. To the degree to which there was interest in this area, much of the philosophical writing was devoted to establishing the thesis that, apart, perhaps, from the analysis of a few concepts, there was here very little that was within the province of the philosopher *qua* philosopher. Considerable attention was directed to showing that most of the language of political philosophy was empty and that the task of the philosopher was to demonstrate the extent to which much that had traditionally been said and thought should be understood to be largely, if not completely, vacuous. The general philosophical mood was somber and the prospects for social and political philosophy especially bleak.

By the early 1960s, if not somewhat earlier, there was a decided change. Within moral philosophy, the interest in metaethical issues was augmented by an interest in what were regarded as problems within normative ethics. Utilitarianism was seen to be one kind of normative ethical theory, and its strengths and weaknesses began to receive much attention. Moral arguments and disagreements were also viewed differently. They were now understood to be genuine in some new sense and hence worthy of a renewed kind of interest and concern.

Social and political philosophy enjoyed a striking renaissance. At least three things played a central role. First, utilitarianism was a general theory that applied to political and social issues as much as to matters of individual conduct. It seemed, for example, to be capable of providing a plausible criterion by which to assess the desirability of laws, as well as other kinds of rules, and to furnish, thereby, a way for the philosopher to examine the justifiability of many social and political practices and institutions. In addition, the legal system was independently seen to be a rich focus for philosophical inquiry of both a conceptual and normative character. The writings of H. L. A. Hart, then the Professor of Jurisprudence at Oxford, especially served to indicate some of the ways in which conceptual analysis of the familiar sort could meaningfully be undertaken in respect to topics such as the nature of law and causation in the law, while normative inquiry could at the same time be pursued in order to examine topics such as those of liberty and responsibility, and to explore the grounds upon which different substantive positions might be defended or criticized. And finally, events occurring within the United States also made a difference. Political activity took a variety of forms and assumed a new kind of importance. The civil rights movement raised pressing theoretical, as well as practical, issues that seemed to need attention. And some analytic philosophers responded by incorporating a number of the normative problems that were central within the corpus of their philosophical inquiries.

These studies are unmistakably creatures of this expanded conception of the domain of academic, analytic philosophy. They are revised and expanded versions of pieces that were written and published over approximately the past fifteen years. The ideas contained in three of them, "Racism and Sexism," "Preferential Treatment," and "The Obligation to Obey the Law," were developed in response to issues raised in one way or another by the civil rights movement. "The Obligation to Obey the Law" was occasioned by the widely discussed concern over the question of whether civil rights activists in the South could justifiably go beyond the limits of what the law permitted in their protests against racial segregation and discrimination. The pieces which were the earlier versions of "Racism and Sexism" and "Preferential Treatment" were written in response to civil rights issues of the late 1960s and the 1970s. The familiar way of thinking about problems of race had focused upon the elimination of formal, legal, racial segregation. Yet, even after legal, racial segregation had been abolished, racial problems seemed more, rather than less, acute. And the concern for the alteration of the system of racial discrimination also spawned a renewed set of interests in other forms of discrimination and oppression. The women's movement became one of the major social movements, and a reexamination of ideas about the nature and status of women became a central theoretical concern within the academy as well as society at large. What racism and sexism are, how they are alike and how they are different, what a nonracist and a nonsexist society might be like, and what the arguments are for different conceptions of the good society in respect to race and sex are the questions examined in "Racism and Sexism." Whether programs of preferential treatment, of the sort that were the subject of constitutional litigation in the *Bakke* case, are defensible, and if so, on what grounds, are the questions addressed in "Preferential Treatment."

The fourth study, "Punishment," reflects both the influence of H. L. A. Hart's identification of important and difficult normative questions that are a part of this topic and the continuing, recurring debate within society over the justifiability of different ways of viewing and responding to crime, criminal laws, and criminals. The focus here is first upon conceptual issues relating to punishment and crime, and second upon the various arguments that can be given in respect to the question of when, if at all, it is defensible to punish persons, and for what reasons.

"Conduct and Responsibility in War" is based upon pieces written in response to issues generated by the Vietnam War. One common way of thinking about the appropriateness of the United States' involvement in Vietnam was to concentrate largely if not exclusively upon the question of whether there were anviolations of the laws of war being committed by United States forces in Vietnam. Another common way of thinking about the Vietnam War was to reject out of hand analogies to the post–World War II war crimes trials and suggestions that the military and civilian leaders of the United States might be culpable in a similar way for their role in that war. Both of these responses seemed to me a good deal more problematic than was often acknowledged. "Conduct and Responsibility in War" endeavors to examine what some of the difficulties with these positions are.

These five studies are most clearly a part of this newer, enlarged corpus of philosophical inquiry in the way in which they share a concern with questions of the justifiability of distinct social practices, laws, and institutions, and an interest in the construction and examination of substantive, normative arguments. They are, however, distinguishable in several respects from much other writing of this same period within moral and social philosophy. There is, for one thing, rather less attention paid to matters of conceptual analysis and relationships among concepts than is characteristic of other recent writing in the area. And in addition, the kinds of arguments considered and the questions of justification examined are somewhat less abstract. The ways the issues are discussed, as well as the issues identified for scrutiny, are both more concrete and in this sense less general than is true of the philosophical discussions of many others working on the same or similar topics. And there is, finally, a greater willingness on my part than may be present in others to move beyond the domain of the philosophical and into other fields of inquiry, such as those of the social sciences, when that seems called for in the discussion of a particular topic or issue. This occurs most notably in my treatment of racism and sexism.

My concern is primarily with substantive moral arguments. My way of proceeding is often to begin by identifying a conclusion or a position that has been, or that might be, held in respect to a reasonably specific issue: that it is never right to disobey the law, or that programs of preferential treatment are indefensible and wrong because they treat the most qualified unjustly. I then try to develop the arguments that might be given in support of that conclusion or position and to state them as clearly and as carefully as I can. Once this is done, I endeavor to examine the strengths and weaknesses of the arguments. Once the premises have been made explicit, it can be asked whether they are clear and unambiguous and, if they are not, how these defects can be remedied. If the premises are clear and unambiguous it is possible to see on what empirical claims, if any, they depend for their truth, and it is then also possible to determine whether the premises, if true, would yield the conclusion in support of which they were offered. What can be produced, I believe, is a kind of map of many of the different arguments that bear most centrally and directly upon the issue under examination, a map which reveals the way the relevant arguments would go, their relationship both to one another and to other more general arguments and premises, their strengths and weaknesses, and, often, even conclusions about their plausibility or implausibility in the light of all that can be said about them.

I do not have a unified, comprehensive, substantive ethical theory or a clearly identifiable set of metaethical positions. The latter do not seem to me essential for the kinds of explorations I conduct, and the former does not seem capable of being fully developed by me in a way that I can find wholly defensible and satisfying. My commitment is to a methodology that I take to be analytic, but the method is an extremely nonesoteric, unpretentious one. It is analytic in that it strives for clarity and explicitness at each point of discussion, and this by itself often seems enough to yield quite definite conclusions—although they are usually of a hypothetical kind. Sometimes the hypothetical conclusion is internal to an argument and is in that sense self-contained. If the claim is, for example, that the quotas that are a part of some programs of preferential treatment are wrong because the institutional racial and sexual quotas of the past were wrong, then inquiry can be undertaken in respect to that claim. If the reasons that most plausibly could be advanced in support of the view that the quotas of the past were wrong do not apply in the same way to the quotas of the present programs, then *that* argument is not a good one with which to criticize the present programs. Sometimes the hypothetical is both less internal and less explicit. Sometimes what can be discovered is not that an argument does not yield the conclusion claimed for it, but that the argument depends upon a premise whose correctness is doubtful, or leads to conclusions it would be hard to defend or accept because of other less controversial or more important matters. What can be learned in such cases is what is involved in depending upon a particular argument, and how that argument fits with other less problematic assumptions, principles, and beliefs about particular cases. In part because the issues discussed are often of great concern to persons outside academic philosophy and outside the academy itself, I have striven to employ nontechnical, nonesoteric language throughout. But I have also sought to use such language because I have found that the things I have wanted to say can be said most adequately without recourse to technical terminology.

I regard as fundamental the distinction between explanation and justification—the difference between the history of a view and its justifiability, the difference between how a position might have come to be held and what is to be said for and against it. Explanatory inquiries and justificatory ones are both important and worth conducting, but they are different and they should not, I believe, be confused. The belief in the centrality of this distinction is one reason why my approach is so largely ahistorical and divorced from a discussion of the views of major philosophers and philosophical positions of the past. To locate a position within a tradition or to relate a position to the views of another is to do little that bears directly on the issue of justifiability and much that has to do with explanations of one sort or another.

Related to this is the fact that a feature of my methodology is to minimize as much as possible the occurrence within the justificatory framework of appeals to authority. The fact that someone else has held a certain view does not by itself shed light upon the question of whether that view is correct or defensible. Justificatory inquiries can go surprisingly far on their own. The danger in not attending sufficiently to the views of others is that one may make mistakes they saw how to avoid and that one may neglect matters they rightly saw to be central. But a danger in attending excessively to the views of others is that the recourse to their writings may become an implicit appeal to authority which functions to remove from the justificatory inquiry a portion of the burden of analysis and criticism that should properly remain there. The views of others are relevant within the context of a justificatory inquiry insofar as they are correct or otherwise instructive, and not because they happen to have been held or believed by any particular person. As between these two dangers, I have tended to worry more about the possibility of covert appeals to authority.

I do not, however, mean to suggest that I have tried to be indifferent to or unconcerned with the ways in which, in thinking about the topics considered in these essays, I might be instructed by attending to the discussions of others on these, as well as related, more abstract, philosophical issues. The one area that has seemed to me most relevant concerns the considerable discussion within philosophy of the strengths and weaknesses of utilitarianism. A dominant theme in the recent literature has been that of the relationship of utilitarian considerations to matters pertaining to the rights of individuals, and one view that has attained appreciable prominence is that which sees the rights of individuals as having a priority of some sort or other over considerations of utility.

I believe that there is much that is both true and important in this general view, although I am often dissatisfied with the way it is presented, and I am often uncertain about its plausibility if stated either too strongly or too simply. Part of the difficulty is that utilitarianism is one normative ethical theory within the class of theories that can be described as consequentialist in character. Utilitarianism has several components that other consequentialist positions need not possess. One such is that the only consequences that matter are consequences of a certain kind, e.g., the pleasures and pains produced in sentient beings. Another is that the relevant consequences are to be taken into account by being directly summed in a certain way. Sometimes utilitarianism is criticized on the ground that things other than pleasure and pain matter morally, or on the ground that pleasure and pain cannot, for one reason or another, be calculated in the way in which utilitarian calculations require. Sometimes utilitarianism is criticized on the ground that to sum directly the relevant consequences will not yield an acceptable result. And sometimes utilitarianism is criticized on the ground that things other than consequences matter morally; namely, considerations of rights, or, more generally, considerations of justice. I regard the latter as the issue of more generic and central concern, and I have endeavored to be sensitive to the insights contained in that critique.

There are, however, aspects and features of this critique that remain for me obscure and uncertain. One is the question of what counts as an appeal to consequences rather than to these other things. For there seem to be consequentialist arguments of quite different kinds. There are, for instance, arguments that turn upon the logical consequences of certain propositions. If one adopts a certain principle or employs a concept analyzable in a certain way, then one may be committed to holding or giving up other principles or other concepts. These are, in a sense, consequentialist arguments, but they are not the type of consequentialist argument which in itself says anything about considerations of justice. And there are also arguments designed to show that if things are done one way rather than another the result will be more just, either in the sense that the change in an institution or rule will render it a more just one or in the sense that the effects upon the individuals affected will, on the whole, be more just, or less unjust, than the alternatives. These, too, seem to me to be capable of being viewed as consequentialist arguments, and I am uncertain whether the critique of consequentialism extends to arguments of this sort.

Then, there are arguments that appeal to a consideration of consequences which are not considerations of justice, i.e., to things such as greater overall efficiency, or the likelihood that persons may be led to misapply certain principles in practice, or that persons will be induced to behave in ways that make it easier or more likely that others will be able to achieve or attain certain goods. Here, too, I am uncertain about the strength of the critique of consequentialism. Consequences, even of this last sort, seem to me always of relevance in moral inquiry. If these consequences were good enough or bad enough, I have trouble understanding exactly why they could never be sufficient to outweigh or override some considerations of justice or rights. I find it more instructive not to try to settle this issue in advance, but rather to endeavor both to specify with care the character of the right or the nature of the injustice at issue and then to determine the arguments or reasons that could be offered in support of the existence and importance of the right or the avoidance of the injustice. The arguments and reasons that can be given within such contexts seem to me to be of appreciably greater significance for moral inquiry than direct, largely unexplicated claims about rights and justice and their invariable priority vis-à-vis consequentialist considerations. In the essays which follow, this is the way in which I have sought to conduct the inquiry.

A related issue which complicates matters further concerns the fact that many arguments about rights and justice depend implicitly upon the justifiability of various practices, roles, and institutions. For example, it might be argued that the most qualified ought to be selected for all positions, that the most qualified have, therefore, a right to be selected, and that an injustice occurs whenever a less qualified person is selected instead of the person who is the most qualified. But if the reason why the most qualified ought to be selected is that things will work best in a society in which this occurs, that tasks will be performed most efficiently or effectively, then here, too, consequentialist considerations of a certain sort appear to play a significant role in the argument, once it is stated with completeness. Arguments which appeal to the existence of roles, practices, and institutions are often implicitly relied upon in critiques of consequentialism and such arguments often neglect to make explicit exactly what the case is for the justifiability of the role, practice, or institution. In many, but not all, instances, the case seems to depend upon a reintroduction of consequentialist considerations. I have tried to identify those arguments whenever they occur and to push the inquiry further in the direction of a fuller examination of the entire set of arguments that is involved.

At other times, arguments about rights seem to depend upon an appeal to the fundamental value and importance of each individual person being able to live a life in which that person's plans, desires, interests, and abilities are accorded a special kind of respect and concern. The centrality of individual autonomy and a concomitant equality of individuals here constitute the reasons for regarding at least some rights as basic and primary vis-à-vis consequentialist considerations and calculations of the typical sort.

I share a belief in the fundamental value of individual autonomy and equality, and in places my arguments make explicit appeal to them. These arguments are incomplete in the sense that I do not defend my recourse to these ideas, or even explicate them very fully. Values such as these are surely not beyond inquiry; they do, however, mark some of the limits of my investigations. Nonetheless, both less and more turns upon this fact than might be thought. Less turns upon it because the arguments that do depend upon these values can, themselves, be construed as hypothetical ones of a more extended sort—given the centrality of the autonomy and equality of persons, other more specific, concrete arguments, positions, institutions, practices, or rules are defensible and others are not. The map can still be drawn, the relationships delineated and explored. More turns upon it, because the possible, defensible, derivative positions are richer and more varied than is often supposed. If individual autonomy is so important, and if each person is equally of such value, then the conditions necessary for the meaningful living of individual lives cannot, themselves, be trivial or beside the point. When claims about rights operate so as to ignore these matters, they lose sight, I believe, of the reasons that made rights seem significant in the first place. Often, but not always, a concern for the consequences derives very plausibly from a proper concern for these reasons. Hence, on this ground, as well, I find it more instructive and attractive not to try to settle the issue in advance but instead to attend to more particular arguments in which consequentialist considerations and considerations of justice can both have the weight that seems most appropriate.

Racism and Sexism

I

Racism and sexism are two central issues that engage the attention of many persons living within the United States today. But while there is relatively little disagreement about their importance as topics, there is substantial, vehement, and apparently intractable disagreement about what individuals, practices, ideas, and institutions are either racist or sexist — and for what reasons. In dispute are a number of related questions concerning how individuals and institutions ought to regard and respond to matters relating to race or sex.

Much of the confusion in thinking and arguing about matters concerning race and sex and in trying to determine which institutions, practices, attitudes, or beliefs are either racist or sexist results, I believe, from a failure to see that there are different domains of inquiry within which any of these matters can be examined. As a result, any inquiry concerned with the question of racism or sexism, or the question of the relevance of persons' race or sex, can most profitably begin by distinguishing these domains and getting clear about which questions one is or is not seeking to answer. What I offer in this essay is, first, a general theory about the proper places or contexts within which to discuss and assess the varieties of issues and arguments which arise within this general topic, and second, a rather detailed examination of the primary questions that arise within several of these contexts. To call the overall structure a general theory is to use a somewhat pretentious phrase for marking what seem to me to be the essentially different and distinct questions that can be asked about such things as the relevance of race or sex and the defensibility or indefensibility of programs, practices, attitudes, or beliefs which take into account or concern a person's race or sex. I call it a general theory chiefly because it provides an analytic framework within which to investigate a large number of issues concerning any characteristic, like race or sex. That is to say, while this inquiry is concerned

11

solely with issues relating to race or sex, it is my belief that this same schema — this same way of marking off questions and contexts — works just as well and in just the same manner for a consideration of comparable issues that might be addressed in respect to socioeconomic class, or religion, or any other comparable characteristic of individuals.

There are four questions, or domains of inquiry, that I think it essential to distinguish and keep separate. The first is what I call the question of the social realities. Within this domain, one is concerned with asking what is the correct, complete description of the existing social arrangements in respect to either the characteristic of race or sex. Under the category of social arrangements I mean to include such things as the existing institutional structures, laws, practices, places in society, attitudes, and ideologies — and within the idea of an ideology I include both beliefs about the facts and beliefs about the appropriateness of the existing set of arrangements.

The second question is devoted to the task of explanation. Given a description of what the social reality at any given time and place is, one can certainly ask how things got that way and by what mechanisms they tend to be perpetuated or changed. There can be, and typically is, an array of competing explanatory theories concerning the causes of the social reality and the determinants of social change and stability. For example, much of the literature about the social relations between men and women is focused upon this question of explanation. Complex and sophisticated theories utilizing the ideas of Freud, Levi-Strauss, and Marx have been developed to explain the past and present oppression of women.[1] Alternative theories, drawing upon such things as the behavior of animals, the nature of early human societies, and the psychological and physiological differences between men and women, have also been offered to explain the dominance of males.[2]

The third question is what I call the question of ideals. Within this domain one is concerned with asking the question of how things ought be arranged: if we had the good or the just society in respect to race or sex, if the social reality were changed so that it in fact conformed to our vision of what the social arrangements ought to be as to these characteristics, what would that society's institutions, practices, and ideology be in respect to matters of racial and sexual differentiation? In other words, what, if anything, would be the social significance of race or sex in a society which got things right as to these two characteristics; when, if at all, would either individuals or institutions ever care about and make social decisions concerning the race or sex of the individuals in that society?

The fourth and final question is that of instrumentalities. Once one has developed the correct account of the social realities, and the most defensible conception of the nature of the good society, and the most adequate theory of how the social realities came about and are maintained, then the remaining question is the broadly instrumental one of the appropriate vehicle of social change. How, given all of this, might a society most effectively and fairly move from the existing state of affairs to a closer approximation of the ideal?

It is a central part of my thesis that many of the debates over matters pertaining to race or sex are less illuminating than they otherwise would be because they neglect to take into account these four different domains, each of which is important and deserving of separate consideration, and to identify clearly which of these four questions is in fact being addressed. While I do not claim that all the significant normative and conceptual questions concerning race and sex can be made to disappear or be rendered uncontroversial once these distinctions are fully grasped, I do believe that an awareness and use of these distinctions can produce valuable insights that contribute to their resolution. In particular, it can, for example, be seen quite readily that the often-asked question of whether race or sex is relevant is not as straightforward or unambiguous as may appear at first. The question may be about social realities, about how the categories of race or sex in fact function in the culture and to what effect. Or the question may be about explanations, about the theory which most adequately explains what has caused the social realities in respect to race or sex, or about the theory which most accurately identifies the features, if any, which underlie the social realities in respect to race or sex. Or the question may be about ideals, about what the good society would make of race or sex. Or the question may be about instrumentalities, about how to achieve a closer approximation of the ideal, given the social realities and the most adequate explanatory theories. When the issues are properly disentangled, one thing that is possible is that what might be an impermissible way to take race or sex into account in the ideal society, may nonetheless be a desirable and appropriate way to take race or sex into account, given the social realities.

It is these different domains and these underlying issues that I endeavor to explore. The framework is employed to clarify a number of central matters that are involved in thinking clearly about the topics of racism and sexism and the relevance of race and sex. Within this structure some of the analogies and disanalogies between racism and sexism, and race and sex, are examined — the ways they are and are not analytically interchangeable phenomena and characteristics.

In this essay I look first and relatively briefly at the social realities in respect to race and to sex. Then, in the remainder of the piece I examine a good deal more fully some competing ideals concerning what the meaning and significance of race and sex would be in the good society. I set out three different conceptions of the way or degree to which any person's race or sex would be viewed as an important characteristic in the good society. I next examine various arguments which purport to establish the relevance and significance of determining whether these characteristics have a natural, as opposed to a socially created, foundation. And I then consider some moral arguments in favor of rendering both race and sex insignificant features of the social existence of persons. In the essay that follows, "Preferential Treatment," I examine, as primarily an issue to be located within the context of instrumentalities, the question of the justifiability of programs of preferential treatment. I view the entire inquiry as providing a map that helps to identify where a number of the key issues and considerations concerning race and sex belong and what further types of investigations need to be undertaken.

II

One way to think and talk about race and sex is, as I have indicated, to concentrate upon the domain of the social realities. Here one must begin by insisting that to talk about either is to talk about a particular social and cultural context.

In our own culture the first thing to observe is that race and sex are socially important categories. They are so in virtue of the fact that we live in a culture which has, throughout its existence, made race and sex extremely important characteristics of and for all the people living in the culture.[3]

It is surely possible to imagine a culture, for instance, in which race would be an unimportant, insignificant characteristic of individuals. In such a culture race would be largely if not exclusively a matter of superficial physiology; a matter, we might say, simply of the way one looked. And if it were, then any analysis of race and racism would necessarily assume very different dimensions from what they do in our society. In such a culture, the meaning of the term "race" would itself have to change substantially. This can be seen by the fact that in such a culture it would literally make no sense to say of a person that he or she was "passing."[4] This is something that can be said and understood in our own culture and it shows at least that to talk of race is to talk of more than the way one looks.[5]

Sometimes, for instance, when people talk about what is wrong with affirmative action programs, or programs of preferential hiring, they say that what is wrong with such programs is that they take a thing as superficial as an individual's race and turn it into something important.[6] They say that a person's race doesn't matter; other things do, such as qualifications. Whatever else may be said of statements such as these, as descriptions of the social realities they seem to be simply false. One complex but correct empirical claim about our society is that the race of an individual is much more than a fact of superficial physiology. It is, instead, one of the dominant characteristics that affects both the way the individual looks at the world and the way the world looks at the individual. That surely need not be the case. It may in fact be very important that we work toward a society in which that would not be the case, but it is the case now and it must be understood in any adequate and complete discussion of racism and the relevance of race. That is why, too, it does not make much sense when people sometimes say, in talking about the fact that they are not racists, that they would not care if an individual were green and came from Mars, they would treat that individual the same way they treat people exactly like themselves. For part of *our* social and cultural history is to treat people of certain races in a certain way, and we do not have a social or cultural history of treating green people from Mars in any particular way. To put it simply, it is to misunderstand the social realities of race and racism to think of them simply as questions of how some people respond to other people whose skins are of different hues, irrespective of the social context.

The point can be put another way: Race does not function in our culture in the way eye color does. Eye color is an irrelevant category; nobody cares what color people's eyes are; it is not an important cultural fact; nothing turns on what eye color you have. It is essential to see that race is not like that at all. This truth affects, among other things, what will and will not count as cases of racism. In our culture to be nonwhite — and especially to be black[7] — is to be treated as and seen to be a member of a group that is different from and inferior to the group of standard, fully developed persons, the adult white males.

In our society, to be black is to be at a disadvantage in terms of virtually every conceivable measure of success or satisfaction — be it economic, vocational, political, or social. To see that this is so one need only conduct a simple thought experiment. If one wanted to maximize one's chances of being wealthy, satisfied with one's employment, politically powerful, secure from arbitrary treatment within the social institutions, and able to pursue one's own goals and develop one's own talents to the fullest, and if one could choose to be born either white or black, which race would one choose to be born?

An emphasis upon the actual character of the social realities was central to Mr. Justice Marshall's analysis of the way to think about the constitutionality of the program of preferential treatment at issue in the *Bakke* case. In his opinion in that case Mr. Justice Marshall sought to remind both his colleagues and the country that

> [t]he position of the Negro today in America is the tragic but inevitable consequence of centuries of unequal treament. Measured by any benchmark of comfort or achievement, meaningful equality remains a distant dream for the Negro.
>
> A Negro child today has a life expectancy which is shorter by more than five years than that of a white child. The Negro child's mother is over three times more likely to die of complications in childbirth, and the infant mortality rate for Negroes is nearly twice that for whites. The median income of the Negro family is only 60% that of the median of a white family, and the percentage of Negroes who live in families with incomes below the poverty line is nearly four times greater than that of whites.
>
> When the Negro child reaches working age, he finds that America offers him significantly less than it offers for his white counterpart. For Negro adults, the unemployment rate is twice that of whites, and the unemployment rate for Negro teenagers is nearly three times that of white teenagers. A Negro male who completes four years of college can expect a median annual income of merely $110 more than a white male who has only a high school diploma. Although Negroes represent 11.5% of the population, they are only 1.2% of the lawyers and judges, 2% of the physicians, 2.3% of the dentists, 1.1% of the engineers and 2.6% of the college and university professors.
>
> The relationship between those figures and the history of unequal treatment afforded to the Negro cannot be denied. At every point from birth to death the impact of the past is reflected in the still disfavored position of the Negro.[8]

In short, to be black is to be a member of what was once a despised minority and what is still a disliked and oppressed one. That is part of the awful truth of our cultural and social history, and a significant feature of the social reality of our culture today.[9]

It is even easier to see that the two sexual categories, male and female, like the racial ones, are also of major social significance. Like one's race, one's sex is not merely or even primarily a matter of physiology. To appreciate this we need only realize that we can understand the idea of a transsexual. A transsexual is someone who would describe himself or herself either as a person who is essentially a female but through some accident of nature is trapped in a male body, or a person who is essentially a male but through some accident of nature is trapped in the body of a female. His (or her) description is some kind of a shorthand way of saying that he (or she) is more comfortable with the role allocated by the culture to people who are physiologically of the opposite sex. The fact that we regard this assertion of the transsexual as intelligible shows something of how deep the notion of sexual identity is in our culture and how little it has to do with physiological differences between males and females. Because people do pass in the context of race and because we can understand what passing means; because people are transsexuals and because we can understand what transsexuality means, we can see that the existing social categories of both race and sex are in this sense fundamentally social rather than natural categories.[10]

It is even clearer in the case of sex than in the case of race that one's sexual identity is a centrally important, crucially relevant category within our culture. If anything, it seems even more important and more fundamental than one's race. It is evident that there are substantially different role expectations and role assignments to persons in accordance with their sexual physiology, and that the positions of the two sexes in the culture are distinct. We have a patriarchal society of sorts in which it matters enormously whether one is a male or a female.[11] Just as with the case of race, by almost all important measures it is more advantageous to be a male rather than a female.

The roles, status, and opportunities of men and women are different. We learn very early and forcefully that we are either males or females and that much turns upon which sex we are. A woman's success or failure in life is still defined largely in terms of her activities within the family. It is important for her that she marry, and when she does she is expected to take responsibility for the wifely tasks: the housework, the child care, and the general emotional welfare of the husband and children.[12] Her status in society is determined in substantial measure by the vocation and success of her husband.[13] Economically, women are substantially worse off than men. They do not receive pay for the work that is done in the home. As members of the labor force their wages are significantly lower than those paid to men, even when they are engaged in similar work and have similar educational backgrounds.[14] The higher the prestige or the salary of the job, the less likely it is that a woman will fill that job. And, of course, women are conspicuously absent from most positions of authority and power in the major political institutions of our society.

In the case of both race and sex the correct description of the social realities is provided through the rendering of a complete, composite account of the role of race or sex in the culture under examination. In this sense, the methodology is identical for the two characteristics. In respect to the particulars of the culture under investigation the resulting analysis may, however, reveal important differences in focus and emphasis. Such seems to be the case for race and sex in our culture. In the case of race, for example, in the case of trying to decide what it means, in terms of the kind of life one is apt to live and to be able to live if one is white or black, the significant variables seem to be such things as: formal legal and institutional rights, access to economic resources, practices relating to racial separation in such things as housing and social interaction, and the significance which the dominant ideology attaches to being black rather than white. And these are also important when it comes to trying to develop a comparable composite picture of the kind of life one is apt to live and to be able to live if one is female or one is male. But there are also other kinds of things which seem important to an answer to this question where sexual identity is concerned that are less significant where race is the relevant characteristic. There are, as has been indicated, important differences in status between males and females just as there are between blacks and whites. Concomitantly, there are important differences in the political, institutional, and economic opportunities readily open to individuals depending upon whether they are male or female. But there are also major differences in role and role expectations in the case of sex that seem less central today in the case of race. There are conventions, idealized models of behavior, and norms of what is appropriate to and expected of persons that have a much more central place in the sexual sphere than they have any longer in the racial one. The significance of race today seems to be maintained primarily through relatively impersonal institutional mechanisms, and its ideological backing and dependence upon a conception of role is weak and changing. That is why, for instance, one can today locate few if any persons who overtly and unashamedly announce themselves to be racists or who refer to the appropriate existence of different roles for blacks and whites. Sexual differences, on the other hand, are much more heavily and directly connected with and fostered by norms of appropriate behavior and the expectations these norms develop and nourish concerning the correct, natural, or proper way for males and females to seek to live their lives and interact with one another. Sex roles are a central part of the society's ideology as well as a part of its formal or material structure.

Closely connected with, and perhaps a part of this idea of sex roles, is the matter of temperament — those personal, largely psychological, attributes and characteristics that are associated with being either male or female and which are thought by the culture to be properly or appropriately displayed, depending upon the sex of the individual and the propriety of the temperament at issue. The evidence seems to be overwhelming and well documented that both sex roles and expectations concerning temperament play a fundamental role in our society in the way persons think of themselves as either male or female.[15] Men and women are socialized to see men as essentially independent, capable, powerful, active, rational, and unemotional. Men and women are socialized to view women as more limited in abilities, passive, emotional, dependent, intuitive, and weak.

Another thing that distinguishes the ideology of sex from the ideology of race is that a female, as opposed to a black, is not conceived of as simply a creature of less worth. That is an important respect in which the sexual categories are differentiated from the racial ones: the ideology of sex, as opposed to the ideology of race, is a good deal more complex and confusing. Women are both put on a pedestal and deemed not fully developed persons. They are idealized; their approval and admiration are sought; and they are at the same time regarded as less competent than men and less able to live fully developed, fully human lives — for that is what men do.[16] Because the sexual ideology is complex, variable, and even inconsistent, it does not unambiguously proclaim the lesser value attached to being female, nor does it as unambiguously correspond to the existing more material parts of the social realities. For these, among other reasons, the sexual categories could plausibly be regarded as deeper than the racial ones. They are more deeply embedded in the culture; hence they are less visible. In a corresponding fashion, sexism may be deeper than racism. Being harder to detect, it is harder to eradicate. Moreover, it is less unequivocally regarded as unjust and unjustifiable. That is to say there is less agreement within the dominant ideology that sexism even implies an unjustifiable practice or attitude.[17] For these and other reasons sexism may be a more insidious evil than racism, but there is little merit, surely, in trying to decide which of two seriously objectionable practices is worse.

Viewed from within the perspective of social reality it should be clear, too, that racism and sexism should not be thought of as phenomena that consist simply in taking a person's race or sex into account, or even simply in taking a person's race or sex into account in an arbitrary way. Instead, racism and sexism consist in taking race and sex into account in a certain way, in the context of a specific set of institutional arrangements and a specific ideology which together create and maintain a *system* of institutions and beliefs and attitudes. That system is and has been one in which political, economic, and social power and advantage are concentrated in the hands of those who are white and male.[18]

One way to bring this out, as well as to show another respect in which racism and sexism are different in their ideologies, concerns segregated bathrooms. We know, for instance, that it is wrong, clearly racist, to have racially segregated bathrooms. There is, however, no corresponding conception that it is wrong, clearly sexist, to have sexually segregated ones. How is this to be understood? The answer to the question of why it was and is racist to have racially segregated bathrooms can be discovered through a consideration of the role that this practice played in that system of racial segregation we had in the United States—from, in other words, an examination of the social realities of race. For racially segregated bathrooms were an important part of that system. That is because a part of that system was its ideology; this ideology was complex and perhaps not even wholly internally consistent. A significant feature of this ideology was that blacks were not only less than fully developed humans, but that they were also dirty and impure. They were the sorts of creatures who could and would contaminate white persons if they came into certain kinds of contact with them—in the bathroom, at the dinner table, or in bed, although it was at the same time appropriate for blacks to prepare and handle food, and even to nurse white infants. This ideology was intimately related to a set of institutional arrangements and power relationships in which whites were politically, economically, and socially dominant. The ideology supported the institutional arrangements, and the institutional arrangements reinforced the ideology. Racially segregated bathrooms were both a part of the institutional mechanism of oppression and an instantiation of this ideology of racial taint. The point of maintaining racially segregated bathrooms was not in any simple or direct sense to keep both whites and blacks from using each other's bathrooms; it was to make sure that blacks would not contaminate bathrooms used by whites. The practice also taught both whites and blacks that certain kinds of contacts were forbidden because whites would be degraded by the contact with the blacks.

The failure to understand the character of these institutions of racial oppression is what makes some of the judicial reasoning about racial discrimination against blacks so confusing and unsatisfactory. At times when the courts have tried to explain what is constitutionally wrong with racial segregation, they have said that the problem is that race is an inherently suspect category. What they have meant by this, or have been thought to mean, is that any differentiation among human beings on the basis of racial identity is inherently unjust, because arbitrary, and therefore any particular case of racial differentiation must be shown to be fully rational and justifiable.[19] But the primary evil of the various schemes of racial segregation against blacks that the courts were being called upon to assess was not that such schemes were a capricious and irrational way of allocating public benefits and burdens. That might be the primary evil of a system of racial segregation in some other society, different in important respects from our own. Within our society, however, the primary evil of *these* schemes was that they designedly and effectively marked off all black persons as degraded, dirty, less than fully developed persons who were unfit for full membership in the political, social, and moral community.[20]

It is worth observing that the social realities of sexually segregated bathrooms appear to be different. The idea behind such sexual segregation seems to have more to do with the mutual undesirability of the use by both sexes of the same bathroom at the same time. There is no notion of the possibility of contamination from use; or even directly of inferiority and superiority. What seems to be involved — at least in part — is the importance of inculcating and preserving a sense of secrecy concerning the genitalia of the opposite sex. What seems to be at stake is the maintenance of that same sense of mystery or forbiddenness about the other sex's sexuality which is fostered by the general prohibition upon public nudity and the unashamed viewing of genitalia.

Sexually segregated bathrooms play a different role in our culture than did racially segregated ones. But that is not to say that the role they play is either benign or unobjectionable — only that it is different. Sexually segregated bathrooms may well be objectionable, but here too, the objection is not on the ground that they are prima facie capricious or arbitrary. Rather, the case against them now would rest on the ground that they are, perhaps, one small part of that scheme of sex-role differentiation which uses the mystery of sexual anatomy, among other things, to maintain the primacy of heterosexual sexual attraction central to that version of the patriarchal system of sexual relationships we have today.[21] Whether sexually segregated bathrooms would be objectionable, because irrational, in the good society depends once again upon what the good society would look like in respect to sexual differentiation.

I do not think the brief description of our society that I have

provided is either inaccurate or especially controversial. It is certainly
the case, though, that the claims I have made have been stated
rather imprecisely and substantiated with comparatively little evidence. Because I take the question of social realities to be a complex
kind of empirical question, the rendering of a detailed, comprehensive answer is not within my purview as a philosopher. In a crude
way, though, we are capable, I believe, both of understanding the
basic assertions and seeing their essential correctness by reflecting seriously and critically upon our own cultural institutions, attitudes
and practices. But in a more refined, theoretical way, I assume that
a more precise and correct description of the social reality would be
rendered by that composite, descriptive account of our society which
utilized the relevant social sciences to examine such things as the society's institutions, practices, attitudes, and ideology — if the social
sciences could be value free and unaffected in outlook or approach
by the fact that they, themselves, are largely pursued and conducted
by persons who are white and male. Such an account would at a minimum include: (1) a description of the economic, political, and
social positions of blacks and whites, and males and females in the
culture; (2) a description of the sexual and racial roles, i.e., the
rules, conventions, and expectations concerning how males and females, blacks and whites, should behave, and the attitudes and responses produced by these roles; and (3) a description of the existing
ideology pertaining to racial and sexual differences. This would include popular beliefs about how males and females, and blacks and
whites, differ, as well as the beliefs as to what accounts for these differences, these roles, and the concomitant economic, political, and
social features.

The problem of empirical objectivity is, however, made difficult by the fact that part of the dominant ideology contains the belief
that white males are the one group in society whose members are
able to be genuinely detached and objective when it comes to things
like an understanding of the place of race and sex in the culture. The
hold of this ideological component is reflected, for example, in the
conduct of a sex-discrimination suit that was brought against a
prominent law firm. The case was assigned to Judge Constance Motley of the Federal District Court. The defendant law firm filed a motion that she be disqualified partly because, as a woman judge, she
would be biased in favor of the plaintiff. Judge Motley denied the
motion. Explaining her decision, Judge Motley pointed out:

> . . . [I]f background or sex or race of each judge were, *by defi-*
> *nition,* sufficient grounds for removal, no judge on this court

could hear this case, or many others, by virtue of the fact that all of them were attorneys, of a sex, often with distinguished law firm or public service backgrounds.[22]

As long as this belief in the detachment and objectivity of white males remains either an explicit or implicit part of the dominant ideology concerning inquiries into issues related to race or sex, many accounts provided by the social sciences will be suspect on this special ground, and not, for example, because of more generic methodological doubts concerning the objectivity of the social sciences. Beliefs and assumptions such as these are themselves a part of the social reality and must be understood as such.[23]

III

Just as we can and must ask what is involved in our or any other culture in being of one race or one sex rather than the other, and how individuals are in fact viewed and treated, we can also ask a different question, namely, what would the good or just society make of an individual's race or sex, and to what degree, if at all, would racial and sexual distinctions ever properly be taken into account there? Indeed, it could plausibly be argued that we could not have a wholly adequate idea of whether a society was racist or sexist unless we had some conception of what a thoroughly nonracist or nonsexist society would look like. This question is an extremely instructive as well as an often neglected one. Comparatively little theoretical literature that deals with either racism or sexism has concerned itself in a systematic way with this issue, but as will be seen it is in some respects both a more important and a more complicated one where sex is concerned than where race is involved.[24] Moreover, as I shall argue, many discussions of sexual differences which touch upon this question do so inappropriately by concentrating upon the relatively irrelevant question of whether the differences between males and females are biological rather than social in origin.

The inquiry that follows addresses and seeks to answer two major questions. First, what are the major, plausible conceptions of what the good society would look like in respect to the race and sex of individuals, and how are these conceptions to be correctly characterized and described? And second, given a delineation of the alternatives, what is to be said in favor or against one or another of them? Here, the focus is upon two more specific issues. One concerns the relevance and force of the various arguments founded upon nature and the occurrence of natural differences for the preservation of sex roles and sexual or racial differences in the good society. The other concerns some of the central moral arguments for the elimination of sex roles and the diminution, if not elimination, of the importance of distinctions connected with one's sex or race.

In order to ask more precisely what some of the possible ideals are of desirable racial or sexual differentiation, it is necessary to ask: Differentiation in respect to what? And one way to do this is to distinguish in a crude way among three levels or areas of social and political arrangements and activities. First, there is the area of basic political rights and obligations, including such things as the rights to vote and to travel, and the obligation to pay taxes. Second, there is the area of important, but perhaps less primary institutional benefits and burdens of both governmental and nongovernmental types. Examples are access to and employment in the significant economic markets, the opportunity to acquire and enjoy housing in the setting of one's choice, the right of persons who want to marry each other to do so, and the duties (nonlegal as well as legal) that persons acquire in getting married. And third, there is the area of individual, social interaction, including such matters as whom one will marry, have as friends, and, perhaps, what aesthetic preferences one will cultivate and enjoy.

As to each of these three areas we can ask, for example, whether in a nonracist or a nonsexist society it would be thought appropriate ever to take the race or sex of an individual into account. It is, for instance, a widely held, but by no means unanimously accepted, view that we would have the good society in respect to race if race were to be a wholly unimportant characteristic of individuals — if, that is, race were to function in the lives of individuals in the way in which eye color now does.

Thus, one conception of a nonracist society is that which is captured by what I shall call the assimilationist ideal: a nonracist society would be one in which the race of an individual would be the functional equivalent of the eye color of individuals in our society today.[25] In our society no basic political rights and obligations are determined on the basis of eye color. No important institutional benefits and burdens are connected with eye color. Indeed, except for the mildest sort of aesthetic preferences, a person would be thought odd who even made private, social decisions by taking eye color into account. It would, of course, be unintelligible, and not just odd, were a person to say today that while he or she looked blue-eyed, he or she regarded himself or herself as really a brown-eyed person. Because eye color functions differently in our culture than does race, there is no analogue to passing for eye color. Were the assimilationist ideal to become a reality, the same would be true of one's race. In short, according to the assimilationist ideal, a nonracist society would be one in which an individual's race was of no more significance in any of these three areas than is eye color today.

What is a good deal less familiar is an analogous conception of the good society in respect to sexual differentiation — one in which an individual's sex were to become a comparably unimportant characteristic. An assimilationist society in respect to sex would be one in which an individual's sex was of no more significance in any of the three areas than is eye color today. There would be no analogue to transsexuality, and, while physiological or anatomical sex differences would remain, they would possess only the kind and degree of significance that today attaches to the physiologically distinct eye colors persons possess.

It is apparent that the assimilationist ideal in respect to sex does not seem to be as readily plausible and obviously attractive here as it is in the case of race. In fact, many persons invoke the possible realization of the assimilationist ideal as a reason for rejecting the Equal Rights Amendment and indeed the idea of women's liberation itself. The assimilationist ideal may be just as good and just as important an ideal in respect to sex as it is in respect to race, but it is important to realize at the outset that this appears to be a more far-reaching proposal when applied to sex rather than race and that many more persons think there are good reasons why an assimilationist society in respect to sex would not be desirable than is true for the comparable racial ideal. Before such a conception is assessed, however, it will be useful to provide a somewhat fuller characterization of its features.

To begin with, it must be acknowledged that to make the assimilationist ideal a reality in respect to sex would involve more profound and fundamental revisions of our institutions and our attitudes than would be the case in respect to race. On the institutional level we would, for instance, have to alter significantly our practices concerning marriage. If a nonsexist society is a society in which one's sex is no more significant than eye color in our society today, then laws which require the persons who are getting married to be of different sexes would clearly be sexist laws.

More importantly, given the significance of role differentiation and ideas about the psychological differences in temperament that are tied to sexual identity, the assimilationist ideal would be incompatible with all psychological and sex-role differentiation. That is to say, in such a society the ideology of the society would contain no proposition asserting the inevitable or essential attributes of masculinity or feminity; it would never encourage or discourage the ideas of sisterhood or brotherhood; and it would be unintelligible to talk about the virtues or the disabilities of being a woman or a man. In addition, such a society would not have any norms concerning the appropriateness of different social behavior depending upon whether one were male or female. There would be no conception of the existence of a set of social tasks that were more appropriately undertaken or performed by males or by females. And there would be no expectation that the family was composed of one adult male and one adult female, rather than, say, just two adults—if two adults seemed the appropriate number. To put it simply, in the assimilationist society in respect to sex, persons would not be socialized so as to see or understand themselves or others as essentially or significantly who they were or what their lives would be like because they were either male or female. And no political rights or social institutions, practices, and norms would mark the physiological differences between males and females as important.[26]

Were sex like eye color, these kinds of distinctions would make no sense. Just as the normal, typical adult is virtually oblivious to the eye color of other persons for all significant interpersonal relationships, so, too, the normal, typical adult in this kind of nonsexist society would be equally as indifferent to the sexual, physiological differences of other persons for all significant interpersonal relationships. Bisexuality, not heterosexuality or homosexuality, would be the typical intimate, sexual relationship in the ideal society that was assimilationist in respect to sex.[27]

To acknowledge that things would be very different is, of course, hardly to concede that they would thereby be undesirable—or desirable for that matter. But still, the problem is, perhaps, with the assimilationist ideal. And the assimilationist ideal is certainly not the only possible, plausible ideal.

There is, for instance, another one that is closely related to, but distinguishable from that of the assimilationist ideal. It can be understood by considering how religion rather than eye color tends to be thought about in our culture today and incorporated within social life today. If the good society were to match the present state of affairs in respect to one's religious identity, rather than the present state of affairs in respect to one's eye color, the two societies would be different, but not very greatly so. In neither would we find that the allocation of basic political rights and duties ever took an individual's religion into account. And there would be a comparable indifference to religion even in respect to most important institutional benefits and burdens — for example, access to employment in the desirable vocations, the opportunity to live where one wished to live, and the like. Nonetheless, in the good society in which religious differences were to some degree socially relevant, it would be deemed appropriate to have some institutions (typically those which are connected in an intimate way with these religions) which did in a variety of ways properly take the religion of members of the society into account. For example, it would be thought both permissible and appropriate for members of a religious group to join together in collective associations which have religious, educational, and social dimensions, and when it came to the employment of persons who were to be centrally engaged in the operation of those religious institutions (priests, rabbis and ministers, for example), it would be unobjectionable and appropriate explicitly to take the religion of job applicants into account. On the individual, interpersonal level, it might also be thought natural and possibly even admirable, were persons to some significant degree to select their associates, friends, and mates on the basis of their religious orientation. So there is another possible and plausible ideal of what the good society would look like in respect to a particular characteristic in which differences based upon that characteristic would be to some degree maintained in some aspects of institutional and interpersonal life. The diversity of the religious beliefs of individuals would be reflected in the society's institutional and ideological fabric in a way in which the diversity of eye color would not be in the assimilationist society. The picture is a more complex, somewhat less easily describable one than that of the assimilationist ideal.

There could be at least two somewhat different reasons why persons might think it preferable to have some ideal different from that of the assimilationist one in respect to religion. They might, for instance, think that heterodoxy in respect to religious belief and practice was a positive good. On this view they would see it as a loss — they would think it a worse society — were everyone to be a member of the same religion. Or they might, instead, view heterodoxy in respect to religious belief and practice more as a necessary, lesser evil. On this view they would see nothing intrinsically better about diversity rather than uniformity in respect to religion, but they might also think that the evils of achieving anything like homogeneity far outweighed the possible benefits. That is to say, persons holding this position might believe, for instance, that there was one correct religion and that it would be good were everyone to accept and be a member of that religion, but they might also believe that it would be undesirable and wrong to try to structure the social and political institutions, or the socialization of persons in the society, in such a way that social benefits and burdens were distributed in accordance with one's religion or that significantly different norms of social behavior ought to be connected with being of one religion or the other. Because persons favoring religious diversity for either reason would desire and expect different religions to exist in the good society, and because religions themselves are composed of and require certain institutional structures of varying degrees of formality and complexity, the good society modeled upon this ideal would necessarily contain some acceptable social and interpersonal differentiation based upon the religious identity of the individuals in the society. As such, the rendering of the precise description of the right degree of differentiation based upon religion would be a more complex and more difficult undertaking than is true for the assimilationist ideal.

Nonetheless, it may be that in respect to sex, and conceivably, in respect to race, too, something more like this ideal of diversity in respect to religion is the right one. But one problem then — and it is a more substantial one than is sometimes realized — is to specify with a good deal of precision and care what that ideal really comes to in the matter of sexual or racial identity and degree of acceptable sexual or racial differentiation. Which institutional and personal differentiations would properly be permissible and which would not be? Which attiudes, beliefs, and role expectations concerning the meaning and significance of being male or female would be properly introduced and maintained in the good society and which would not be? Which attitudes, beliefs, and practices would continue in the good society to constitute the meaning of ethnicity as a racial concept and which would have to be purged? Part, but by no means all, of the attractiveness of the assimilationist ideal is its clarity and simplicity. In the good society of the assimilationist sort we would be able to tell easily and unequivocally whether any law, practice, attitude, or form of socialization was in any respect either racist or sexist. Part, but by no means all, of the unattractiveness of any more pluralistic ideal concerning sex or race is that it makes the question of what is racist or sexist a much more difficult and complicated one to answer. But although simplicity and lack of ambiguity may be virtues, they are not the only virtues to be taken into account in deciding among competing ideals. We quite appropriately take other considerations to be relevant to an assessment of the value and worth of alternative, possible conceptions of nonracist and nonsexist societies. What has been said so far by no means settles the question.

Nor do I even mean to suggest that all persons who reject the assimilationist ideal in respect to sex would necessarily embrace something like the kind of pluralistic ideal I have described as matching something like our present arrangements and ideas concerning the relevance of religious identity—although these do seem to exhaust the plausible ideals in respect to race. Some persons might think the right ideal was one in which substantially greater sexual differentiation and sex-role identification were retained than would be the case within a good society of that general type. Thus, someone might believe, for instance, that the good society was, perhaps, essentially like the one they think we now have in respect to sex: equality of basic political rights, such as the right to vote, but all of the sexual differentiation in both legal and nonlegal, formal and informal institutions, all of the sex-role socialization and all of the differences in matters of temperament that are characteristic of the way in which our society has been and still is ordered. And someone might also believe that the prevailing ideological concomitants of these arrangements are the correct and appropriate ones to perpetuate.[28]

This could, of course, be regarded as a version of the pluralistic ideal described above, with the emphasis upon the extensive character of the institutional, normative, and personal differences connected with sexual identity. Whether it is a form of this pluralistic ideal or a different ideal altogether turns, I think, upon two things: first, how pervasive the sexual differentiation is in terms of the number, importance, and systemic interconnectedness of the institutions and role expectations connected with being of one sex or the other, and, second, whether the ideal contains within it a conception of the appropriateness of significant institutional and interpersonal inequality, e.g., that the woman's job is in large measure to serve and be dominated by the male. The more either or both of these features is present, the clearer is the case for regarding this as an ideal, distinctively different from either of the other two described so far. I shall indicate later why I think these two features make such a difference.

But the next question is that of how a choice is rationally to be made among these different, possible ideals. One general set of issues concerns the empirical sphere, because the question of whether something is a plausible and attractive ideal does turn in part on the nature of the empirical world. If it is true, for example, that any particular characteristic, such as an individual's race or sex, is not only a

socially significant category in our culture but that it is largely a socially created one as well, then for many people a number of objections to the assimilationist ideal appear immediately to disappear.
The other general set of issues concerns the relevant normative considerations. Here the key questions concern the principles and considerations by which to assess and evaluate different conceptions of
how persons ought to be able to live and how their social institutions
ought to be constructed and arranged. I begin with the empirical
considerations and constraints, although one heuristic disadvantage
in doing so is that this decision may appear to give them greater
weight than, as I shall argue, they in fact deserve.

What opponents of assimilationism and proponents of schemes
of strong sexual differentiation seize upon is that sexual difference
appears to be a naturally occurring category of obvious and inevitable relevance for the construction of any plausible conception of the
nature of the good society.[29] The problems with this way of thinking
are twofold. To begin with, a careful and thorough analysis of the social realities would reveal, I believe, that it is the socially created sexual differences which constitute most of our conception of sex differences and which tend in fact to matter the most in the way we live
our lives as persons of one sex or the other. For, it is, I think, sex-role
differentiation and socialization, not the physiological and related
biological differences — if there are any — that make men and women
as different as they are from each other, and it is these same sex-role-
created differences which are invoked to justify the necessity or the
desirability of most sexual differentiation proposed to be maintained
at any of the levels of social arrangements and practices described
earlier.[30]

It is important, however, not to attach any greater weight than
is absolutely necessary to the truth or falsity of this causal claim
about the source of the degree of sexual distinctions that exist in our
or other cultures. For what is significant, although seldom recognized, is the fact that the answer to that question almost never goes
very far in settling the question of what the good society should look
like in respect to any particular characteristic of individuals. And the
answer certainly does not go as far as many persons appear to believe
it does to settle that question of the nature of the good society.

Let us suppose that there are what can be called "naturally occurring" sexual differences and even that they are of such a nature
that they are in some sense of direct prima facie social relevance. It is
essential to see that this would by no means settle the question of
whether in the good society sex should or should not be as minimally

significant as eye color. Even if there are major or substantial biological differences between men and women that are in this sense "natural" rather than socially created, this does not determine the question of what the good society can and should make of these differences — without, that is, begging the question by including within the meaning of "major" or "substantial" or "natural" the idea that these are things that ought to be retained, emphasized, or otherwise normatively taken into account. It is not easy to see why, without begging the question, it should be thought that this fact, if it is a fact, settles the question adversely to anything like the assimilationist ideal. Persons might think that truths of this sort about nature or biology do affect, if not settle, the question of what the good society should look like for at least two different reasons.

In the first place, they might think the differences are of such a character that they substantially affect what would be *possible* within a good society of human persons. Just as the fact that humans are mortal necessarily limits the features of any possible good society, so, they might argue, the fact that males and females are physiologically or biologically different limits in the same way the features of any possible good society.[31]

In the second place, they might think the differences are of such a character that they are relevant to the question of what would be *desirable* in the good society. That is to say, they might not think that the differences determine or affect to a substantial degree what is possible, but only that the differences are appropriately taken into account in any rational construction of an ideal social existence.

The second reason seems to be a good deal more plausible than the first. For there appear to be very few, if any, respects in which the ineradicable, naturally occurring differences between males and females *must* be taken into account. The industrial revolution has certainly make any of the general differences in strength between the sexes capable of being ignored by the good society for virtually all significant human activities.[32] And even if it were true that women are naturally better suited than men to care for and nurture children, it is also surely the case that men can be taught to care for and nurture children well.[33] Indeed, the one natural or biological fact that seems *required* to be taken into account is the fact that reproduction of the human species requires that the fetus develop *in utero* for a period of months. Sexual intercourse is not necessary, for artificial insemination is available. Neither marriage nor the nuclear family is necessary either for conception or child rearing. Given the present state of medical knowledge and what might be termed the natural realities of female pregnancy, it is difficult to see why any important institutional or interpersonal arrangements are constrained to take the existing biological differences as to the phenomenon of *in utero* pregnancy into account.

But to say all this is still to leave it a wholly open question to what degree the good society *ought* to build upon any ineradicable biological differences, or to create ones in order to construct institutions and sex roles which would thereby maintain a substantial degree of sexual differentiation. The way to answer that question is to consider and assess the arguments for and against doing so. What is significant is the fact that many of the arguments for doing so are less persuasive than they appear to be upon the initial statement of this possibility.

It might be argued, for instance, that the fact of menstruation could be used as a premise upon which to base the case for importantly different social roles for females than for males. But this could only plausibly be proposed if two things were true: first, that menstruation would be debilitating to women and hence relevant to social role even in a culture which did not teach women to view menstruation as a sign of uncleanliness or as a curse;[34] and, second, that the way in which menstruation necessarily affected some or all women was in fact necessarily related in an important way to the role in question. But even if both of these were true, it would still be an open question whether any sexual differentiation ought to be built upon these facts. The society could still elect to develop institutions that would nullify the effect of these natural differences and it would still be an open question whether it ought to do so. Suppose, for example, what seems implausible—that some or all women will not be able to perform a particular task while menstruating, e.g., guard the border of a country. It would be possible, even easy, if the society wanted to, to arrange for substitute guards for the women who were incapacitated. We know that persons are not good guards when they are sleepy, and we make arrangements so that persons alternate guard duty to avoid fatigue. The same could be done for menstruating women, even given the implausibly strong assumptions about menstruation.

The point that is involved here is a very general one that has application in contexts having nothing to do with the desirability or undesirability of maintaining substantial sexual differentiation. It has to do with the fact that humans possess the ability to alter their natural and social environment in distinctive, dramatic, and unique ways. An example from the nonsexual area can help bring out this too seldom recognized central feature. It is a fact that some persons born in human society are born with congenital features such that they cannot walk or walk well on their legs. They are born naturally crippled or lame. However, humans in our society certainly possess the capability to devise and construct mechanical devices and institutional arrangements which render this natural fact about some persons relatively unimportant in respect to the way they and others will live together. We can bring it about, and in fact are in the process of bringing it about, that persons who are confined to wheelchairs can move down sidewalks and across streets because the curb stones at corners of intersections have been shaped so as to accommodate the passage of wheelchairs. And we can construct and arrange buildings and events so that persons in wheelchairs can ride elevators, park cars, and be seated at movies, lectures, meetings, and the like. Much of the environment in which humans live is the result of their intentional choices and actions concerning what that environment shall be like. They can elect to construct an environment in which the natural incapacity of some persons to walk or walk well is a major difference or a difference that will be effectively nullified vis-à-vis the lives that they, too, will live.

Nonhuman animals cannot do this in anything like the way humans can. A fox or an ape born lame is stuck with the fact of lameness and the degree to which that will affect the life it will lead. The other foxes or apes cannot change things. This capacity of humans to act intentionally and thereby continuously create and construct the world in which they and others will live is at the heart of what makes studies of nonhuman behavior essentially irrelevant to and for most if not all of the normative questions of social, political, and moral theory. Humans can become aware of the nature of their natural and social environment and then act intentionally to alter the environment so as to change its impact upon or consequences for the individuals living within it. Nonhuman animals cannot do so. This difference is, therefore, one of fundamental theoretical importance. At the risk of belaboring the obvious, what it is important to see is that the case against any picture of the good society of an assimilationist sort — if it is to be a defensible critique — ought to rest on arguments concerned to show why some other ideal would be preferable; it cannot plausibly rest in any significant respect upon the claim that the sorts of biological differences typically alluded to in contexts such as these require that the society not be assimilationist in character.

There are, though, several other arguments based upon nature, or the idea of the "natural" that also must be considered and assessed. First, it might be argued that if a way of doing something is natural, then it ought to be done that way. Here, what may be meant by "natural" is that this way of doing the thing is the way it would be done if culture did not direct or teach us to do it differently. It is not clear, however, that this sense of "natural" is wholly intelligible; it supposes that we can meaningfully talk about how humans would behave in the absence of culture. And few if any humans have ever lived in such a state. Moreover, even if this is an intelligible notion, the proposal that the natural way to behave is somehow the appropriate or desirable way to behave is strikingly implausible. It is, for example, almost surely natural, in this sense of "natural," that humans would eat their food with their hands, except for the fact that they are, almost always, socialized to eat food differently. Yet, the fact that humans would naturally eat this way, does not seem in any respect to be a reason for believing that that is thereby the desirable or appropriate way to eat food. And the same is equally true of any number of other distinctively human ways of behaving.

Second, someone might argue that substantial sexual differentiation is natural not in the sense that it is biologically determined nor in the sense that it would occur but for the effects of culture, but rather in the sense that substantial sexual differentiation is a virtually universal phenomenon in human culture. By itself, this claim of virtual universality, even if accurate, does not directly establish anything about the desirability or undesirability of any particular ideal. But it can be made into an argument by the addition of the proposition that where there is a widespread, virtually universal social practice or institution, there is probably some good or important purpose served by the practice or institution. Hence, given the fact of substantial sex-role differentiation in all, or almost all, cultures, there is on this view some reason to think that substantial sex-role differentiation serves some important purpose for and in human society.

This is an argument, but it is hard to see what is attractive about it. The premise which turns the fact of sex-role differentiation into any kind of a strong reason for sex-role differentiation is the premise of conservatism. And it is no more or less convincing here than elsewhere. There are any number of practices or institutions that are typical and yet upon reflection seem without significant social purpose. Slavery was once such an institution; war perhaps still is.

More to the point, perhaps, the concept of "purpose" is ambiguous. It can mean in a descriptive sense "plays some role" or "is causally relevant." Or, it can mean in a prescriptive sense "does something desirable" or "has some useful function." If "purpose" is used descriptively in the conservative premise, then the argument says nothing about the continued desirability of sex-role differentiation or the assimilationist ideal. If "purpose" is used prescriptively in the conservative premise, then there is no reason to think that premise is true.[35]

To put it another way, the question that seems fundamentally to be at issue is whether it is desirable to have a society in which sex-role differences are to be retained in the way and to the degree they are today—or even at all. The straightforward way to think about the question is to ask what would be good and what would be bad about a society in which sex functioned like eye color does in our society; or alternatively, what would be good and what would be bad about a society in which sex functioned in the way in which religious identity does today; or alternatively, what would be good and what would be bad about a society in which sex functioned in the way in which it does today. We can imagine what such societies would look like and how they might work. It is hard to see how thinking about answers to this question is substantially advanced by reference to what has typically or always been the case. If it is true, for instance, that the sex-role-differentiated societies that have existed have tended to concentrate power and authority in the hands of males, have developed institutions and ideologies that have perpetuated that concentration, and have restricted and prevented women from living the kinds of lives that persons ought to be able to live for themselves, then this, it seems to me, says far more about what may be wrong with any strongly nonassimilationist ideal than does the conservative premise say what may be right about any strongly nonassimilationist ideal.

This does not, however, exhaust the reasons why persons might think that the question of whether sex differences are naturally occurring differences is an important or relevant one. There are at least two others. First, if the differences are natural, rather than socially created, it might be thought that there is less of an obligation to correct or alter the impact or effect that those differences will play in the lives people will be able to live in the society. That is to say, if it is nature, or biology, that accounts for the differences that result, then the society is not causally responsible and for that reason is not to blame for or accountable for those differences. The cause is not society, but nature. If society were the cause, and if the differences produced arrangements that seemed unequal or unfair, then the fault would be society's and its obligation to remedy the situation would be clearer, more direct, and more stringent. But since it is not, the causal chain is different and society is, for this reason, off the hook of accountability. An argument such as this one is seldom made explicit, but it underlies, I suspect, much of the motivation for the belief in the relevance of the search for natural as opposed to social causation.

The difficulty here is that only if the question is cast in terms of a certain very particular conception of compensatory justice does the causal issue assume genuine relevance or importance. What remains unexplained is why that perspective should be seen to be the obviously correct or appropriate one from which to look at matters. For if the question were to be cast, instead, in terms of a conception of distributive justice — one that was, say, founded upon the importance of a *resulting* equality of distributional treatment — then the cause of the initial differences or inequalities becomes a substantially less significant issue. And, if the focus were to be on the more general question of what kind of society it would be desirable to have, then the correct causal explanation would be still less important. Consider again the fact that some persons are born lame while others are not. Even though social institutions did not cause the lameness at all, it is difficult to understand how that is at all decisive to the question of what the good society would do in the way of seeking to nullify the natural consequences of lameness through having certain institutions and arrangements rather than others. If the cause of undesirable existing inequalities or differences is socially created, then there is an additional argument of a compensatory sort for requiring that the society make the alterations necessary to change the operative social mechanisms. But the absence of such an argument in no way implies that things may therefore be appropriately or justly left the way nature has produced them.

The other argument is that if the differences are natural, then there are considerations of efficiency that come into play. If some persons are naturally less equipped or suited to do some things, then it will be less efficient than would otherwise be the case to bring it about that they will end up being able to do those things — either because they will not be able to do them as well as others, or because it will be most costly to bring it about that they will be able to do them as well as others who are differently endowed can do them. Here, too, there is, I think, something to the argument, but not as much as is typically supposed. If it is possible to arrange things so that the natural differences can be nullified, and if there are reasons of justice (or reasons of morality) for doing so, then it is as hard here, as elsewhere, to see why considerations of efficiency should necessarily be thought overriding.

There are, in fact, several different issues and arguments that may be involved here, and it is worthwhile trying to disentangle them. One issue is whether what underlies this line of thought is the view that all persons ought to be *required* to do whatever it is they are naturally endowed to do, and that, therefore, the social institutions should be designed so as to bring that state of affairs into being. On this view, if a person were naturally endowed to be a brain surgeon, or a garbage collector, the social institutions ought to at least direct if not require the person to end up in that role or place—irrespective of the person's desires and irrespective of the kind and quality of life allotted to the persons with differing natural endowments. A society organized in this fashion would, doubtless, be highly efficient in terms of the correspondence between natural endowments and places in society and the degree to which each person was living the life he or she was "naturally" suited for, but I do not see how one could easily argue that such a "naturally" ordered society would be either just or morally desirable. Apart from everything else, if one wanted a nice philosophical example of a case of viewing persons wholly as a means—a case of using persons as objects—a society organized and justified along these lines would seem to be an obvious candidate.

But the argument about nature and efficiency may not be this sweeping. Perhaps instead the claim is only that in the good society at least those persons who are especially able or competent ought to be permitted to do what they are naturally able or competent to do. This is a substantially weaker thesis, and I shall assume for purposes of argument that it is defensible. This thesis is not, however, fundamentally at issue. The primary question is whether the society ought to be organized so that the less well endowed will be able to do things, live their lives, in a way that is more fully adequate and satisfactory. If some are naturally able to do certain things well, while others are less able naturally to do them, one complaint the better endowed could have about attempts to increase the abilities and opportunities of the less well endowed is that based upon the overall social cost involved in doing so. But the better endowed do not have a claim that, just because they happen to be better endowed by nature, they *alone* should have the opportunity to participate in institutions that depend upon or require certain abilities, talents, dispositions, and the like. They can claim that different social structures may be less efficient in terms of overall cost of having those social structures than ones in which they alone participate. But if there are considerations of justice or morality that favor these alternative "more expensive" arrangements, it seems plausible that considerations of efficiency should at least to some degree give way.

Perhaps, though, they have one other argument, namely, that

if alternative social arrangements are to be preferred, then the society will be one in which the institutions do not permit them to utilize their natural talents to the fullest extent. This may be just a restatement of the argument from efficiency, or it may be an argument that the better endowed deserve to be able always to utilize their natural talents to the fullest.[36]

I do not think they can claim to deserve to be able always to utilize their natural talents to the fullest. They cannot claim this because, *ex hypothesi* since these are natural talents or capabilities, they manifestly did nothing to deserve these natural attributes.[37] And while it may be good to permit them to utilize their talents — in terms of the happiness of those who are naturally better endowed — there is no reason to give their claims any greater weight than the claims of others on the ground that their talents or characteristics are naturally rather than socially produced. And it even seems plausible, for reasons analogous to those offered by Rawls for the difference principle, that if there are sacrifices of any sort to be made, it is fairer that they be made or borne by the naturally better rather than naturally worse off.

So, even supposing that there is a clear sense of natural endowments or capabilities based on sexual physiology, and even supposing that the natural differences between males and females were as strongly present "in nature" as the preceding arguments require, the conclusions to be drawn vis-à-vis the character of the good society would be appreciably weaker and more indeterminate than is typically supposed by those who focus upon the possible existence of biological differences between the sexes. The primary point that emerges is that the question of whether there are natural differences (in any of the above senses) between males and females (or even persons of different races) tends to get disputed on the wrong grounds. The debate tends to focus upon whether biology or society is the cause of the differences. The debate ought to attend instead to the question of why it matters. The debaters ought to address first the unasked question of within what theoretical inquiry the issue is even relevant. When the question is one of ideals, of what the good society would make of sexual or racial characteristics, the issue of natural as opposed to social causation is a strikingly irrelevant one. There do not, therefore, appear to be any very powerful, let alone conclusive, arguments against something like the assimilationist society that can be based on any of the different, possible appeals to nature and the natural.

If the chief thing to be said in favor of something like the assimilationist society in respect to sex is that some arguments against it are not very relevant, that does not by itself make a very convincing case. Such is not, however, the way in which matters need be left. There is an affirmative case of sorts for something like the assimilationist society.

One strong, affirmative moral argument on behalf of the assimilationist ideal is that it does provide for a kind of individual autonomy that a substantially nonassimilationist society cannot provide. The reason is because any substantially nonassimilationist society will have sex roles, and sex roles interfere in basic ways with autonomy. The argument for these two propositions proceeds as follows.

Any nonassimilationist society must have some institutions and some ideology that distinguishes between individuals in virtue of their sexual physiology, and any such society will necessarily be committed to teaching the desirability of doing so. That is what is implied by saying it is nonassimilationist rather than assimilationist. And any substantially nonassimilationist society will make one's sexual identity an important characteristic so that there will be substantial psychological, role, and status differences between persons who are male and those who are female. That is what is implied by saying that it is substantially nonassimilationist. Any such society will necessarily have sex roles, a conception of the places, characteristics, behaviors, etc., that are appropriate to one sex or the other but not both. That is what makes it a *sex* role.

Now, sex roles are, I think, morally objectionable on two or three quite distinct grounds. One such ground is absolutely generic and applies to all sex roles. The other grounds are less generic and apply only to the kinds of sex roles with which we are familiar and which are a feature of patriarchal societies, such as our own. I begin with the more contingent, less generic objections.

We can certainly imagine, if we are not already familiar with, societies in which the sex roles will be such that the general place of women in that society can be described as that of the servers of men. In such a society individuals will be socialized in such a way that women will learn how properly to minister to the needs, desires, and interests of men; women and men will both be taught that it is right and proper that the concerns and affairs of men are more important than and take precedence over those of women; and the norms and supporting set of beliefs and attitudes will be such that this role will be deemed the basic and appropriate role for women to play and men to expect. Here, I submit, what is objectionable about the connected set of institutions, practices, and ideology — the structure of the prevailing sex role — is the role itself. It is analogous to a kind of human slavery. The fundamental moral defect — just as is the case with slavery — is not that women are being arbitrarily or capriciously assigned to the social role of server, but that such a role itself has no legitimate place in the decent or just society. As a result, just as is the case with slavery, the assignment on *any* basis of individuals to such a role is morally objectionable. A society arranged so that such a role is a prominent part of the structure of the social institutions can be properly characterized as an *oppressive* one. It consigns some individuals to lives which have no place in the good society, which restrict unduly the opportunities of these individuals, and which do so in order improperly to enhance the lives and opportunities of others.

But it may be thought possible to have sex roles and all that goes with them without having persons of either sex placed within a position of general, systemic dominance or subordination. Here, it would be claimed, the society would not be an oppressive one in this sense. Consider, for example, the kinds of sex roles with which we are familiar and which assign to women the primary responsibilities for child rearing and household maintenance. It might be argued first that the roles of child rearer and household maintainer are not in themselves roles that could readily or satisfactorily be eliminated from human society without the society itself being deficient in serious, unacceptable ways. It might be asserted, that is, that these are roles or tasks that simply must be filled if children are to be raised in a satisfactory way. Suppose this is correct, suppose it is granted that society would necessarily have it that these tasks would have to be done. Still, if it is also correct that, relatively speaking, these are unsatisfying and unfulfilling ways for humans to concentrate the bulk of their energies and talents, then, to the degree to which this is so, what is morally objectionable is that if this is to be a *sex* role, then women are unduly and unfairly allocated a disproportionate share of what is unpleasant, unsatisfying, unrewarding work. Here the objection is the degree to which the burden women are required to assume is excessive and unjustified vis-à-vis the rest of society, i.e., the men. Unsatisfactory roles and tasks, when they are substantial and pervasive, should surely be allocated and filled in the good society in a way which seeks to distribute the burdens involved in a roughly equal fashion.

Suppose, though, that even this feature were eliminated from sex roles, so that, for instance, men and women shared more equally in the dreary, unrewarding aspects of housework and child care, and that a society which maintained sex roles did not in any way have as a feature of that society the systemic dominance or superiority of one sex over the other, there would still be a generic moral defect that would remain. The defect would be that any set of sex roles would necessarily impair and retard an individual's ability to develop his or her own characteristics, talents, capacities, and potential life-plans to the extent to which he or she might desire and from which he or she might derive genuine satisfaction. Sex roles, by definition, constitute empirical and normative limits of varying degrees of strength — restrictions on what it is that one can expect to do, be, or become. As such, they are, I think, at least prima facie objectionable.

To some degree, all role-differentiated living is restrictive in this sense. Perhaps, therefore, all role differentiation in society is to some degree troublesome, and perhaps all strongly role-differentiated societies are objectionable. But the case against sex roles and the concomitant sexual differentiation they create and require need not rest upon this more controversial point. For one thing that distinguishes sex roles from many other roles is that they are wholly involuntarily assumed. One has no choice about whether one shall be born a male or female. And if it is a consequence of one's being born a male or a female that one's subsequent emotional, intellectual, and material development will be substantially controlled by this fact, then it is necessarily the case that substantial, permanent, and involuntarily assumed restraints have been imposed on some of the most central factors concerning the way one will shape and live one's life. The point to be emphasized is that this would necessarily be the case, even in the unlikely event that substantial sexual differentiation could be maintained without one sex or the other becoming dominant and developing oppressive institutions and an ideolgy to support that dominance and oppression. Absent some far stronger showing than seems either reasonable or possible that potential talents, abilities, interests, and the like are inevitably and irretrievably distributed between the sexes in such a way that the sex roles of the society are genuinely congruent with and facilitative of the development of those talents, abilities, interests, and the like that individuals can and do possess, sex roles are to this degree incompatible with the kind of respect which the good or the just society would accord to each of the individual persons living within it. It seems to me, therefore, that there are persuasive reasons to believe that no society which maintained what I have been describing as *substantial* sexual differentiation could plausibly be viewed as a good or just society.

What remains more of an open question is whether a society in which sex functioned in the way in which eye color does (a strictly assimilationist society in respect to sex) would be better or worse than one in which sex functioned in the way in which religious identity does in our society (a nonoppressive, more diversified or pluralistic one). For it might be argued that especially in the case of sex and even in the case of race much would be gained and nothing would be lost if the ideal society in respect to these characteristics succeeded in preserving in a nonoppressive fashion the attractive differences between males and females and the comparably attractive differences among ethnic groups. Such a society, it might be claimed, would be less bland, less homogeneous and richer in virtue of its variety.

I do not think there is any easy way to settle this question, but I do think the attractiveness of the appeal to diversity, when sex or race are concerned, is less alluring than is often supposed. The difficulty is in part one of specifying what will be preserved and what will not, and in part one of preventing the reappearance of the type of systemic dominance and subservience that produces the injustice of oppression. Suppose, for example, that it were suggested that there are aspects of being male and aspects of being female that are equally attractive and hence desirable to maintain and perpetuate: the kind of empathy that is associated with women and the kind of self-control associated with men. It does not matter what the characteristic is, the problem is one of seeing why the characteristic should be tied by the social institutions to the sex of the individuals of the society. If the characteristics are genuinely ones that all individuals ought to be encouraged to display in the appropriate circumstances, then the social institutions and ideology ought to endeavor to foster them in all individuals. If it is good for everyone to be somewhat empathetic all of the time or especially empathetic in some circumstances, or good for everyone to have a certain degree of self-control all of the time or a great deal in some circumstances, then there is no reason to preserve institutions which distribute these psychological attributes along sexual lines. And the same is true for many, if not all, vocations, activities, and ways of living. If some, but not all persons would find a life devoted to child rearing genuinely satisfying, it is good, surely, that that option be open to them. Once again, though, it is difficult to see the argument for implicitly or explicitly encouraging, teaching, or assigning to women, as opposed to men, that life simply in virtue of their sex. Thus, while substantial diversity in individual characteristics, attitudes, and ways of life is no doubt an admirable, even important feature of the good society, what remains uncertain is the necessity or the desirability of continuing to link attributes or behaviors such as these to the race or sex of individuals. And for the reasons I have tried to articulate there are significant moral arguments against any conception of the good society in which such connections are pursued and nourished in the systemic fashion required by the existence and maintenance of *sex* roles.

NOTES

1. For an example of this kind of theory see Rubin, "The Traffic in Women" in Reiter (ed.), *Toward an Anthropology of Women* (New York: Monthly Review Press, 1975), pp. 157–210.

2. For an example of this kind of theory see Tiger, *Men in Groups* (New York: Random House, 1969).

3. In asserting the importance of one's race and sex in our culture I do not mean to deny the importance of other characteristics — in particular, socioeconomic class. I do think that in our culture race and sex are two very important facts about a person, and I am skeptical of theories which "reduce" the importance of these features to a single, more basic one, *e.g.*, class. But apart from this one bit of skepticism I think that all of what I have to say is compatible with several different theories concerning why race and sex are so important — including, for instance, most versions of Marxism. *See, e.g.*, the account provided in Mitchell, *Woman's Estate* (New York: Pantheon Books, 1971).

As I have indicated, the correct causal explanation for the social realities is certainly an important question, both in its own right and for some of the issues I address. It is particularly significant for the development of an adequate program for altering the social realities to bring them closer to the ideal. Nonetheless, I have limited the scope of my inquiry to exclude a consideration of this large, difficult topic.

4. Passing is the phenomenon in which a person who in some sense knows himself or herself to be black "passes" as white because he or she looks white. A version of this is described in Sinclair Lewis' novel, *Kingsblood Royal* (New York: Random House, 1947), where the protagonist discovers when he is an adult that he, his father, and his father's mother are black (or, in the idiom of the late 1940s, Negro) in virtue of the fact that his great grandfather was black. His grandmother knew this and was consciously passing. When he learns about his ancestry, one decision he has to make is whether to continue to pass or to acknowledge to the world that he is in fact "Negro."

5. That looking black is not in our culture a necessary condition for being black can be seen from the phenomenon of passing. That it is not a sufficient condition can be seen from the book *Black Like Me* (Boston: Houghton Mifflin, 1961) by John Howard Griffin, where "looking black" is easily understood by the reader to be different from being black. I suspect that the concept of being black is, in our culture, one which combines both physiological and ancestral criteria in some fairly complex, yet imprecise fashion.

6. Justice Douglas suggests something like this in his dissent in *DeFunis*: "The consideration of race as a measure of an applicant's qualification normally introduces a capricious and irrelevant factor working an invidious discrimination." DeFunis v. Odegaard, 416 U.S. 312, 333 (1974).

7. There are significant respects in which the important racial distinction is between being *white* and being *nonwhite,* and there are other significant respects in which the fact of being *black* has its own special meaning and importance. My analysis is conducted largely in terms of what is involved in being black. To a considerable extent, however, what I say directly applies to the more inclusive category of being nonwhite. To the extent to which what I say does not apply to the other nonwhite racial distinctions, the analysis of those distinctions should, of course, be undertaken separately.

One unsatisfactory aspect of the position of the dissenters in the *Bakke* case is their failure to discuss the social realities in respect to the other nonwhite groups included in the Davis Medical School preferential treatment program. See, "Preferential Treatment," *infra,* note 8, pp. 78-79.

8. Regents of the University of California v. Bakke, 98 S. Ct. 2733 (1978).

9. *See, e.g.,* Baldwin, *The Fire Next Time* (New York: The Dial Press, 1963); DuBois, *The Souls of Black Folks* (Chicago: A. C. McClurg & Co., 1903); Ellison, *Invisible Man* (New York: Random House, 1952); Franklin, *From Slavery to Freedom,* 3d ed. (New York: Alfred A. Knopf, 1967); Carmichael and Hamilton, *Black Power* (New York: Random House, 1967); *Report of the National Advisory Commission on Civil Disorders* (Washington, D.C.: U.S. Government Printing Office, 1968); Kilson, "Whither Integration?" 45 *Am. Scholar* 360 (1976); and many other sources such as these that describe a great variety of features of the black experience in America: such things as the historical as well as the present-day material realities and the historical as well as present-day ideological realities—the way black people have been and are thought about within the culture. In *Kingsblood Royal,* Lewis provides a powerful account of what he calls the "American Credo" about the Negro, circa 1946. *Supra* note 4, at 194-97.

10. I discuss the meaning and significance of "social" versus "natural" categories further in Part III *infra,* pp. 30-38.

11. One very good general account of the structure of patriarchy and of its major dimensions and attributes is that found in the chapter, "Theory of Sexual Politics," in Millett, *Sexual Politics* (Garden City, N.Y.: Doubleday & Co., 1970), pp. 23-58. The essay seems to me to be a major contribution to an understanding of the subject. I draw upon Millett's analytic scheme in my description of the social realities of sex.

Something of the essence of the thesis is contained in the following: "[A] disinterested examination of our system of sexual relationship must point out that the situation between the sexes now, and throughout history, is a case of that phenomenon Max Weber defined as *herrschaft,* a relationship of dominance and subordinance. What goes largely unexamined, often even unacknowledged (yet is institutionalized nonetheless) in our social order, is the birthright priority whereby males rule females. Through this system a most ingenious form of 'interior colonization' has been achieved. It is one which tends moreover to be sturdier than any form of segregation and more rigorous than class stratification, more uniform, certainly more enduring. However muted its present appearance may be, sexual dominion obtains nevertheless as perhaps the most pervasive ideology of our culture and provides its most fundamental concept of power.

"This is so because our society, like all other historical civilizations, is a patriarchy. The fact is evident at once if one recalls that the military, industry, technology, universities, science, political office, and finance—in short, every avenue of power within the society, including the coercive force of the police, is entirely in male hands. . . .

"Sexual politics obtains consent through the 'socialization' of both sexes to basic patriarchal politics with regard to temperament, role, and status. As to status, a pervasive assent to the prejudice of male superiority guarantees superior status in the male, inferior in the female. The first item, temperament, involves the formation of human personality along stereotyped lines of sex category ('masculine' and 'feminine'), based on the needs and values of the dominant group and dictated by what its members cherish in themselves and find convenient in subordinates: aggression, intelligence, force and efficacy in the male; passivity, ignorance, docility, 'virtue,' and ineffectuality in the female. This is complemented by a second factor, sex role, which decrees a consonant and highly elaborate code of conduct, gesture and attitude for each sex. In terms of activity, sex role assigns domestic service and attendance upon infants to the female, the rest of human achievement, interest and ambition to the male. . . . Were one to analyze the three categories one might designate status as the political component, role as the sociological, and temperament as the psychological — yet their interdependence is unquestionable and they form a chain." *Id.* at 24–26 (footnotes omitted).

12. "For the married woman, her husband and children must always come first; her own needs and desires, last. When the children reach school age, they no longer require constant attention. The emotional-expressive function assigned to the woman is still required of her. Called the 'stroking function' by sociologist Jessie Bernard, it consists of showing solidarity, raising the status of others, giving help, rewarding, agreeing, concurring, complying, understanding, and passively accepting. The woman is expected to give emotional support and comfort to other family members, to make them feel like good and worthwhile human beings." Deckard, *The Women's Movement* (New York: Harper and Row, 1975), p. 59.

"Patriarchy's chief institution is the family. It is both a mirror of and a connection with the larger society; a patriarchal unit within a patriarchal whole. Mediating between the individual and the social structure, the family effects control and conformity where political and other authorities are insufficient." K. Millett, *supra* note 11, at 33.

13. "Even if the couple consciously try to attain an egalitarian marriage, so long as the traditional division of labor is maintained, the husband will be 'more equal.' He is the provider not only of money but of status. Especially if he is successful, society values what he does; she is just a housewife. Their friends are likely to be his friends and co-workers; in their company, she is just his wife. Because his provider function is essential for the family's survival, major family decisions are made in terms of how they affect his career. He need not and usually does not act like the authoritarian paterfamilius [*sic*] of the Victorian age. His power and status are derived from his function in the family and are secure so long as the traditional division of labor is maintained." Deckard, *supra* note 12, at 62.

14. In 1970, women workers were, on the average, paid only 59 percent of men's wages. And when wages of persons with similar educational levels are compared, women still were paid over 40 percent less than men. *Id.* at 79–81.

15. *See, e.g.,* Hochschild, "A Review of Sex Role Research," 78 *Am. J. Soc.* 1011 (1973), which reviews and very usefully categorizes the enormous volume of literature on this topic. *See also* Stewart, "Social Influences on Sex Differences in Behavior," in Teitelbaum (ed.) *Sex Differences* (Garden City, N.Y.: Anchor Press/

Doubleday, 1976); Weitzman, "Sex-Role Socialization" in Freeman (ed.), *Women: A Feminist Perspective* (Palo Alto, Cal.: Mayfield Publishing Co., 1975), p. 105. A number of the other pieces in *Women: A Feminist Perspective* also describe and analyze the role of women in the culture, including the way they are thought of by the culture.

The Women's Room by Marilyn French (New York: Harcourt Brace Jovanovich, 1977) is a powerful literary portrayal of a number of these same matters.

16. "It is generally accepted that Western patriarchy has been much softened by the concepts of courtly and romantic love. While this is certainly true, such influence has also been vastly overestimated. In comparison with the candor of 'machismo' or oriental behavior, one realizes how much of a concession traditional chivalrous behavior represents—a sporting kind of reparation to allow the subordinate female certain means of saving face. While a palliative to the injustice of woman's social position, chivalry is also a technique for disguising it. One must acknowledge that the chivalrous stance is a game the master group plays in elevating its subject to pedestal level. Historians of courtly love stress the fact that the raptures of the poets had no effect upon the legal or economic standing of women, and very little upon their social status. As the sociologist Hugo Beigel has observed, both the courtly and the romantic versions of love are 'grants' which the male concedes out of his total powers. Both have the effect of obscuring the patriarchal character of Western culture and in their general tendency to attribute impossible virtues to women, have ended by confining them in a narrow and often remarkable conscribing sphere of behavior. It was a Victorian habit, for example, to insist the female assume the function of serving as the male's conscience and living the life of goodness he found tedious but felt someone ought to do anyway." Millett, *supra* note 11, at 36-37.

17. I discuss the reasons for this in Part III, *infra*.

18. I return to this point, too, in Part III, *infra*, pp. 39-43.

19. Thus, in Bolling v. Sharpe, 347 U.S. 497 (1953), the Supreme Court said that what was wrong with preventing black children from attending the all white schools of the District of Columbia was that "[s]egregation in public education is not reasonably related to any proper governmental objective, and thus it imposes on Negro children of the District of Columbia a burden that constitutes an arbitrary deprivation of their liberty in violation of the Due Process Clause." *Id.* at 500.

20. Others have made this general point about the nature of the evil of racial segregation in the United States. *See, e.g.,* Ely, "The Constitutionality of Reverse Discrimination," 41 *U. Chi. L. Rev.* 723 (1974); Fiss, "Groups and Equal Protection," 5 *Phil. & Pub. Aff.* 107 (1976); Thalberg, "Reverse Discrimination and the Future," 5 *Phil. Forum* 268 (1973).

The failure fully to understand this general point seems to me to be one of the things wrong with Professor Wechsler's famous article, "Toward Neutral Principles of Constitutional Interpretation," 73 *Harv. L. Rev.* 1 (1959). Near the very end of the piece Wechsler reports, "In the days when I joined with Charles H. Houston [a well-known black lawyer] in a litigation in the Supreme Court, before the present building was constructed, he did not suffer more than I in knowing that we had to go to Union Station to lunch together during the recess." *Id.* at 34. If the stress in that sentence is wholly on the fact of *knowing,* no one can say for certain that Professor Wechsler is wrong. But what is certain is that Charles H. Houston suffered more than Professor Wechsler from living in a system in which he, Charles H. Houston, could only lunch at Union Station because *he* was black.

21. This conjecture about the role of sexually segregated bathrooms may well be inaccurate or incomplete. The sexual segregation of bathrooms may have more to do with privacy than with patriarchy. However, if so, it is at least odd that what the institution makes relevant is the sex of the individuals rather than merely the ability to perform the eliminatory acts in private.

22. Blank v. Sullivan and Cromwell, 418 F. Supp. 1, 4 (S.D.N.Y. 1975) writ of mandamus denied sub nom. Sullivan and Cromwell v. Motley No. 75-3045 (2d Cir. Aug. 26, 1975) (emphasis added).

23. I discuss one respect in which this phenomenon is relevant to the justifiability of programs of preferential treatment in "Preferential Treatment," *infra* pp. 57-60.

24. One of the few thorough and valuable explorations of this question as it relates to sexual difference is Jaggar's "On Sexual Equality," 84 *Ethics* 275 (1974). The article also contains a very useful analysis of the views of other feminist writers who have dealt with this topic.

25. There is a danger in calling this ideal the "assimilationist" ideal. That term often suggests the idea of incorporating oneself, one's values, and the like into the dominant group and its practices and values. No part of that idea is meant to be captured by my use of the term. Mine is a stipulative definition.

26. Jaggar describes something fairly close to the assimilationist view in this way:

"The traditional feminist answer to this question [of what the features of a non-sexist society would be] has been that a sexually egalitarian society is one in which virtually no public recognition is given to the fact that there is a physiological sex difference between persons. This is not to say that the different reproductive function of each sex should be unacknowledged in such a society nor that there should be no physicians specializing in female and male complaints, etc. But it is to say that, except in this sort of context, the question whether someone is female or male should have no significance. . . .

". . . In the mainstream tradition, the nonsexist society is one which is totally integrated sexually, one in which sexual differences have ceased to be a matter of public concern." Jaggar, *supra* note 24, at 276-77.

27. In describing the assimilationist society in this fashion, I do not mean thereby to be addressing the question of how government and laws would regulate all of these matters, or even whether they would. I am describing what laws, practices, attitudes, conventions, ideology, behavior, and the like one would expect to find. These might be reasons, for example, why it would be undesirable to have laws that regulated interpersonal relationships and personal preferences. We have no such laws concerning eye color and interpersonal relationships and yet it is generally irrelevant in this area. If the entire cultural apparatus were different from what it now is in respect to race or sex, we can imagine that race and sex would lose their significance in the analogous ways, even in the absence of laws which regulated all dimensions of social life.

28. Thus, for example, a column appeared a few years ago in the *Washington Star* concerning the decision of the Cosmos Club to continue to refuse to permit women to be members. The author of the column (and a member of the club) defended the decision on the ground that women appropriately had a different status in the society. Their true distinction was to be achieved by being faithful spouses and devoted mothers. The column closed with this paragraph:

"In these days of broken homes, derision of marriage, reluctance to bear children, contempt for the institution of the family—a phase in our national life when it seems more honorable to be a policewoman, or a model, or an accountant than to be a wife or mother — there is a need to reassert a traditional scale of values in which the vocation of homemaker is as honorable and distinguished as any in political or professional life. Such women, as wives and widows of members, now enjoy in the club the privileges of their status, which includes [sic] their own drawing rooms, and it is of interest that they have been among the most outspoken opponents of the proposed changes in club structure." Groseclose, "Now—Shall We Join the Ladies?" *Washington Star,* Mar. 13, 1975.

29. This is not to deny that certain people believe that race is linked with characteristics that prima facie are relevant. Such beliefs persist. They are, however, unjustified by the evidence. *See, e.g.,* Block & Dworkin, "IQ, Heritability and Inequality," 3 *Phil & Pub. Aff.* 331 (1974); 4 *id.* 40 (1974). More to the point, even if it were true that such a linkage existed, none of the characteristics suggested would require that political or social institutions, or interpersonal relationships, would have to be structured in a certain way.

30. *See, e.g.,* authorities cited in note 15, *supra;* Mead, *Sex and Temperament in Three Primitive Societies* (New York: Morrow, 1935).

"These three situations [the cultures of the Anapesh, the Mundugumor, and the Tchambuli] suggest, then, a very definite conclusion. If those temperamental attitudes which we have traditionally regarded as feminine — such as passivity, responsiveness, and a willingness to cherish children — can so easily be set up as the masculine pattern in one tribe, and in another to be outlawed for the majority of women as well as for the majority of men, we no longer have any basis for regarding such aspects of behaviour as sex-linked. . . .

". . . We are forced to conclude that human nature is almost unbelievably malleable, responding accurately and contrastingly to contrasting cultural conditions. . . . Standardized personality differences between the sexes are of this order, cultural creations to which each generation, male and female is trained to conform." *Id.,* at 190–91.

A somewhat different view is expressed in Sherman, *On the Psychology of Women* (Springfield, Ill.: C. C. Thomas, 1975). There the author suggests that there are "natural" differences of a psychological sort between men and women, the chief ones being aggressiveness and strength of sex drive. *See id.* at 238. However, even if she is correct as to these biologically based differences, this does little to establish what the good society should look like. *See* pp. 30–38 *infra.*

Almost certainly the most complete discussion of this topic is Macoby & Jacklin, *The Psychology of Sex Differences* (Stanford, Cal.: Stanford U. Press, (1974). The authors conclude that the sex differences which are, in their words, "fairly well established," are: (1) that girls have greater verbal ability than boys; (2) that boys excel in visual-spacial ability; (3) that boys excel in mathematical ability; and (4) that males are aggressive. *Id.* at 351–52. They conclude, in respect to the etiology of these psychological sex differences, that there appears to be a biological component to the greater visual-spacial ability of males and to their greater aggressiveness. *Id.* at 360.

31. As H. L. A. Hart has observed in a different context, if humans had a different physical structure such that they were virtually invulnerable to physical attack or assault by other humans, this would alter radically the character or role of substantial segments of the criminal and civil law. Hart, *The Concept of Law* (Oxford: At the Clarendon Press, 1961), p. 190. But humans are, of course, not like this at all. The fact that humans are vulnerable to injury by others is a natural fact that affects the features of any meaningful conception of the good society.

32. As Sherman observes, "Each sex has its own special physical assets and liabilities. The principal female liability of less muscular strength is not ordinarily a
handicap in a civilized, mechanized, society. . . . There is nothing in the biological
evidence to prevent women from taking a role of equality in a civilized society."
Sherman, *supra* note 30, at 11.

There are, of course, some activities that would be sexually differentiated in the
assimilationist society, namely, those that were specifically directed toward, say,
measuring unaided physical strength. Thus, I think it likely that even in this ideal
society, weight-lifting contests and boxing matches would in fact be dominated,
perhaps exclusively so, by men. But it is hard to find any significant activities or institutions that are analogous. And it is not clear that such insignificant activities
would be thought worth continuing, especially since sports function in existing patriarchal societies to help maintain the dominance of males. *See* Millett, *supra* note
11, at 48–49.

It is possible that there are some nontrivial activities or occupations that depend
sufficiently directly upon unaided physical strength that most if not all women
would be excluded. Perhaps being a lifeguard at the ocean is an example. Even
here, though, it would be important to see whether the way lifeguarding had traditionally been done could be changed to render such physical strength unimportant.
If it could be changed, then the question would simply be one of whether the increased cost (or loss of efficiency) was worth the gain in terms of equality and the
avoidance of sex-role differentiation. In a nonpatriarchal society very different
from ours, where sex was not a dominant social category, the argument from efficiency might well prevail. What is important, once again, is to see how infrequent
and peripheral such occupational cases are.

33. Once again, though, I believe there is substantial evidence that to sex-role
socialization and not to biology is far more plausibly attributed the dominant causal
role in the relative child-rearing capacities and dispositions of men and women in
our and other societies.

34. *See, e.g.*, Paige, "Women Learn to Sing the Menstrual Blues," in C. Tavis
(ed.), *The Female Experience* (Del Mar, Cal.: CRM, Inc., 1973), p. 17.

"I have come to believe that the 'raging hormones' theory of menstrual distress
simply isn't adequate. All women have the raging hormones, but not all women
have menstrual symptoms, nor do they have the same symptoms for the same reasons. Nor do I agree with the 'raging neurosis' theory, which argues that women
who have menstrual symptoms are merely whining neurotics, who need only a kind
pat on the head to cure their problems.

"We must instead consider the problem from the perspective of women's subordinate social position, and of the cultural ideology that so narrowly defines the behaviors and emotions that are appropriately 'feminine.' Women have perfectly
good reasons to react emotionally to reproductive events. Menstruation, pregnancy
and childbirth—so sacred, yet so unclean—are the woman's primary avenues of
achievement and self-expression. Her reproductive abilities define her femininity;
other routes to success are only second-best in this society. . . .

". . . My current research on a sample of 114 societies around the world indi-
cates that ritual observances and taboos about menstruation are a method of con-
trolling women and their fertility. Men apparently use such rituals, along with those
surrounding pregnancy and childbirth, to assert their claims to women and their
children.

". . . The hormone theory isn't giving us much mileage, and it's time to turn it
in for a better model, one that looks to our beliefs about menstruation and women.

It is no mere coincidence that women get the blue meanies along with an event they consider embarrassing, unclean — and a curse." *Id.* at 21.

35. *See also,* Joyce Trebilcot, "Sex Roles: The Argument from Nature," 85 *Ethics* 249 (1975).

36. Thomas Nagel suggests that the educationally most talented deserve, as a matter of "educational justice," the opportunity to develop their talents to the fullest. Thomas Nagel, "Equal Treatment and Compensatory Discrimination," 2 *Phil. & Pub. Aff.* 348, 356 (1973).

I do not find the concept of educational justice a clear or even wholly intelligible one. Nor, I think, has Nagel adequately explained why this is a matter of desert at all.

37. What, if anything, the most qualified deserve because they are the most qualified is an issue I discuss more fully in the next essay, "Preferential Treatment," at pp. 68–77.

Preferential Treatment

There are few issues of contemporary institutional morality which have engendered more controversy than that of whether programs variously called programs of "affirmative action," "preferential treatment" or "reverse discrimination" are justifiable. Some are convinced that such programs in virtually all of their forms are indefensible — often on the ground that they are racist and sexist in the same way in which earlier, discriminatory practices were.[1] The programs are causally explicable, perhaps, but morally reprehensible. Other persons — perhaps a majority — are sorely troubled by these programs. They are convinced that some features of some programs, e.g., quotas, are indefensible and wrong. Other features and programs are tolerated, but not with fervor or enthusiasm. They are seen as a kind of moral compromise, as, perhaps, a lesser evil among a set of unappealing options.[2] They are perceived and reluctantly implemented as a covert, euphemistic way to do what would clearly be wrong — even racist or sexist — to do overtly and with candor. And still a third group has a very different view. They think these programs are important and justifiable. They do not see these programs, quotas included, as racist, sexist, or otherwise wrong; they see much about the dominant societal institutions that is objectionable, and they think the programs appropriate and important.[3]

I agree with the persons in the last group, and in this essay I present a defense of such programs. More specifically, I articulate and defend a set of arguments for the view that it is both right and good to have programs that take a particular characteristic of individuals — their race or sex — into account in order to increase the number of nonwhites or females in institutions such as the university, the legal system, various occupations and corporate structures. I argue for the appropriateness even of quotas of the sort that were involved in the

Bakke case[4] and declared by the majority opinion in that case to be unconstitutional.[5]

Any endeavor to justify these programs of preferential treatment, if it is to succeed, must, of course, take into account the arguments that can be mounted against these programs. Hence, I both examine the nature and strength of some of the central arguments for those programs and assess the character and force of the major arguments against them. My concern is with the moral justifiability of these programs, rather than their statutory authority or their constitutionality. However, because moral argument is an integral part of much, if not all, constitutional adjudication, I do consider some of the underlying moral arguments advanced by Mr. Justice Mosk in his majority opinion for the California Supreme Court in the *Bakke* case,[6] and some of the arguments offered by the Justices of the United States Supreme Court in their consideration of the *Bakke* case.

It is a central part of my thesis that any adequate examination of the justifiability of programs of preferential treatment must begin by locating the issues that arise in connection with this topic within the appropriate context of inquiry. It is also a central part of my thesis that most of the issues concerning the justifiability of programs of preferential treatment belong in a very general way within the context of what I have called the question of instrumentalities. That is to say, as was indicated in the preceding essay, the question of instrumentalities is the question of the permissible and appropriate way by which to alter the social reality in order to bring about a greater congruence between it and the relevant social ideal. Once one has developed the correct account of the social reality, the most defensible conception of the nature of the good society, and the most adequate theory of how the features of the social reality came about and are maintained, then the remaining question is what I term the instrumental one of the appropriateness of different programs of social change. The general issue is that of how, given the answers to these other questions, might a society both effectively and fairly move from the existing state of affairs to a closer approximation of the ideal.

Programs of preferential treatment should be viewed and assessed as instrumentalities in the sense just described. And, even if this sense of "instrumentality" is not wholly clear, it is essential to understand that such programs are instrumentalities rather than ideals. Whenever they have been proposed and defended the fundamental justificatory claim is not that they should be made a part of the *ongoing* institutional life of the good society, but rather that they should be introduced because they are a way to help bring that society into being. As I shall endeavor to make clear in what follows, if such programs are construed in this light there is much to be said on their behalf, and few, if any, of the dominant arguments against them in fact apply.

The analysis builds upon the discussion in "Racism and Sexism." I take the social reality to be the one there described — one of black disadvantage and oppression, and one of female disadvantage and oppression. I take the most attractive picture of a nonracist and nonsexist society to be one that is captured by the assimilationist ideal or one that is close to it. In this sense the structure of the entire argument that follows is an extended hypothetical one of the form: If the social reality is as described, and if the conception of the good society is the one that is in fact the desirable one to have in respect to race and sex, then the case for preferential treatment programs is as follows.[7]

It is particularly appropriate in this context to take some version of the assimilationist ideal as the one that is to be presupposed. This so because most opponents of preferential treatment programs appear to believe that such an ideal is the right one (at least in respect to race), and, further, that acceptance of this ideal is a ground for rejecting these programs. Hence, there is a special heuristic advantage in assuming the attractiveness of such an ideal and showing that programs of this type are nonetheless defensible.[8]

As is the case in respect to the justifiability of many social policies and programs, the relevant considerations and arguments can to some degree be divided into two major groups. There are, first, those that are more or less consequentialist in nature. These look primarily to the effects of these programs in terms of the goal or ideal that is sought to be attained. And there are, in addition, those that are essentially nonconsequentialist in nature and which focus largely upon what can be called considerations and arguments of justice. The latter concern such things as the rights of individuals, the fairness of institutional arrangements, distributions in accordance with what individuals deserve, and the consistent application of relevant general principles. It is a complicated, complex, and disputed issue within philosophy to what degree considerations of justice (in this general sense) properly function as a constraint upon consequentialist justifications (in this general sense), i.e., to what degree and under what conditions the fact that a given procedure, practice, or program treats persons unjustly requires the conclusion that the procedure, practice or program is unjustifiable — no matter how good or beneficial in other respects the consequences of such procedures, practices, or programs may be for others affected by them. This issue does not, however, have to be confronted directly in thinking about preferential treatment programs. For, despite what many persons believe, the arguments that programs of preferential treatment are unjust to white males are much weaker, and hence less decisive, than is commonly thought to be the case. Much of the burden of my analysis is, in fact, devoted to trying to make explicit the confusions which lead persons erroneously to conclude that these programs are ultimately unjustifiable because they are in some important sense unjust in any of the relevant respects.

Nor is this the only respect in which issues of justice enter into the debate over programs of preferential treatment. In what follows I am concerned primarily to refute the view that justice prohibits preferential treatment and to argue that consequentialist considerations combine with other considerations of justice to justify these programs as instrumentalities. Others, however, have maintained that particular aspects of justice go further and require such programs. They have, more particularly, sought to construe these programs as schemes by which compensation or restitution in the form of more desirable and valuable places in the social institutions is paid to minorities to which it is owed by the whites who owe it and who pay it through their replacement in the relevant social slot by the minority group member.

Much of the philosophical literature on preferential treatment is devoted to this issue.[9] The question is a complicated and difficult one, in part at least because there are neither in law nor philosophy very clearly worked out principles and theories of compensation and restitution for situations such as these. While there may, in fact, be arguments of considerable power derivable from considerations of compensatory and rectificatory justice,[10] none of what constitutes my defense of the justifiability of preferential treatment programs turns on such arguments or considerations. If, as many have argued, these programs are justifiable — if not required — on grounds of compensatory justice, then there is an independent case, parallel to the one I construct, for their desirability.

I begin with the main arguments that constitute the case to be made for such programs and then turn to the arguments of justice that are thought to count so decisively against them.

II

One primary argument for preferential treatment programs is that these programs can and do function so as directly to alter the social realities in ways that are both important and desirable. There is, at present, a maldistribution of power and authority along racial and sexual lines that is a part of the social structure. Within the major political and social institutions, such as the university, the bench and the bar, the state and federal executive and legislative branches, and the corporate world, the great majority of positions are held by those who are white and male. One thing to be said for programs of preferential treatment is that by their operation they directly alter the composition of these institutions by increasing the number of nonwhites and women who in fact fill these positions of power and authority. This is desirable in itself because it is a redistribution of positions in a way that creates a new social reality—one which more nearly resembles the one captured by the conception of the good society. For, if what is sought is a society in which the places of significance will be held to a substantially greater degree than they are at present by persons who are nonwhite and female, then these programs quite directly and necessarily make alterations in this direction. They produce a social reality in which these individuals are present in a way in which they previously were not. To be sure, the ideal invoked contains within it the expectation that these positions will eventually be distributed without regard to either race or sex as relevant characteristics. But the argument is not inconsistent with that expectation; its claim is that such an ideal can be plausibly brought more fully into being only if there is first a redistribution of the place holders within the existing institutional arrangements.

Although the argument has the air of paradox to it, it is rather plausible. For one thing, such a reallocation of status puts members of these groups into positions where they can provide services which directly enrich and benefit the lives of other members of these groups in a way which is not done by the institutions as presently constituted. To the degree to which the present distribution of services and goods is unfair to members of these groups, the distributional change is justifiable simply because it is now a more just distribution. Furthermore, to the degree to which this occurs the social reality is altered so as to make it more likely that all members of these groups will be in a position to participate more fully in the important social institutions. This is something that the existing social reality now makes difficult; the programs help to break the systemic, exclusionary character of the present arrangement and in this way make additional, desirable change easier and more probable.

Concomitantly, the ideological component of the social reality is altered. The presence of nonwhites and women in positions from which they have historically been excluded or in which they have been vastly underrepresented aids in altering the conception of the kinds of individuals who are seen as appropriately the holders of such positions of prestige and influence. Members of the excluded or underrepresented groups are more inclined to see themselves as potential holders of such positions. They are, by the operation of these programs, provided with role models which make becoming a lawyer, doctor, corporate executive, university professor, and the like, now a more plausible aspiration. And the prevailing conception, held implicitly to some degree or other by most members of the society, that these positions are appropriately held in large numbers by white males is also to some degree transformed. Once again, the claim is that in these ways the programs serve as a mechanism which by its presence alters the self-perpetuating character of the existing social reality.[11]

In addition, there is an important respect in which the programs in some contexts can have a different kind of effect upon ideology—upon the way in which issues and problems are themselves thought about within the society. This can be seen most clearly in the case of institutions such as the university and the legal system. Consider, for example, one of the more traditional conceptions of the function of the university, the search for truth. One argument for programs of preferential treatment is that the addition of minority persons and women to the student body and the faculty will, *ceteris paribus,* increase substantially the likelihood that important truths, which would otherwise have gone undiscovered, will be discovered. To the degree to which this occurs, minority group membership is by itself a good although not sufficient reason for admitting a minority group student or appointing a minority group faculty member.

The crucial premise of this argument is the second one. The question it raises is whether it is reasonable to suppose that minority group membership is connected in a significant, special way with the success of the university's ongoing search for truth.

One way to see that it might be so connected is to see that in many, if not all, disciplines the ways in which the problems of that discipline get defined have a substantial effect upon what eventually comes to be known and believed to be true. Now, again, it is hardly a radical suggestion to observe that substantial progress in inquiry often occurs when someone succeeds in rendering problematic what was hithertofore deemed an obvious truth or what was not even previously seen to be an assumed fact. The link between minority group membership and significant, intellectual inquiry is forged, on this argument, through the special likelihood that minority group persons (and especially minority group academicians) will tend to define conventional intellectual problems in new and different ways and will tend to perceive more easily unnoticed assumptions that would otherwise have gone unexamined and unchallenged.

The next step in the argument consists in making out the case that women and members of minorities would, within the university, tend to probe received wisdom and unnoticed assumptions. And here, once again, the analysis of the existing social reality is what makes this belief plausible. Because of the significance of race and sex,[12] it is reasonable to believe that persons from these groups will tend to look at the world and will tend to define problems differently from the way white males are inclined to do so.

Although the evidence is of necessity impressionistic, in the two fields I know best — law and philosophy — I think there is no question but that both academic and nonacademic theoreticians do now look at any number of problems and issues differently because of the recent addition of members of these groups to the student body and the faculty that has come about in response to the complaints made about the previous composition of the university. A new awareness of the many and peculiar ways in which the legal system has treated the offense of rape is one obvious example;[13] a more critical recognition of the United States Supreme Court's dependence on a conception of the importance of white interests and dominant white values in cases involving the most familiar type of racial discrimination is another;[14] and a reassessment of the moral problems of abortion is still a third.[15] The general claim seems, of course, more plausible in the case of the humanities and the social sciences than it does in some of the natural sciences. So it cannot hold across the board, but where it does, it is an independent argument for these programs.

Two features of this claim are worth special mention. In the first place, for reasons already discussed,[16] it may be difficult to get the thesis taken seriously because part of the characteristic white male point of view consists in the belief that reasonably well-educated, well-intentioned white males possess the capacity to view both social and natural phenomena in a detached, objective, nondistorted fashion. Sometimes, of course, this view derives simply from a more general one concerning the comparable objectivity of all persons similarly situated. More often and more interestingly, however, the view is one that white males tend to hold exclusively about themselves. That is to say, they are quite ready and eager to acknowledge that others — members of various racial groups, or women — do look at the world, approach problems, define issues, etc., through particular, nonobjective points of view. But while this is something others do, it is not something that they do, for they possess the capacity and the detachment to look at things fairly, comprehensively, and completely — in short, to view things as they really are.

If this often is a part of the white male outlook, then this creates a metaproblem at the outset. For among the assumptions of the white male point of view that it will be hardest to call into question is the assumption of the typical detachment, neutrality, and objectivity of the white, middle-class males — and they are the ones who in overwhelming numbers do make up the faculties of our universities.

In the second place, it is important to be clearer about how extensive the thesis is. Some might be inclined to accept it only because they interpret it in an unduly restrictive fashion, as the claim that the race or sex of the persons involved will make a substantial difference in the way issues get thought about only where the matters under consideration themselves directly involve race or sex. That is to say, the thesis might be deemed plausible only in circumstances where one's interest as a member of a minority group is somehow directly relevant. I think, however, that this is an unnecessarily cramped conception of the general point. A more ambitious interpretation of the thesis certainly seems both possible and plausible; it regards the race or sex of the relevant individuals as affecting their points of view in respect to many matters that are not directly racial or sexual.

An example drawn from the law can be instructive. Consider the question of whether it is important for different minorities to be present on juries and, if so, why it is important. One view which is both dominant and overly simplistic is that minority representation is important only if, or because, all jurors will tend to act upon straightforward prejudices as jurors. White jurors will, for instance, tend to vote against black defendants and black jurors will tend to vote in favor of them — irrespective, to some degree, of the evidence. Within this view minority representation makes sense as the way to cancel the unfair voting of other interests.[17] Because this is by no means the most obvious or sensible way to think about the behavior of jurors, it is not, therefore, surprising that judges act unsympathetically toward demands for minority representation on juries in cases in which the defendants are members of a minority. If this were all there were to the claim that white jurors cannot, say, give a black person a fair trial, it would be a rather unconvincing, highly limited claim.

But the point is that this is not the only way to think about things. A black person may not be able to get a fair trial from an all white jury even though the jurors are disposed to be fair and impartial, because the whites may unknowingly bring into the jury box a view about a variety of matters, which affects in very fundamental respects the way they will look at and assess the facts. Thus, for example, it is often not a part of the experience of most white persons who serve on juries that police lie in their dealings with people and the courts. Indeed, it is probably not part of their experience that persons lie about serious matters except on rare occasions. And they themselves tend to take truth telling very seriously. As a result, white persons for whom these facts about police and lying are a part of their explicit beliefs and implicit assumptions about the world will have very great difficulty taking seriously the possibility that the inculpatory testimony of a police witness is a deliberate untruth. However, it may also be a part of the social reality that many black persons, just because they are black, have had encounters with the police in which the police were at best indifferent to whether they, the police, were speaking the truth. And even more black persons may have known a friend or a relative who has had such an experience. As a result, a black juror might be appreciably more likely than his or her white counterpart to approach skeptically the testimony of ostensibly neutral, reliable witnesses such as police officers. The point is not that all police officers lie; nor is the point that all whites always believe everything police say and blacks never do. The point is that because the world we live in is the way it is, it is likely that whites and blacks may on the whole be disposed to view the credibility of police officers very differently. If this is so, the legal system's election to ignore this reality, and to regard as fair and above reproach the familiar occurrence of all-white juries (and white judges) deciding cases, provided only there was no intentional or otherwise systematic exclusion of blacks from the selection process, directly affects the way in which issues of credibility will be determined and justice dispensed in a wide variety of cases.[18]

It is this same kind of argument that applies to the university as well as to the legal system and other institutions. If there are distinctive points of view that are typically connected with minority group membership, then the case for programs which make this identity relevant is in part the case for a useful and valuable type of intellectual pluralism which advances the pursuit of knowledge and the fair resolution of social issues. Here, too, the programs are instrumentally justified in that they are not offered as constituents of the good society, but as one means by which to more nearly bring it into being.

Sometimes opponents of programs of preferential treatment do oppose them on the ground that they will have bad consequences and that they do not or will not work very efficiently or well, although, as will be seen, that is seldom the core of their objection. For example, near the conclusion of his opinion for the majority of the California Supreme Court in the *Bakke* case, Justice Mosk asserted that there were forceful policy reasons against preferential treatment programs based on race. "The divisive effect of such preferences," he said, "needs no explication and raises serious doubts whether the advantages obtained by the few preferred are worth the inevitable cost to social harmony. The overemphasis upon race as a criterion will undoubtedly be counterproductive. . . . Pragmatic problems are certain to arise in identifying groups which should be preferred or in specifying their numbers, and preferences once established will be difficult to alter or abolish. . . ."[19] And Mr. Justice Powell in his opinion in the *Bakke* case pointed to similar matters when he observed both that ". . . preferential programs may only reinforce common stereotypes holding that certain groups are unable to achieve success without special protection based on a factor having no relationship to individual worth," and that "[d]isparate constitutional tolerance of such classifications well may seem to exacerbate racial and ethnic antagonisms rather than alleviate them."[20]

While I do not believe that most opponents of these programs base their opposition primarily on the ground that such programs cannot or will not bring about or create the kinds of desirable changes described above, it must, however, certainly be conceded, that if it were to turn out, as the Justices and others have predicted, that programs of this sort will in fact exacerbate prejudice and hostility, thereby making it harder rather than easier to alter the social reality so as to achieve something like an assimilationist society, that would be a reason which would count quite directly against the instrumental desirability of these programs. This would still not settle the matter, of course, for these undesirable features would still have to be balanced against all of the respects in which preferential treatment programs would advance the occurrence of the assimilationist society. They are relevant aspects of what is a complicated empirical inquiry of sorts.[21]

But there is reason to think that at least most critics of these programs do not believe these programs to be ineffective in the ways in which I have suggested they might be effective. The reason is simply that most of their arguments are concerned to make one of two rather different points. Sometimes, what looks to be an argument of this sort is in reality an argument about the undesirability of such programs within the good society. Such an objection misses the mark. For as I have indicated, the programs are not offered as constituents of the good society. Indeed, they would make no sense whatsoever within a good society of the assimilationist sort.[22] The objection is miscast and the appropriate question is whether, viewed in the ways I have suggested, such programs could be plausibly regarded as on balance effective in helping to create or bring that society about. Judgment on this matter must, therefore, be restricted to the good and bad changes included within the scope of that question.

Far more often, the core of the objection to programs of preferential treatment is that a consideration of issues of this type is not enough. The essence of the argument in opposition is instead something like this: What these programs are trying to do makes sense; it would be good if we could have the kinds of results, the kinds of alterations in the social reality, these programs do help to bring into being. It would, for example, be a good thing if somehow blacks and women were more substantially present throughout the dominant institutions; it is even a good thing that they are more present today than they have been in the past. In this sense, the changes that have occurred and that are occurring in the social reality are also a good thing. The problem, though, is that such programs go about doing so in an impermissible way. It is not that these programs are not in this sense effective or their results desirable; rather it is that efficacy or effectiveness is just not all there is to it. And when we look to these other considerations—considerations of justice—we see what is fundamentally wrong with programs of preferential treatment. They are unjust; they violate persons' rights.[23]

It is these arguments against programs of preferential treatment which must be examined in some detail.

III

One very common criticism of preferential treatment programs goes something like this: There are more questions to be asked about these programs than whether they will work reasonably well to bring about a certain result. There is also the question of the *way* they will work to bring about that end. And once one sees this then one also has to face the fact that it is simply wrong in principle ever to take a person's race into account. Or, to put what may be the same point differently, persons have a right never to have race taken into account. These programs, by definition, do just that, and that is what makes them impermissible.

A version of this position was taken by Justice Mosk in the *Bakke* case. What is impermissible, said Justice Mosk, is taking race into account where that has the effect of depriving nonminority group members of benefits they would otherwise have enjoyed.

"We cannot agree with the proposition that deprivation *based* upon race is subject to a less demanding standard of review under the 14th Amendment if the race discriminated against is the majority rather than the minority. We have found no case so holding, and we do not hesitate to reject the notion that racial discrimination may be more easily justified against one race than another. . . ."[24]

A similar view was expressed by Mr. Justice Powell in his opinion in *Bakke*. "The guarantee of equal protection cannot mean one thing when applied to one individual and something else when applied to a person of another color. If both are not accorded the same protection, then it is not equal."[25]

One difficulty with statements such as these, whether they occur in a moral or a legal context, is that without more they are incomplete as arguments. What are missing are the reasons for regarding the claim as a sound one. If persons have a right, for example, never to have race taken into account, it is important to be presented with an argument for why they ought to be viewed as having such a right. What is to be said in support of thinking about them and acting toward them in that way? If no reasons are given, it is extremely difficult to decide whether the claim that they have that right is correct. It is certainly not obvious that one just knows that persons have this particular right. When trying to think about the issue of preferential treatment it is difficult simply to "see" or to intuit the existence of this right. Claims about rights in unproblematic contexts are sometimes like descriptions of the world based upon what we directly perceive to be true; in less clear cases, however, they are more properly the conclusions of arguments. Intuitions about rights may be useful points from which to begin or even to test moral arguments, but unsupported by reasoning and analysis they run the great risk of being both ad hoc and inconclusive. In the case of preferential treatment I find it difficult to understand how an unsupported appeal to the right in question can be an intellectually satisfying determination of the issue.

There are, however, reasons and arguments that can be offered in support of this claim about this right. An opponent of programs of preferential treatment might argue that any proponent of these programs is guilty of intellectual inconsistency, if not racism or sexism itself. For, at times past, it might be pointed out, employers, universities, and many other social institutions did have racial and sexual quotas (when they did not practice overt racial or sexual exclusion), and it was clear that these quotas were pernicious. What is more, the argument might continue, many of those who were concerned to bring about the eradication of those racial quotas now seem untroubled by the new programs which reinstitute them. And this is just a terrible sort of intellectual inconsistency which at worst panders to the fashion of the present moment and at best replaces intellectual honesty and integrity with understandable but misguided sympathy. More to the point, even, if it was wrong to take race into account when blacks were the objects of racial policies and practices of exclusion, then it is wrong to take race into account when the objects of the policies have their race reversed. Simple considerations of intellectual consistency—of what it means to have had a good reason for condemning these social policies and practices—require that what was a good reason then is still a good reason now.

An argument such as this one is, I think, both common and closer to the core of the cluster of objections that many persons have to programs of preferential treatment. I think that it is a mistaken one and that recourse to the general mode of analysis I have proposed can show how it is mistaken.

It is certainly correct that the racial quotas and the practices of racial exclusion that were an integral part of the fabric of a culture, and which are still to some degree part of it, were pernicious. They were and are a grievous wrong and it was and is important that all individuals concerned to be moral work for their eradication from our social universe. Yet, one can grant all of this and still believe that the kinds of racial and sexual quotas that are a part of contemporary preferential treatment programs are commendable and right. There is no inconsistency involved in holding both views. For even if contemporary schemes that take race and sex into account are wrong, they must, I believe, be wrong for reasons different in kind from those that made quotas and the like against blacks and women wrong. The reason why depends, once again, upon an analysis of the social realities.

A fundamental feature of programs that discriminated against blacks and women was that these programs were a part of a larger social universe which systematically maintained a network of institutions which concentrated power, authority, and goods in the hands of white male individuals. This same social universe contained a complex ideology which buttressed this network of institutions and at the same time received support from it. Practices which excluded or limited the access of blacks or women into the desirable institutions were, therefore, wrong both because of the direct consequences of these practices on the individuals most affected by them and because the system of racial and sexual superiority of which they were constituents was an immoral one in that it severely and without any adequate justification restricted the capacities, autonomy, and happiness of those who were members of the less favored categories.

Whatever may be wrong with today's programs of preferential treatment, even those with quotas, it should be clear that the evil, if any, is simply not the same. Neither women nor blacks constitute the dominant social group. Nor is the conception of who is a fully developed member of the moral and social community one of an individual who is either black or female. Quotas which prefer blacks or women do not add to an already overabundant supply of resources and opportunities at the disposal of members of these groups in the way in which exclusionary practices of the past added to an already overabundant supply of resources and opportunities at the disposal of white males. If preferential treatment programs are to be condemned or abandoned, it cannot, therefore, be because they seek either to perpetuate an unjust society in which all the desirable options for living are husbanded by and for those who already have the most, or to realize a corrupt ideal of distinct classes and grades of political, social, and moral superiority and inferiority. When viewed and offered as instrumentalities for social change they do neither.

The same point can be made in a somewhat different way. Sometimes people say that what was wrong with the system of racial discrimination in the South was that it took an irrelevant characteristic, namely race, and used it systematically to allocate social benefits and burdens of various sorts. The defect was the irrelevance of the characteristic used, i.e., race, for that meant that individuals ended up being treated in a manner that was arbitrary. On this view, the chief defect of the system of racial segregation was its systemic capriciousness.

That does not seem to me to have been the central flaw at all. Consider, for instance, the most hideous of the practices, human slavery. The primary thing that was wrong with that institution was not that the particular individuals who were assigned the place of slaves were assigned that place arbitrarily because the assignment was made in virtue of an irrelevant characteristic, i.e., their race. Rather, the fundamental thing that was and is wrong with slavery is the practice itself—the fact that some human beings were able to own other human beings and all that goes with that practice and that conception of permissible interpersonal relationships. If one wants a clear case of the violation of the Kantian Categorical Imperative, if one wants a clear case of what it is to treat a person wholly as a means rather than an end in itself, human slavery is the historically real paradigm. It would not matter by what criterion persons were assigned within that institution, human slavery would still be wrong. And a comparable criticism can be made of most if not all of the other discrete practices and institutions which comprised the system of racial discrimination even after human slavery was abolished. The practices were unjustifiable—they were oppressive—and they would have been so no matter how the assignment of the victims had been made. In particular, very few of the institutions were involved in allocating either social positions or other resources in a way such that a concern for the arbitrariness of the method of selection was even an issue. As I have tried to indicate, what made it worse, still, was that the institutions and ideology were a part of a comprehensive system. The parts interlocked and that is what made it a *system* of human oppression whose effects on those living under it were as devastating as they were unjustifiable. For women and for blacks the system is less firm than at times past, but it still exists and its presence is still a central reality.

One flaw in Mr. Justice Powell's opinion is his failure to understand this. He says: The so-called white majority "itself is composed of various minority groups most of which can lay claim to a history of prior discrimination at the hands of the state and private individuals. Not all of these groups can receive preferential treatment and corresponding tolerance of distinctions drawn in terms of race and nationality. . . . There is no principled basis for deciding which groups would merit 'heightened judicial solicitude' and which would not."[26] This is wrong as a matter of history and wrong as a matter of present realities. The treatment of blacks and women was different historically from the treatment of white minority groups, even when those groups were subject to discriminatory practice. But, historical analysis to one side, the more central consideration is that there does not seem to be any way in which the contemporary programs of preferential treatment can plausibly be construed as even beginning to consign whites to the kind of oppressive status characteristically and systemically bestowed upon blacks by the dominant social institutions and the connected ideology.

Nor is the fact that contemporary programs have quotas an obvious defect. In his opinion in *Bakke,* Justice Mosk says at one point ". . . it is difficult to avoid considering the University scheme as a form of an educational quota system, benevolent in concept, perhaps, but a revival of quotas nevertheless. No college admission policy in history has been so thoroughly discredited in contemporary times as the use of racial percentages. Originated as a means of exclusion of racial and religious minorities from higher education, a quota becomes no less offensive when it seems to exclude a racial majority."[27] The history is right, the conclusion is not. Perhaps the quotas of today's program are objectionable because they do serve to restrict somewhat the access by whites to some of the positions and options that would have been open to them in the absence of the quotas. This is an issue to be discussed shortly. But the offensiveness must surely be less, not the same. When the racial majority has the great bulk of the political, economic, and social power, when members of the majority group still have the greatest access to most of the places within the desirable social institutions, when they are not in any respect systemically oppressed, then the quotas of today are not properly subjected to the same kind or degree of moral condemnation appropriately directed toward those quotas that were a part of the social system of the past.

Still another common objection is that, when used in programs of preferential treatment, race or sex is a category that is too broad in scope. Categories such as these, it is claimed, include some persons who do not have the appropriate characteristic and excludes some persons who do. Thus, Justice Mosk, for instance, thought it perfectly appropriate to give special weight to the applications for admission of those who are disadvantaged. In his view programs of preferential treatment for the disadvantaged would be constitutionally and morally permissible. "Disadvantaged applicants of all races must be eligible for sympathetic consideration, and no applicant may be rejected because of his race, in favor of another who is less qualified, as measured by standards applied without regard to race."[28] And Mr. Justice Powell said much the same when he insisted that the university examine each applicant to see what he or she can contribute to the diversity of the student body.[29] Perhaps Justices Mosk and Powell think that the problem is in part one of fit—that race, for instance, is not correlated very well with disadvantage or diversity of outlook and approach.

An objection such as this presupposes that whatever the appropriate or relevant characteristic, it is not that of being black or female. Yet, for reasons I have already tried to make clear, I cannot see why, given the social realities, it is not an appropriate characteristic to take into account directly in order to deal with the effects of the system of racial and sexual oppression. The nature of the society is such that to be black rather than white and to be female rather than male itself makes a difference in the way one can and will live.

Mr. Justice Marshall, I think, sought to make this point when he reminded his colleagues and the world that

> . . . it is more than a little ironic that, after several hundred years of class-based discrimination against Negroes, the Court is unwilling to hold that a class-based remedy for that discrimination is permissible. In declining to so hold, today's judgment ignores the fact that for several hundred years Negroes have been discriminated against, not as individuals, but rather solely because of the color of their skins. It is unnecessary in 20th century America to have individual Negroes demonstrate that they have been victims of racial discrimination; the racism of our society has been so pervasive that none, regardless of wealth or position, has managed to escape its impact. The experience of Negroes in America has been different in kind, not just in degree, from that of other ethnic groups. It is not merely the history of slavery alone but also that a whole people were marked as inferior by the law. And that mark has endured. The dream of America as the great melting pot has not been realized for the Negro; because of his skin color he never even made it into the pot.[30]

It is also important to see that this objection to the over- or underinclusiveness of race as a category is no different in kind from that which applies to much legislation and many rules. For example, in restricting the franchise to those who are eighteen and older, some who have all the other relevant qualifications for voting are excluded and some who lack them are included. The fit can seldom be precise. Suppose universities were to reconstitute their programs of preferential treatment so as to give a preference to those who were disadvantaged or who were likely to contribute to the existence of diversity, rather than to those who were black or female. They would still have to select general criteria which were to be deemed the indicia of disadvantage, e.g., family income below a certain amount or quality of

school attended. Given any usable set of criteria, there would be
some who did not meet these criteria and who were nonetheless disadvantaged. The defect, if there is one, is generic and not peculiar to
programs of racial or sexual preferential treatment.[31]

The discussion so far may appear to have avoided what is to
many a central defect of all preferential treatment programs: that
these programs are wrong because they take race or sex into account
rather than the only thing that does matter, namely, an individual's
qualifications. What all such programs have in common and what
makes them all objectionable, so the argument goes, is that they necessarily do give a preference to those who are less qualified in virtue
of their being black or female over those who are more qualified.

There are, I think, a number of features of this objection based
on qualifications that require careful examination, and the first
thing that merits notice is the implicit background assumption that
our society is one in which persons occupy positions of substantial
power and authority in virtue of their being the most qualified for
the positions. They do not. Nor, more significantly is it even a part of
the social ideology that in many cases they should be the most qualified. For example, there is no general expectation that the persons
who comprise the judiciary are either the most qualified lawyers or
the most qualified persons to be judges. The expectation here, typically, is only that they be qualified. Similarly, it would be difficult
for anyone to claim that a person such as Henry Ford II is the head of
the Ford Motor Company because among all the persons interested
in the job he is the most qualified for the job. Or that the 100 persons
who are Senators of the United States are the most qualified persons
to be Senators. Part of what is wrong with the context in which discussion about qualifications and merit usually occurs is that the argument against programs of preferential treatment derives some of
its force from the erroneous notion that we would have a meritocracy
were it only not for programs such as these. In reality, the higher the
position in terms of prestige, power, and the like, the less being the
most qualified seems ever to be a central concern. Rather, it is only
for certain classes of jobs and places that qualifications are used to do
more than establish the possession of certain minimum competencies. And, of course, all of the preferential treatment programs
which have been proposed or implemented also contain minimum
competency requirements that must be satisfied by all.

But this contextual difficulty to one side, there are also theoretical difficulties which cut much more deeply than is often recognized into the argument about qualifications. To begin with, it is im-

portant to establish what the ground of the argument is for making selections based solely upon who is the most qualified. One such argument for the exclusive relevance of qualifications — although it is seldom stated explicitly — is that the most qualified persons should be selected to perform the relevant social tasks because those tasks will then be done in the most economical and efficient manner. Now, there is nothing wrong in principle with an argument based upon the good results that will be produced by maintaining a social practice of selection based solely upon qualifications. Certainly such an argument cannot be ruled out *a priori* on the ground that it is an argument about the consequences or results. But there is a serious problem that many opponents of preferential treatment programs must confront. It may be impermissible for them to attach too much weight to an exclusive preoccupation with qualifications *on this ground,* if it was an analogous appeal to the good consequences of programs of preferential treatment that the opponent of preferential treatment thought was wrong in the first place with viewing these programs in instrumentalist terms. That is to say, as was indicated, one plausible argument offered for these programs was that they would have desirable consequences. They were in this sense potentially effective means by which to bring about a society more consonant with the appropriate conception of the good society. A central objection to that way of thinking about things was that it was concerned with consequences or effects rather than with other things that really mattered, such as considerations of justice. If, therefore, the chief thing to be said in favor of always preferring the most qualified is that this is the most efficient way of getting things done, then the inquiry has returned to an instrumental assessment of the different consequences that will flow from different programs. To be sure, programs of preferential treatment may in some areas produce a certain loss of efficiency. And if that is the case, that is a consideration of a consequentialist sort appropriately taken into account in deciding upon the justifiability of the particular program in question. It is, however, just one of the bad effects of the programs that has to be considered in conjunction with all of the other good and bad consequences of this same type that are produced by programs of this sort. What is central is that the objection fails completely to shift inquiry to a different, nonconsequentialist mode of analysis. And it was such a shift that the objection originally promised.

Nor is that all there is to be said about the argument for selection based only upon qualifications. It is important to note that qualifications, at least in the educational context, are often not even connected very closely with any plausible conception of social effectiveness. To admit the most qualified students to law school, for instance—given the way qualifications are now determined—is primarily to admit those who have the greatest chance of achieving the highest grades in law school. This says nothing directly about efficiency except perhaps that these students are the easiest for the faculty to teach. Since so little is known about what constitutes being a good, or even a successful, lawyer, and since even less is known about the correlation between being a good law student and being a good lawyer, it can hardly be claimed with the degree of confidence often exhibited by opponents of preferential treatment that the legal system will operate most effectively if those deemed the most qualified, in virtue of their test scores and the like, are alone admitted to law school.

What is more, the university situation is not even representative in its use of what might be termed "objective qualifications," such as test scores or grade point averages. When it comes to the alleged qualifications for many desirable social positions—in particular, jobs—the qualifications claimed to be required are not capable of anything resembling systematic or statistical measurement or assessment. Yet, a number of programs of preferential treatment are directed at increasing directly the number of minorities in careers such as the police force, the building trades, and the corporate structures. Traditionally, they were excluded from these desirable vocations by exclusionary policies. Today, many minority applicants are as qualified for the positions as the whites who obtained them in the past and obtain them still. The difficulty is that there are often no agreed upon, or objectively defensible, measures of relative qualification for these positions. The accepted and prevailing method of entry into these vocations can and does depend instead to some degree upon such factors as whom one knows, how one presents oneself, and the subjective, ill-defined evaluations of qualification made by those already engaged in the management and control of the activity. When conditions such as these obtain, programs of preferential treatment can be defended both because they break the chain of interlocking factors which trade upon the favored place of white males in the society and because the white males who make the subjective evaluations concerning whom to hire are not likely to do so in a wholly fair and impartial manner. Once again, this may not be because these individuals are in any deliberate or intentional fashion seeking to implement exclusionary policies, but because in a variety of subtle and unsuspected ways the lives they have lived and the ways they have been socialized will lead them to view as more qualified those who are and who act most like themselves. Both objective and subjective determinations of who is the most qualified are, therefore, often properly subject to the charge that what will count as evidence of superior qualification will have embedded within it an appreciable degree of preference for the perpetuation within institutions of those persons whose attitudes, attributes, and ways of behaving are most like those of the persons doing the selection and which have nothing much at all to do with any set of genuinely definable qualifications for the job. When this phenomenon occurs, programs of preferential treatment can be defended on the quite conventional grounds that they make it more likely than would otherwise have been the case that positions will be filled with equally or more qualified persons than would have been so in their absence. When this state of affairs exists, programs of preferential treatment are not even subject to the charge that they necessarily impair rather than promote efficiency.

The analysis cannot, however, rest upon considerations such as these. For it may surely be the case that for some social places and in some important respects there are neutral, objective, and defensible notions of qualification and of being the most qualified that are connected to the role, job, or place in question. Where such is the case, the considerations just discussed do not apply. What still remains unspecified, however, is the reason why, apart from matters of overall efficiency, selection in terms of the most qualified should be thought the fundamental, if not decisive, issue.

The argument, perhaps, is this: Selection should be made in terms of who is the most qualified because those who are the most qualified *deserve* to receive the benefits (the job, the place in law school, etc.) because they are the most qualified. The introduction of the concept of desert does make the argument a thoroughly nonconsequentialist one of the sort promised by the original objection to the programs. But now the question is whether there are grounds for thinking that the most qualified deserve anything in virtue of their being the most qualified. The grounds are more elusive than may be thought.

Consider, for example, the case of preferential treatment in respect to admission to college or graduate school. There is a gap in the inference from the claim that a person is most qualified to perform a task, e.g., be a good student, to the conclusion that he or she deserves to be admitted as a student. Even if it be conceded that those who deserve to be admitted should be admitted, it is far from clear why the most qualified students thereby deserve to be admitted.

They might deserve it if there were a discoverable general and necessary connection between the idea of being the most qualified and the idea of deserving something. But such a connection is neither as general nor as obvious as might be thought.

Suppose, for instance, that there is only one resource of a certain sort in a community and that some people are more qualified to use it than are others. That means, it seems, that they are better at using it than are others, or that they will use it better than will others. Suppose it is a tennis court. Is it clear that the two best tennis players ought to be the ones permitted to use it? Why not those who were there first? Or those who will enjoy playing the most? Or those who are the worst and therefore need the greatest opportunity to practice? Or those who have the chance to play least frequently? Each of these criteria appears to be as plausible a candidate for allocation as this idea of being the most qualified.

There might, of course, be a rule that provides that the best tennis players get to use the court before the others. If there were, it could then be said that under such a rule the best players deserve the court rather than the poorer ones. But that is primarily just to push the inquiry back one stage. There should then be a reason to think that there ought to be a rule giving good tennis players such a preference. The arguments that might be advanced for or against such a rule are many and varied, and surprisingly few of the arguments that might be offered as a justification for this rule would depend upon a connection between competence as a tennis player and deserving to use the court.

Perhaps, however, the claim is that at least in many of the relevant contexts the most able do deserve the benefits and opportunities because they are the most qualified. Apart from matters of efficiency, so the argument might go, a system based upon merit is clearly desirable. And for substantial segments of the social system the merit to be rewarded is that which manifests itself in superior ability. That, it might be concluded, is certainly the way the university is—or would be—operating were it not for these programs.

The difficulty with this argument is that it is in part tautological and in part incomplete. The tautology occurs because of the meaning of "merit." The concept of merit almost surely implies the idea of what is deserved. It is, therefore, analytic that merit is at least an appropriate condition (and perhaps the sole appropriate condition) for deserving something positive or good. If so, then it is also analytic that a system based upon merit is desirable.

This, though, says nothing so far about the connection between merit and the idea of being the most qualified in terms of ability. What is there about ability that permits an identification with the idea of merit? There is a sense in which there is tension rather than compatibility between the two concepts. For part of the idea of merit (or, to put it somewhat differently, one idea of merit) is the idea that the only kinds of things which can lead appropriately to persons meriting goods, or to the idea of personal merit, are those things which persons can claim responsibility for having brought into being, created, developed, brought to fruition, and the like. This may not be all there is to the idea of merit but it is a familiar and substantial, if not essential, component.

If this feature is given prominence, then the argument has doubtful applicability to the university and to many other institutions. Many of what are regarded as the most important characteristics for higher education have a great deal to do with things over which the individual has neither control nor responsibility: natural talent, home environment, socioeconomic class of parents, race, and the quality of the primary and secondary schools attended. Since individuals do not, therefore, merit having had any of these things vis-à-vis other individuals, they do not, for the most part, merit their qualifications. And since they do not merit their qualifications they do not in either a strong or direct sense deserve to be admitted because of their qualifications.

It is, in fact, more than a little ironic that members of the Supreme Court, among others, have failed to notice that the received view about merit and about the evil of racism also cut so deeply against most general connections between qualifications and desert.

Justice Brennan, for example, described the received view this way:

> . . . race, like gender and illegitimacy, is an immutable characteristic which its possessors are powerless to escape or set aside. . . . [Divisions resulting from such a characteristic] are contrary to our deep belief that 'legal burdens should bear some relationship to individual responsibility or wrongdoing' and that advancement sanctioned, sponsored, or approved by the State should ideally be based on individual merit or achievement, or at the least on factors within the control of an individual.[32]

If what is wrong with assigning benefits or burdens on the basis of race is that race is a characteristic which is immutable and one for which an individual is not responsible, then it is also wrong to assign benefits or burdens on the basis of any other characteristic which is immutable and for which an individual is not responsible. The theory that connects merit with the things for which an individual is responsible, or at least could partially control, has implications of a kind not often appreciated.

It is possible, to be sure, that some of the most qualified students can claim that they do deserve to be admitted to school because their qualifications are merited in virtue of the extra effort they expended in comparison with the others who also seek admission. Effort is clearly a more plausible condition for merit within this view than is, say, I.Q. or race, although there are problems with the idea of effort, too.[33] But even if effort is appropriately linked with merit and, hence, with desert, there is no general congruence between, for instance, being the most qualified applicant to the university and having been the applicant who expended the greatest amount of effort. In our society, surely, it is seldom thought relevant, and almost never decisive, to the determination of who are the most qualified that the effort expended by the applicants be first ascertained.

Effort might, however, be thought indirectly to be present and taken into account in the following way. If persons have developed reasonable expectations concerning the connection between their qualifications and their selection by an institution, and if they have relied upon these expectations, they have an additional claim of desert, deriving from the effort manifested in their reliance, to be selected on this ground as well. This claim can, however, only be made by those who reasonably developed these expectations and relied upon them. In the case of higher education, it is rather unconvincing for many applicants to maintain that the grades, test scores, and the like that they present as the qualifications in virtue of which they deserve admission over others are causally connected with their earlier reliance upon the announced criteria for admission. This is so because in the past colleges and universities almost always had announced criteria which disclosed that things other than qualifications (in this sense) would be taken into account, e.g., athletic ability, relationships with alumni, even geographical location of the applicant. As a result, it could not have been reasonable in respect to most colleges and universities for persons to have expected selection to have been made *solely* on the basis of qualifications. In addition, the appearance of preferential treatment programs itself makes a difference. After these programs have a public existence there must come a time at which continued reliance on the existence of some other selection process is no longer reasonable. The claim of mere *de facto* reliance, and of the additional effort thereby engendered, is both implausibly derived from the educational system of the past and wholly unavailable to those whose expectations were formed after the announced implementation of preferential treatment programs of admission.

The general point is that if the only thing that is known of an individual is that he or she is the most qualified in the sense of the most able, nothing necessarily follows about what that individual deserves except, perhaps, the description of being the most qualified or the most able. More must be known about the context or the situation before determinations of desert can appropriately be made.

In a race, or in any other comparable activity the point of which is to determine the winner, there is certainly a sense in which the person who wins deserves the prize—assuming, that is, that the competition was fairly conducted and the winner fairly determined. If, in a situation such as this, we mean by "the most qualified," "the person who won the competition," then here, too, it is analytic that the most qualified deserved the prize.[34]

It might be argued, therefore, that the most able students deserve to be admitted to the university because all of their earlier schooling was part of a pure competition, with university admission being the prize awarded to the winners. On this view they deserve to be admitted simply because that is what the rule of this competition provides. Preferential treatment programs of admission, which do prefer some who are less qualified over some who are more qualified, it might be concluded, all ignore this logically required claim of desert.

For reasons already given, it is doubtful that our system of education can reasonably be construed as a pure competition of this kind. But if there is or has been a rule or a practice which connects in the requisite way performance at high school with admission to college, then there is, I think, a weak sense in which those who do well at high school deserve, for that reason alone, to be admitted—to get the prize.

The difficulty, however, is that this is a wholly intrasystemic claim of desert and, as such, is insufficient by itself to settle other questions of desert and most questions of justice. Even in cases of "pure competitions" where there is an analytic connection between being the most qualified and deserving the prize, there are further justificatory inquiries appropriately undertaken. One very important one is whether it is desirable to continue to have such competitions; another is how much significance ought to be attached to them — either because of short- and long-term effects that they have on the individuals directly involved, or because of the way they affect a society's view of itself and its view of the value of these and other forms of human activity and interaction. For any intrasystemic claim of desert, the genuine strength of the claim depends in substantial measure upon the defensibility of the system which makes the intrasystemic claim possible. Thus, rule-based claims of desert are always incompletely defended or justified unless and until the rule which creates the claim is itself shown to be justifiable. For this reason, unless one has a strong preference for the status quo, and unless one can defend that preference, the existence of a practice of allocating places within a system in a certain way does not by itself go very far at all in showing that that is the genuinely right, just, or desirable way to continue to allocate those places. By itself it certainly is not a strong enough kind of claim to defeat either morally based claims of justice or all claims based upon consequences of a morally relevant sort.

It is also evident that there are other kinds of cases which are manifestly not pure competitions. These cases are distinguished by the fact that the sole point is not to determine, within the confines of the competition, who the winner is and who thereby deserves the prize. The educational system falls unmistakably within this category rather than within the class of pure competitions. What, then, of the relevance of qualifications in these more complex situations? In some of the cases it will surely be very important that great weight be attached to the determination of who in fact is the most qualified, and it will be both reasonable and important to allocate the places within these activities very largely, if not exclusively, on the basis of the qualifications of the individuals seeking the positions. As among the applicants who desire to be neurosurgeons or commercial airline pilots, it seems defensible to make the process of selection depend heavily, if not solely, on their respective abilities. But the argument for doing so is not that they *deserve* to be selected because they are the most qualified. Instead, the argument for doing so is that, all things considered, it is good to make the selection on that basis. The severity of the risks to others, as well as considerations of efficiency, are what justify attaching so much importance to the selection of those who are the most qualified in terms of ability or competence.

Yet, even in cases such as these, it is in principle still an open and contingent question whether qualifications determined solely by ability ought to be the only relevant criteria. Where the differences in ability are very slight so that, for instance, the differences in levels of performance are correspondingly small, there is no reason in principle why other criteria, such as the race or sex of the individuals could not justifiably be taken into account in order to achieve a better result overall.

What is significant for any well-founded appraisal of programs of preferential treatment is how dissimilar are most of the social activities with which those programs are typically concerned from the sorts of cases just described. To be a member of a student body, even to be a member of a faculty, to say nothing of being a banker, lawyer, policeman, or corporate executive, is not in the usual case very much like being a violinist in the Philadelphia Orchestra, a neurosurgeon, or the pilot of a commercial 747. What the former do have in common is the need for certain, identifiable competencies. What differentiates them from the latter cases is that many persons may be fully competent to perform the task or assume the role and not be the most able of applicants.

Preferential treatment programs typically, if not invariably, do regard qualifications, specified in terms of competency or ability, as decidedly relevant, and it is inacccurate to suppose that they do not. They do so for several reasons. In the first place, given the existing structure of any institution, there is almost always some minimal set of qualifications without which one cannot participate meaningfully within the institution. In addition, there is no question but that the degree of competence of those involved in the enterprise or institution will affect the way the institution works and the way it affects others in the society. The consequences will vary depending upon the particular institution. Considerations such as these are always, therefore, an appropriate part of the calculus. But all of this only establishes that qualifications are relevant, not that they are decisive. Thus, this concern for qualifications is wholly consistent with the claim that race or sex is today also properly relevant when it comes to matters such as admission to college or law school, or entry into the more favored segments of the job market. And that is all that any preferential treatment program—even one with the kind of quota involved in the *Bakke* case—has ever sought to establish. The general case against such programs has, in short, yet to be made, while the case for them remains persuasive.

NOTES

1. *See, e.g.*, Brief for the Anti-Defamation League of the B'nai B'rith as Amicus Curiae on Appeal, DeFunis v. Odegaard, 416 U.S. 312 (1974); Graglia, "Special Admission of the 'Culturally Deprived' to Law School," 119 *U. Pa. L. Rev.* 351 (1970); Gross, *Discrimination in Reverse: Is Turnabout Fair Play?* (New York: New York U. Press, 1978); Lavinsky, "DeFunis v. Odegaard: The Non-Decision with a Message," 75 *Colum. L. Rev.* 520 (1975).

A number of the relevant philosophical articles are collected in Gross (ed.), *Reverse Discrimination* (Buffalo, N.Y.: Prometheus Books, 1977).

2. *See, e.g.*, Nagel, "Equal Treatment and Compensatory Discrimination," 2 *Phil. & Pub. Aff.* 348, 362 (1973).

3. Among those who have defended such programs, in one form or another, are Askin, "The Case for Compensatory Treatment," 24 *Rut. L. Rev.* 65 (1964); Bell, "In Defense of Minority Admissions Programs: A Reply to Professor Graglia," 119 *U. Pa. L. Rev.* 364 (1970); Ely, "The Constitutionality of Reverse Discrimination," 41 *U. Chi. L. Rev.* 723 (1974); Hughes, "Reparations for Blacks," 43 *N.Y.U. L. Rev.* 1063 (1968). Some, but by no means all, of the relevant philosophical articles are collected in *Reverse Discrimination, op. cit., supra* note 1. The precise programs vary greatly, as do the reasons offered to justify them.

4. Regents of the University of California v. Bakke, 98 S. Ct. 2733 (1978).

5. They are quotas in the sense that they set aside a certain number of places for minorities or women and, provided the applicants possess the requisite minimum abilities, they are preferred for those places over those white male applicants who present higher qualifications.

6. Bakke v. Regents of the University of California, 18 Cal. 3d 34 (1976).

7. The antecedents of the hypothetical are incomplete because I do not specify any general explanatory theory concerning the fundamental causes of the social reality. Without such a theory of what causes and maintains the social reality, there appears to be no way to decide whether any programs of social change (instrumentalities in my nomenclature) will be effective or not. If a particular program leaves the fundamental causes unaffected, it could be argued that there is surely a sense in which the program is at best cosmetic, probably irrelevant, and perhaps counterproductive. Thus, if it were thought that the correct, fundamental explanation of the social reality of racial and sexual oppression was a Marxist one, then programs not directed at the material, economic relations of the society might be so viewed.

I do not think an objection such as this affects substantially my analysis. As I shall argue, programs of preferential treatment do change the character of the social reality in respect at least to some of the racial and sexual features of the social reality. They may be less important programs than others which work more directly at altering the less epiphenomenal, more basic features of the social reality, *e.g.*, ownership of the means of production, but that is a different matter.

My own view is that the racial and sexual features of the social reality are not reducible in any direct, or even very illuminating, way to more fundamental, nonracial and nonsexual phenomena. At a minimum, the racial and sexual features of the social reality are surely important enough phenomena (even if they are in some sense ultimately epiphenomenal) to be attacked and altered directly with significant effect. That is all my analysis requires.

8. In my discussion of preferential treatment, I shall discuss quite indiscrimi-

nately the case for preferential treatment as it relates to those who are black and to those who are female. I do not think that the arguments vary substantially depending upon which of these two characteristics is considered, and my focus upon either one to the exclusion of the other is, therefore, a matter largely of expository convenience. Others do, however, sometimes suggest that there are significant differences between the two cases. *See, e.g.,* the opinion of Justice Powell in Regents of the University of California v. Bakke, 98 S. Ct. 2733, 2755 (1978).

Sometimes, also for reasons of convenience, I will refer simply to members of minority groups. Here I am somewhat less confident whether the discussion applies without further qualification to all of the other nonwhite groups which are also often included within such programs. As I indicated in "Racism and Sexism," *supra* note 7, p. 44, whether or not they do depends upon a detailed examination of the social realities, one that is more detailed than I have undertaken. Hence, the applicability of my analysis to these groups is more clearly hypothetical in character.

I do think it a defect of the opinions of the Justices Marshall and Brennan, both of whom thought the preferential treatment program in the *Bakke* case to be constitutional, that they discussed only the position of blacks in our society. To the degree to which the justifiability of such programs does depend upon an analysis of the social realities, it is necessary that one be provided for each of the designated groups. In the case of the program at issue in *Bakke,* those groups were Blacks, Asians, American Indians, and Chicanos.

9. Much of the relevant literature is collected in *Reverse Discrimination, op. cit., supra* note 1, and in Cohen, Nagel, and Scanlon (eds.) *Equality and Preferential Treatment* (Princeton, N.J.: Princeton U. Press, 1976).

10. One major difficulty with arguments of a straightforwardly compensatory sort is that of identifying the individuals who owe compensation to the members of the groups who have been injured by the past or present system of racial or sexual oppression. That is to say, if preferential treatment programs are to be defended as compensatory schemes which award compensation to the eligible members of the relevant minority groups, then the most plausible principles of compensatory justice for injuries sustained require a fairly direct causal connection between the acts of persons causing the injury and the sufferers of the injury. It is the absence of this causal connection that critics of a compensatory rationale often focus upon.

I am uncertain whether the appropriate causal nexus can be shown to exist. I suspect there is more to be said for its existence than the critics sometimes suppose. Nonetheless, a stronger argument of a compensatory character can surely be constructed. It would depend not upon ordinary principles of compensation for injury but upon principles of unjust enrichment. Within the law there are moderately well-developed ideas of unjust enrichment which do not depend upon the person from whom a benefit or good is taken having caused injury to another. In some cases it is a sufficient justification for the transfer of a good or a benefit from one person to another that it would be unjust to allow the "innocent" possessor of the good to retain it rather than have it restored to another with a better claim to it. Cases and other materials that deal with situations of this general sort are collected in, *e.g.,* Dawson and Palmer, *Cases on Restitution* (Indianapolis: Bobbs-Merrill, 1958.) Were I to develop a defense of programs of preferential treatment within the general framework of something like compensatory justice, I would seek to make it along lines such as these.

11. An argument such as the above reveals the difficulty of classifying all arguments as either consequentialist or nonconsequentialist. It is consequentialist in the

sense that the change in the composition of the institutions is a result of the operation of the programs. It is an argument from justice both in the sense that the
changed composition of the institutions makes the institutions operate in a way that
is more just and in the sense that the distribution of places is itself a more just
distribution.

12. Here, I draw upon the analysis in "Racism and Sexism," *supra*, pp. 14–23.

13. *See, e.g.,* Wood, "The Victim in a Forcible Rape Case: A Feminist View,"
11 *Am. Crim. L. Rev.* 335 (1973); Shafer and Frye, "Rape and Respect" in
Vetterling-Braggin, Elliston, and English (eds.), *Feminism and Philosophy*
(Totowa, N. J.: Littlefield, Adams & Co., 1977), p. 333; Foa, "What's Wrong with
Rape," *id.,* p. 347.

14. *See, e.g.,* Bell "School Litigation Strategies for the 1970's: New Phases in
the Continuing Quest for Quality Schools," 1970 *Wis. L. Rev.* 247; Steel, "Nine
Men in Black Who Think White," *New York Times Magazine,* Oct. 13, 1968, p. 56;
and *see,* especially, the rich set of legal and nonlegal materials collected in Bell,
Race, Racism and American Law (Boston: Little, Brown and Co., 1973).

15. *See, e.g.,* English, "Abortion and the Concept of a Person" 5 *Canadian J.
Phil.* 233 (1975); Jaggar, "Abortion and a Woman's Right to Decide" 5 *Phil. Forum*
347 (1973-74); Thomson, "A Defense of Abortion" 1 *Phil. & Pub. Aff.* 47 (1971);
and Warren, "On the Moral and Legal Status of Abortion" 57 *The Monist* 43
(1973).

16. *See,* "Racism and Sexism," *supra.* pp. 22–23.

17. *See, e.g.,* the position of Mr. Chief Justice Burger in his dissent in Peters v.
Kiff, 407 U.S. 493, 508–09 (1972).

18. An analysis, similar to the above, was offered by Justice Marshall to explain
why a *white* defendant could challenge the systematic exclusion of blacks from the
jury rolls. The defendant could complain, Justice Marshall argued, because "[W]e
are unwilling to make the assumption that the exclusion of Negroes has relevance
only for issues involving race. When any large and identifiable segment of the community is excluded from jury service, the effect is to remove from the jury room
qualities of human nature and varieties of human experience, the range of which is
unknown and perhaps unknowable. It is not necessary to assume that the excluded
group will consistently vote as a class in order to conclude, as we do, that its exclusion deprives the jury of a perspective on human events that may have unsuspected
importance in any case that may be presented." *Id.* at 503–04 (footnote omitted).

Given an argument such as the one I have presented, it would be the case that
any defendant is disadvantaged by the absence of blacks from the jury, where, for
instance, the testimony of a police officer is a significant part of the prosecution
case. Because police are more apt to lie about black defendants, and because black
jurors are more apt to be sensitive to this possibility, black defendants are, I think,
especially likely to be tried unfairly by many all-white juries. What matters in terms
of fairness is that blacks be represented on particular juries; nonexclusion from the
jury rolls is certainly not obviously sufficient to guard against this evil.

19. Bakke v. Regents of the University of California, 18 Cal. 3d 34, 61–62
(1976).

20. Regents of the University of California v. Bakke, 98 S. Ct. 2733, 2753
(1978).

21. Although largely empirical, the questions of whether, how, and to what extent preferential treatment programs "work" also have a substantial nonempirical
component. There are many variables that can plausibly be taken into account,

and many differing weights to be assigned to these variables. Consequently, how one marshalls and assesses the "evidence" concerning which programs "work" and which do not, has at least as much to do with whether one believes that the programs are or are not justifiable on other grounds as it does with a disinterested marshalling of the "facts." It is partly on these grounds that I find unconvincing the ostensibly empirical arguments against the programs offered by writers such as Sowell [*Affirmative Action Reconsidered* (Washington, D.C.: American Enterprise Institute, 1975), pp. 34-40] and Glazer [*Affirmative Discrimination: Ethnic Inequality and Public Policy* (New York: Basic Books, 1976)]. This is also a feature of Justice Mosk's analysis where he asserts, for example, that "[t]he over-emphasis upon race as a criterion will undoubtedly be counter-productive." Bakke v. Regents of the University of California, 18 Cal. 3d 34, 62 (1976). To the degree to which my arguments are empirical they are, of course, also subject to the same potential for distortion.

22. They would, perhaps literally, make no sense. If race and sex were like eye color, one's race and sex would necessarily lack the significance they now possess, and none of the things that are today true of race and sex, except the physiological features, would still be true of them.

23. To an appreciable degree the opinions of Justice Mosk and Justice Powell both have precisely this ring to them. *See, e.g.,* Bakke v. Regents of the University of California, 18 Cal. 3d 34, 53-57, 61·(1976) and Regents of the University of California v. Bakke, 98 S. Ct. 2733, 2757-60 (1978).

24. Bakke v. Regents of the University of California, 18 Cal. 3d 34, 50 (1976).

25. Regents of the University of California v. Bakke, 98 S. Ct. 2733, 2748 (1978).

26. *Ibid.,* p. 2751.

27. Bakke v. Regents of the University of California, 18 Cal. 3d 34, 62 (1976).

28. *Ibid.,* p. 55.

29. Regents of the University of California v. Bakke, 98 S. Ct. 2733, 2761-64 (1978).

30. *Ibid.,* p. 2805.

31. In this connection, it is interesting to speculate about how a preferential treatment program based upon disadvantage or diversity might operate. Would it be permissible, for instance, to take the fact that a person was black into account in determining disadvantage or diversity? If so, it is hard to see how the programs declared unconstitutional in the *Bakke* case are significantly different. If it were not permissible to regard being black as relevant to disadvantage, then programs of preferential treatment based upon disadvantage would be required to close their eyes to what is probably the greatest single factor in producing disadvantage in our culture—being black. It would be especially paradoxical, to say the least, to require universities—institutions committed to some significant degree to rationality and truth—to pretend in this crucial respect that the social world was not at all the way it really was.

32. Regents of the University of California v. Bakke, 98 S. Ct. 2733, 2784-85 (1978).

33. The problems arise because it is not clear to what extent or in what respects the effort expended is something for which the individual is fully responsible. One is not, for instance, always in a position to have chosen to have the motivations that are constitutive of effort.

34. Even in this context there are other senses of "most qualified" and of "de-

sert" in which the connection may be contingent rather than analytic. For we also have the sense of "most qualified" that permits us to say that the most able (and in that sense the most qualified) sometimes do not win the race. And there is, correspondingly, a sense of "desert" in which the person who deserved the prize because he or she was the winner also did not really deserve to win in this other sense of "desert" and in which the person who was the most able did deserve to win. Here, what seems to be meant is that, but for certain adventitious circumstances, the most able individual would have won the competition rather than the less able individual who did.

The Obligation to Obey the Law

I

The question of what is the nature and extent of one's obligation to obey the law is one of those relatively rare philosophic questions which can never produce doubts about the importance of theory for practice. To ask under what circumstances, if any, one is justified in disobeying the law is to direct attention to problems which all would acknowledge to be substantial. Concrete, truly problematic situations are as old as civil society.

The general question was posed — though surely not for the first time — well over two thousand years ago in Athens when Crito revealed to Socrates that Socrates' escape from prison could be easily and successfully accomplished. The issue was made a compelling one — though once again surely not for the first time — by Crito's insistence that escape was not only possible but also *desirable,* and that disobedience to law was in *this* case at least, surely justified. And the problem received at the hand of Socrates — here perhaps for the first time — a sustained theoretical analysis and resolution.

Just as the question of what is the nature and extent of one's obligation to obey the law demanded attention then — as it has throughout social life within the body politic — it has been no less a problem in recent times. The freedom rides and sit-ins of the civil rights movement raised for many the question of whether the immorality of segregation justified disobeying the law, while at the same time the rightness of disobedience to law in the face of court-ordered school integration was insisted upon by the citizens and executives of several states. The all too awesome horrors of nuclear war seemed to some to justify responsive action including the deliberate trespass upon government-owned property. And the Vietnam War led many to propose and carry out strategies for opposing it which often included clearly illegal actions. The Vietnam War, in fact, invited consideration of a different, stronger claim: that in the light of the

Nuremberg principles one may have a duty to disobey the law of the state and that one may even be properly punished for having obeyed the law.[1]

The problem is one of continuing concern and the questions it necessarily raises are real. But even if the exigencies of contemporary life were not such as to make this topic one of continuing concern, it is one which would still be ripe for critical inquiry. In part this is so because despite their significance many of the central issues have been relatively neglected by legal or political theorists. Some of the important questions which bear upon the nature and extent of one's obligation to obey the law have been dealt with summarily and uncritically; distinguishable issues have been indiscriminately blurred and debatable conclusions gratuitously assumed.

More important is the fact that historically the topic has generally been examined from only one very special aspect of the problem. Many political philosophers who have seriously considered questions relating to one's obligation to obey the law have considered them only in the context of revolution. They have identified the conditions under which one would, if ever, be justified in disobeying the law with the conditions under which revolution would, if ever, be justified; and they have, perhaps not surprisingly, tended thereby to conclude that one would be justified in disobeying the law if, and only if, revolution itself would in that case be justified.[2]

To view the problem in a setting of obedience or revolution is surely to misconstrue it. It is to neglect, among other things, something that is obviously true — that most people who disobey the law are not revolutionaries and that most acts of disobedience of the law are not acts of revolution. Many who disobey the law are, of course, ordinary criminals: burglars, kidnappers, embezzlers, and the like. But even of those who disobey the law under a claim of justification, most are neither advocates nor practitioners of revolution.[3]

If the traditional, philosophical treatment of this subject has sometimes been unduly simplistic and restrictive, the writings of legal theorists have also often been uninstructive. Those whose daily intellectual concern is the legal system have had comparatively little to say on this subject. And many of those who have addressed the topic appear to embrace the view that justified disobedience of the law is a rare, if not impossible, occurrence. This conclusion, which I think is a mistaken one, is often assumed, rather than argued for in any extended fashion.[4]

There is still another way in which attention to the obligation to obey the law has been distorted. Much of the recent literature touching on the issue has centered upon a consideration of the topic of civil disobedience. Civil disobedience is a special way in which the law can be disobeyed. It involves public, rather than covert, disobedience; it involves peaceful behavior, rather than behavior that is violent or seriously injurious to other persons; and it is often, if not always, thought to require the willing submission to punishment for having broken the law.[5] Civil disobedience in virtue of its peaceful character and its requirement of submission to punishment may be thought to be justifiable in situations in which other types of disobedience are not. If it is taken to be the paradigm, there is a tendency to assume that civil disobedience can be the only kind of disobedience, short of revolution, that may be justifiable. To some degree civil disobedience is a discrete phenomenon that merits its own analysis. To an appreciable extent, however, it is a derivative problem within the more generic one of the obligation to obey the law. As such a preoccupation with civil disobedience can distract attention from other, more fundamental issues.

My concern in what follows is not to document the claims just made concerning either historical or contemporary thought. Rather, in very general terms I am concerned with an examination of the arguments which have been or which might be given in support of the claim that one does have an obligation to obey the law, and because there is such an obligation it is never right to disobey the law. My thesis is in some respects a weak one. It is to show that no arguments of this strength are convincing, that no matter how the context is refined there are no adequate arguments of a general sort for the proposition that it is never right to disobey the law.

To state the thesis in this manner is, however, to leave ambiguous several crucial matters. Before the relevant arguments can be properly considered, some things must be clarified.

First, there are different views which could be held concerning the nature of the stringency of one's obligation to obey the law. One such view, and the one which I shall be most concerned to show to be false, can be characterized as holding that one has an *absolute* obligation to obey the law. I take this to mean that a person is never justified in disobeying the law; to know that a proposed action is illegal is to know all one needs to know in order to conclude that the action ought not to be done;[6] to cite the illegality of an action is to give a sufficient reason for not having done it. A view such as this is not uncommon. The late President Kennedy, for example, expressed a version of the position when he said in the midst of his presidency and the earlier part of the civil rights movement:

. . . [O]ur nation is founded on the principle that obser-
vance of the law is the eternal safeguard of liberty and defiance
of the law is the surest road to tyranny.

The law which we obey includes the final rulings of the
courts as well as the enactments of our legislative bodies. Even
among law-abiding men few laws are universally loved.

But they are universally respected and not resisted.

Americans are free, in short, to disagree with the law, but
not to disobey it. For in a government of laws and not of men,
no man, however prominent or powerful, and no mob, however
unruly or boisterous, is entitled to defy a court of law.

If this country should ever reach the point where any man or
group of men, by force or threat of force, could long deny the
commands of our court and our Constitution, then no law
would stand free from doubt, no judge would be sure of his writ
and no citizen would be safe from his neighbors.[7]

A more moderate or weaker view is that which holds that,
while one does have an obligation to obey the law, the obligation is a
prima facie rather than absolute one. If one knows that a proposed
course of conduct is illegal then one has a good — but not necessarily
a sufficient — reason for refraining from engaging in that course of
conduct. Under this view, a person may be justified in disobeying the
law, but an act which is in disobedience of the law does have to be
justified, whereas an act in obedience of the law does not have to be
justified.

There is, though, a further ambiguity in this notion of a prima
facie obligation. For the claim that one has a prima facie obligation
to obey the law can come to one of two different things. On the one
hand, the claim can be that the fact that an action is an act of disobedience is something which always does count against the performance of the action. If one has a prima facie obligation to obey the
law, one always has that obligation — although, of course, it may be
overridden by other obligations in any particular case. Thus the fact
that an action is illegal is a relevant consideration in every case and it
is a consideration which must be outweighed by other considerations
before the performance of an illegal action can be justified.

On the other hand, the claim can be weaker still. The assertion
of a prima facie obligation to obey the law can be nothing more than
the claim that as a matter of fact it is *generally* right or obligatory to
obey the law. As a rule the fact that an action is illegal is a relevant
circumstance. But in any particular case, after deliberation, it might
very well turn out that the illegality of the action was not truly rele-

vant. For in any particular case the circumstances might be such that there simply was nothing in the fact of illegality which required over- riding, e.g., there were no bad consequences at all which would flow from disobeying the law in this case.[8]

Thus there are at least three different positions which might be taken concerning the character of the obligation to obey the law or the rightness of disobedience to the law. They are: (1) One has an absolute obligation to obey the law; disobedience is never justified. (2) One has an obligation to obey the law but this obligation can be overridden by conflicting obligations; disobedience can be justified, but only by the presence of overriding circumstances. (3) One does not have a special obligation to obey the law, but it is in fact usually obligatory, on other grounds, to do so; disobedience to law often does turn out to be unjustified.

Second, it must also be made clear that when I talk about the obligation to obey the law or the possibility of actions which are both illegal and justified, I am concerned solely with *moral obligations* and *morally justified* actions. I shall be concerned solely with argu- ments which seek to demonstrate that there is some sort of a connec- tion between the legality or illegality of an action and its morality or immorality. Concentration on this general topic necessarily renders a number of interesting problems irrelevant. Thus, I am not at all con- cerned with the question of why, in fact, so many people do obey the law. Nor, concomitantly, am I concerned with the nonmoral reasons which might and do justify obedience to law—the fact, for instance, that highly unpleasant consequences of one form or another are typi- cally inflicted upon those who disobey the law. Also, there are many actions which are immoral irrespective of whether they also happen to be illegal. And I am not, except in one very special sense, con- cerned with this fact either. I am not concerned with the fact that the immorality of the action itself may be a sufficient reason for con- demning it regardless of its possible illegality.

And third, my last preliminary clarification relates to the fact that there is a variety of kinds of legal rules or laws and that there is a variety of ways in which actions can be related to these rules. This is an important point because many moral philosophers, in particular, have tended to assimilate all legal rules to the model of a law that is enforced through the direct threat of the infliction by the govern- ment of a severe sanction. They have thereby tended to assume that all laws and all legal obligations can be broken or disobeyed only in the manner in which penal laws can be broken or disobeyed. That this assimilation is a mistake can be demonstrated quite readily.

There are many laws that, unlike the typical penal law, do not require or prohibit the performance of any acts at all. They cannot, therefore, be disobeyed. There are laws, for example, that make testamentary dispositions of property ineffective, unenforceable, or invalid, if the written instrument was not witnessed by the requisite number of disinterested witnesses. Yet a law of this kind obviously does not impose an obligation upon anyone to make a will. Nor, more significantly, could a person who executed a will without the requisite number of witnesses be said to have disobeyed the law. Such a person has simply failed to execute a valid will.[9] Thus, to talk about disobeying the law or about one's obligation to obey the law is usually to refer to a rather special kind of activity, namely, that which is exemplified most characteristically by actions in violation or disobedience of a penal law. It is this special type of activity which alone is the concern of my inquiry.

II

One kind of argument in support of the proposition that one cannot be justified in disobeying the law is that which asserts the existence of some sort of logical or conceptual relationship between disobeying the law and acting immorally.[10] If the notion of illegality entails that of immorality then one is never justified in acting illegally just because part of the meaning of *illegal* is *immoral*; just because describing an action as illegal is — among other things — to describe it as unjustified.[11]

A claim such as this is extremely difficult to evaluate. For one has great difficulty in knowing what is to count as truly relevant — let alone decisive — evidence of its correctness. There is, nevertheless, a supporting argument of sorts which can be made. It might go something like this:

It is a fact which is surely worth noticing that people generally justify action that *seems to be* illegal by claiming that the action *is not really* illegal. Typically an actor who is accused of having done something illegal will not defend himself or herself by pointing out that, while illegal, the conduct was nevertheless morally justified. Instead, the actor will endeavor to show in one way or another that it is really inaccurate to call the conduct illegal at all. Now it looks as though this phenomenon can be readily accounted for. People try to resist the accusation of illegality, it might be argued, for the simple reason that they wish to avoid being punished. But what is interesting and persuasive is the fact that people try as hard as they do to evade a charge of illegality even in those situations where the threat of punishment is simply not an important or even relevant consideration.

This was common during the civil rights movement. To be sure, the claim was that the preservation of segregated lunchcounters, waiting rooms, and the like was morally indefensible. But an important justification for the rightness of the actions employed in integrating these facilities in the fashion selected rested upon the insistence that the perpetuation of segregation in these circumstances was itself illegal because unconstitutional. One primary claim for the rightness of freedom rides was that these were not instances of disobeying the law. They were instead attempts to invoke judicial and executive protection of legal, indeed constitutional, rights. While there were some, no doubt, who might have insisted upon the rightness of sit-ins even if they were clearly illegal, most people were confident of the blamelessness of the participants just because it was plain that their actions were not, in the last analysis, illegal. Were it evident that sit-ins were truly illegal many were prepared to hold a different view about the rightness of sitting-in as a means to bring about integrated facilities.

Language commonly invoked in the course of disputes between nations furnishes another equally graphic illustration of the same point. In many controversies between countries the countries have relied heavily upon claims of legality and have been very sensitive to charges of illegality. They have attended to these matters to an appreciably greater extent than one would otherwise have supposed. Indeed, the character of much discussion of the Vietnam War reflected just this concern. The focus was quite directly upon whether the United States or North Vietnam were behaving illegally in pursuit or conduct of that war. Now if nations which have so little to fear in the way of the imposition of sanctions for acting illegally are nevertheless extraordinarily sensitive to charges of illegal conduct, this also may be taken as evidence of the fact that *illegality* implies *immorality*.

A similar feature was present in the controversy over the Eichmann trial. To some, the fact that the seizure and trial of Eichmann by Israel was illegal was sufficient to cast grave doubts upon the justifiability of the proceedings. To others, the charge of illegality made it necessary to demonstrate that nothing really illegal had occurred. What is significant about all this is the fact that all of the disputants implicitly acknowledged that illegality, even in this setting, was something which did have to be worried about.

Such in brief is the argument which might be advanced and the evidence of sorts which might be adduced to support it. Whether or not it is persuasive depends upon how the argument is construed.

The argument is not persuasive if it is interpreted to mean that an action can never be both illegal and morally justified. Consider, for example, the Fugitive Slave Law. That law made it a crime for anyone who came upon a slave who had escaped to fail to apprehend the slave and return the slave to his or her "owner." It seems not only possible but fully correct to say that persons who violated that law did the morally right, if not obligatory, thing—even though what they did was unmistakably illegal. I, at least, can see nothing logically odd or inconsistent about recognizing both that there was a law prohibiting this conduct and that further questions concerning the rightness of obedience were relevant and, perhaps, decisive. Thus I can see nothing logically odd about describing this as a case in which refusing to return an escaped slave was both illegal and morally justified.

There is, no doubt, a heroic defense which can be made to the above. It would consist of the insistence that the activity simply cannot have been both illegal and justified. Two alternatives are possible. First, one might argue that failing to return a slave would indeed have been justified if the law had not been otherwise. But since it was, violations were wrong. Now if this is a point about the appropriateness of kinds of reasons, I can only note that referring the action to a valid law does not seem to preclude asking meaningful questions about the obligatoriness or rightness of the action. If this is a point about language or concepts it does seem to be perfectly intelligible to say that the conduct was both illegal and morally justified. And if this is, instead, an argument for the immorality of ever disobeying a valid law, then it surely requires appreciable substantiation and not mere assertion.

Second, one might take a different line and agree that other questions can be asked about the conduct, but that is because failing to return a slave simply cannot have been illegal. The difficulty here, however, is that it is hard to understand what is now meant by *illegal*. The problem is that were we to satisfy all the usual tests that we do invoke when we determine that a given course of conduct is illegal, and were someone still to maintain that because it was morally justifiable not to have returned escaped slaves it cannot have been illegal, then the burden is on the proponent of this view to make clear how we are to decide when conduct is or was illegal.[12] And it would further be incumbent upon such a person to demonstrate what seems to be highly dubious, namely, that greater clarity and insight could somehow be attained through a radical change in our present terminology. It appears to be a sufficient refutation to observe that there has never been a legal system whose criteria of validity — no matter how sophisticated, how rational and how well-defined — themselves guaranteed that morally justified action would never be illegal.

Thus, construed as an argument of this strength, it fails. There is, however, a weaker version which is more appealing. If it is true that there is something disturbing about justifying actions that are conceded to be illegal, then one way to account for this is to insist that there is a logical connection between the concepts involved, but it is something less than the kind of implication already discussed. Perhaps it is correct that *illegal* does not entail *immoral; illegal* might nevertheless entail *prima facie immoral.* The evidence adduced tends to show that among one's moral obligations is the prima facie duty to obey the law.[13] Or, to put the matter somewhat differently, the illegality of an action is on conceptual grounds always a moral reason that counts against its rightness.

Once again, I find it exceedingly difficult to know precisely what to make of such a claim. It is hard to know how one is to decide what is to count as genuinely relevant or convincing evidence and, therefore, whether the evidence is persuasive. At a minimum, it is not difficult to imagine several equally plausible alternative explanations of the disturbing character of accusations of illegal activity, and to construct alternative theories all of which appear able to take the relevant, unproblematic cases into account.[14] In addition, to know only that one has a prima facie duty to obey the law is not to know a great deal. In particular, one does not know how or when that obligation can be overridden. And, of course, even if it is correct that acting illegally logically implies acting prima facie immorally, this in no way shows that people may not often be morally justified in acting illegally. At most, it demands that they have some good reason for acting illegally; at most, it requires what has already been hypothesized, namely, that the action in question, while illegal, be morally justified.

What is clear, I believe, is that if the case against *ever* acting illegally is to be made out, conceptual analysis alone cannot do it. Arguments of quite another sort must be forthcoming. And it is to these that I now turn.

III

One such argument, and it is probably the most common argument advanced, goes something like this: The reason why one ought never to disobey the law is simply that the consequences would be disastrous if everybody disobeyed the law. The reason why disobedience is never right becomes apparent once we ask the question "But what if everyone did that?"

Consider the case of a person who has to decide whether he or she is justified in disobeying the law in a particular case. If there is only a prima facie obligation (even of the strong sort) to obey the law, it is certainly possible that the person could justifiably decide that in this case the prima facie obligation is overridden by more stringent conflicting obligations. Or, if the person is a consequentialist, he or she might rightly conclude in any particular case that the consequences of disobedience would on the whole be less deleterious than those of obedience. These possibilities are inevitable if the obligation to obey the law is thought of in any nonabsolute way. And this shows what is mistaken about them. They neglect the most crucial factor of all, namely, that one is disobeying the law. Just imagine what would happen if everyone went around disobeying the law. The alternatives are obedience to the law or general disobedience. The choice is between social order and chaos. As President Kennedy correctly observed, if any law is disobeyed, then no law can be free from doubt, no citizen safe from his neighbor.

Such an argument, while perhaps overdrawn, is, as I have suggested, by no means uncommon.[15] Yet, as it stands, it is an essentially confused one. Its claims, if they are to be fairly evaluated, must be delineated with some care.

At a minimum, the foregoing attack upon the possibility of justified disobedience might be either one or both of two radically different kinds of objection. The first, which relates to the consequences of an act of disobedience, is essentially a *causal* argument. The second questions the *principle* that any proponent of justified disobedience invokes. As to the causal argument, it is always relevant to point out that any act of disobedience may have certain consequences simply because it is an act of disobedience. Once the occurrence of the act is known, for example, expenditure of the state's resources may become necessary. The time and energy of the police will probably be turned to the task of discovering who it was who did the illegal act and in gathering evidence relevant to the offense. And other resources might be expended in the prosecution and adjudication of the case against the perpetrator of the illegal act. Illustrations of this sort could be multiplied, no doubt, but I do not think either that considerations of this sort are very persuasive or that they have been uppermost in the minds of those who make the argument now under examination. Indeed, if the argument is a causal one at all, it consists largely of the claim that any act of disobedience will itself cause, to some degree or other, general disobedience of all laws; it will cause or help to cause the overthrow or dissolution of the state. And while it is possible to assert that any act of disobedience will tend to further social disintegration or revolution, it is much more difficult to see why this must be so.

The most plausible argument would locate this causal efficacy in the kind of example set by any act of disobedience. But how plausible is this argument? It is undeniable, of course, that the kind of example that will be set is surely a relevant factor. Yet, there is nothing that precludes any proponent of justified disobedience from taking this into account. If, for example, others will somehow infer from a particular act of otherwise justifiable disobedience that they are justified in disobeying *any* law under *any* circumstances, then the actor ought to consider this fact. This is a consequence — an unfortunate one in this case — of the act of disobedience. Similarly, if others will extract the proper criterion from the act of disobedience, but will be apt to misapply it in practice, then this too ought to give the actor pause. It, too, is a consequence of acting.[16] But if the argument is that disobedience would be wrong even if no bad example were set and no other deleterious consequences were likely, then the argument must be directed against the principle the actor appeals to in disobeying the law, and not against the consequences of the disobedience at all.

As to the attack upon a principle of justified disobedience, as a principle, the response "But what if everyone disobeyed the law?" does appear to be a good way to point up both the inherent inconsistency of almost any principle of justified disobedience and the manifest undesirability of adopting such a principle. Even if one need not worry about what others will be led to do by one's disobedience, there is surely something amiss if one cannot consistently defend one's right to do what one is claiming one is right in doing.

In large measure, such an objection is unreal. The appeal to "But what if everyone did that?" loses much, if not all, of its persuasiveness once we become clearer about what precisely the "did that" refers to. If the question "But what if everyone did that?" is simply another way of asking "But what if everybody disobeyed the law?" or "But what if people generally disobeyed the laws?" then the question is surely quasi-rhetorical. To urge general or indiscriminate disobedience to laws is to invoke a principle that, if coherent, is very difficult to defend. It is equally plain, however, that with few exceptions such a principle has never been seriously espoused. Anyone who claims that there are actions that are both illegal and justified surely need not be thereby asserting that it is right generally to disobey all laws or even any particular law. It is surely not inconsistent to assert both that indiscriminate disobedience is indefensible and that discriminate disobedience is morally right and proper conduct. Nor, analogously, is it at all evident that a person who claims to be justified in performing an illegal action is thereby committed to or giving endorsement to the principle that the entire legal system ought to be overthrown or renounced. At a minimum, therefore, the appeal to "But what if everyone did that?" cannot by itself support the claim that one has an absolute obligation to obey the law—that disobeying the law can never be fully justified.

There is, however, a distinguishable but related claim which merits very careful attention—if for no other reason than the fact that it is widely invoked by philosophers who discuss in a very general way issues of this sort. The claim is simply this: While it may very well be true that there are situations in which a person will be justified in disobeying the law, it is surely not true that disobedience can ever be justified solely on the grounds that the consequences of disobeying the particular law were in that case on the whole less deleterious than those of obedience.[17]

This claim is particularly relevant at this juncture because one of the arguments most often given to substantiate it consists of the purported demonstration of the fact that any principle must itself be incoherent if it contains a proviso permitting a general appeal to consequences. One of the more complete statements of the argument reads as follows:

> Suppose, . . . that I am contemplating evading the payment of income taxes. I might reason that I need the money more than the government does, that the amount I have to pay is so small in comparison with the total amount to be collected that the government will never miss it. Now I surely know perfectly well that if I evade the payment of taxes this will not cause others to do so as well. For one thing, I am certainly not so foolish as to publicize my action. But even if I were, and the fact became known, this would still not cause others to do the same, unless it also became known that I was being allowed to get away with it. In the latter case the practice might tend to become widespread, but this would be a consequence, not of my action, but of the failure of the government to take action against me. Thus there is no question of my act being wrong be-

cause it would set a bad example. It would set no such example, and to suppose that it must, because it would be wrong, is simply a confusion. . . . Given all this, then, if the reasons mentioned would justify me in evading the payment of taxes, they would justify everyone whatsoever in doing the same thing. For everyone can argue in the same way — everyone can argue that if he breaks the law this will not cause others to do the same. The supposition that this is a justification, therefore, leads to a contradiction.

I conclude from this that, just as the reply "Not everyone will do it" is irrelevant to the generalization argument, so is the fact that one knows or believes that not everyone will do the same; and that, in particular, the characteristic of knowing or believing that one's act will remain exceptional cannot be used to define a class of exceptions to the rule. One's knowledge or belief that not everyone will act in the same way in similar circumstances cannot therefore be regarded as part of the circumstances of one's action. One's belief that not everyone will do the same does not make one's circumstances relevantly different from the circumstances of others, or relevantly different from those in which the act is wrong. Indeed, on the supposition that it does, one's circumstances could never be specified, for the specification would involve an infinite regress.[18]

This argument is open to at least two different interpretations. One quite weak interpretation is this: A person cannot be morally justified in acting as he or she does unless the person is prepared to acknowledge that everyone else in the identical circumstances would also be right in acting the same way. If the person insists that he or she is justified in performing a certain action because the consequences of acting in that way are more desirable than those of acting in any alternative fashion, then that person must be prepared to acknowledge that anyone else would also be justified in doing that action whenever the consequences of doing that action were more desirable than those of acting in any alternative fashion. To take Singer's own example: A person, A, could not be morally justified in evading the payment of her taxes on the grounds that the consequences of nonpayment were in her case more beneficial, all things considered, than those of payment, unless A were prepared to acknowledge that any other person, X, would also be justified in evading his, i.e., X's taxes, if it is the case that the consequences of X's nonpayment would in X's case be more beneficial, all things considered, than those of payment. If this is Singer's point, it is, for reasons already elaborated, unobjectionable.[19]

But Singer seems to want to make a stronger point as well. He seems to believe that even a willingness to generalize in this fashion could not justify acting in this way. In part his argument appears to be that this somehow will permit everyone to justify nonpayment of taxes; and in part his argument appears to be that there is a logical absurdity involved in attempting to make the likelihood of other people's behavior part of the specification of the relevant consequences of a particular act. Both of these points seem to me to be wrong. To begin with, on a common sense level it is surely true that the effect which one's action will have on other people's behavior is a relevant consideration. For as was pointed out earlier, if A determines that other people will be, or may be, led to evade *their* taxes even when the consequences of nonpayment will in their cases be less beneficial than those of payment, then this is a consequence of A's action which A must take into account and attempt to balance against the benefits which would accrue from A's nonpayment. Conversely, if for one reason or another A can determine that her act of nonpayment will not have this consequence, this, too, must be relevant. In this sense, at least, other people's prospective behavior is always a relevant consideration.

More importantly, it is also a mistake to suppose that permitting a general appeal to consequences would enable everyone to argue convincingly that they are justified in evading their taxes. Even if I adopt the principle that everyone is justified in evading their taxes whenever the consequences of evasion are on the whole less deleterious than those of payment, this in no way entails that I or anyone else will always, or ever, be justified in evading my taxes. It surely need not turn out to be the case—even if no one else will evade their taxes—that the consequences will on the whole be beneficial if I succeed in evading mine. It might surely be the case that I will spend the money saved improvidently or foolishly; it might very well be true that the government will make much better use of the money. Indeed, the crucial condition which must not be ignored and which Singer does ignore is the condition which stipulates that the avoidance of one's taxes in fact be optimific, that is, more desirable than any other course of conduct.

The general point is simply that it is an empirical question—at least in theory—what the consequences of any action will be. And it would surely be a mistake for me or anyone else to suppose that that action whose consequences are most pleasing to me—in either the short or long run—will in fact be identical with that action whose consequences are on the whole most beneficial over all. Where the demands of self-interest are strong, as in the case of the performance of an unpleasant task like paying taxes, there are particular reasons for being skeptical of one's conclusion that the consequences of non-payment would in one's own case truly be beneficial. But once again there is no reason why there might not be cases in which evasion of taxes would be truly justified, nor is there any reason why someone could not consistently and defensibly endorse nonpayment whenever these circumstances were in fact present.

There is one final point which Singer's discussion suggests and which does appear to create something of a puzzle. Suppose that I believe that I am justified in deliberately trespassing on an atomic test site, and thereby disobeying the law, because I conclude that this is the best way to call attention to the possible consequences of continued atmospheric testing or nuclear war. I conclude that the consequences of trespassing will on the whole be more beneficial than any alternative action I can take. But suppose I also concede—what very well may be the case—that if everyone were to trespass, even for this same reason and in the same way, the consequences would be extremely deleterious. Does it follow that there is something logically incoherent about my principle of action? It looks as though there is, for it appears that I am here denying others the right to do precisely what I claim I am right in doing. I seem to be claiming, in effect, that it is right for me to trespass on government property in order to protest atomic testing only if it is the case that others, even under identical circumstances, will not trespass. Thus, it might be argued, I appear to be unwilling or unable to generalize my principle of conduct.

But this argument, too, is unsound, for there is a perfectly good sense in which I am acting on a principle which is coherent and which is open to anyone to adopt. It is simply the principle that one is justified in trespassing on government property whenever—among other things—it happens to be the case that one can say accurately that others will not in fact act on that same principle. Whether anyone else will at any given time act on any particular principle is also an empirical question. It is, to repeat what has already been said, one of the possible circumstances which can be part of the description of a class of situations. There is, in short, nothing logically self-contradictory or absurd about making the likelihood of even identical action one of the relevant justifying considerations. And there is, therefore, no reason why the justifiability of any particular act of disobedience cannot depend, among other things, upon the probable conduct of others.

IV

It would not be at all surprising if at this stage one were to feel considerable dissatisfaction with the entire cast of the discussion so far. In particular, one might well believe that the proverbial dead horse has received still another flaying for the simple reason that no one has ever seriously argued that people are never justified in disobeying the law. One might insist, for instance, that neither Socrates nor President Kennedy were talking about all law in all legal systems everywhere. And one might urge, instead, that their claims concerning the unjustifiability of any act of disobedience rest covertly, if not overtly, on the assumption that the disobedience in question was to take place in a society in which the lawmaking procedures and other political institutions were those which are characteristic of an essentially democratic, or free, society. This is, of course, an important and plausible restriction upon the original claim, and the arguments which might support it must now be considered.

While there are several things about a liberal, democratic, or free society which might be thought to preclude the possibility of justified disobedience, it is evident that the presence of all the important constitutive institutions *cannot* guarantee that unjust or immoral laws will not be enacted. For the strictest adherence to principles of representative government, majority rule, frequent and open elections, and, indeed, the realization of all of the other characteristics of such a society, in no way can insure that laws of manifest immorality will not be passed and enforced.[20] And if even the ideal democratic society might enact unjust laws, no existing society can plausibly claim as much. Thus, if the case against the possibility of justified disobedience is to depend upon the democratic nature of the society in question, the case cannot rest simply on the claim that the only actions which will be made illegal are those which on independent grounds it would be wrong to do.

What then are the arguments which might plausibly be advanced? One very common argument goes like this: It is, of course, true that even democratically selected and democratically constituted legislatures can and do make mistakes. Nevertheless, a person is never justified in disobeying the law as long as there exist alternative, "peaceful" procedures by which to bring about the amendment or repeal of undesirable or oppressive laws. The genuine possibility that rational persuasion and argument can bring a majority to favor any one of a variety of competing views, both requires that disapproval always be permitted and forbids that disobedience ever be allowed. This is so for several reasons.

First, it is clearly unfair and obviously inequitable to accept the results of any social decision-procedure only in those cases in which the decision reached was one of which one approves, and to refuse to accept those decisions which are not personally satisfying. If there is one thing which participation, and especially voluntary participation, in a decision procedure entails, it is that all of the participants must abide by the decision regardless of what it happens to be. If the decision procedure is that of majority rule, then this means that any person must abide by those decisions in which he or she was in a minority just as much as it means that he or she can insist that members of the minority abide when he or she is a member of the majority.

As familiar as the argument is, its plausibility is far from assured. On one reading, at least, it appears to be one version of the universalization argument. As such, it goes like this. Imagine any person, A, who has voted with the majority to pass a law making a particular kind of conduct illegal. A surely would not and could not acknowledge the right of any person voting with the minority justifiably to disobey that law. But, if A will not and cannot recognize a right of justified disobedience here, then A certainly cannot consistently or fairly claim any right of justified disobedience on his or her part in those cases in which A happened to end up being in a minority. Thus, justified disobedience can never be defensible.

This argument seems fallacious. For a person who would insist that justified disobedience was possible even after majoritarian decisionmaking could very plausibly and consistently acknowledge the right of any person to disobey the law under appropriate circumstances regardless of how that person had voted on any particular law. Consider, once again, the case of the Fugitive Slave Law. A person could surely be consistent in claiming both that circumstances made the violation of that law justified and that any comparable violation of that law would also have been right irrespective of how the actor, or anyone else, happened to have voted on the Fugitive Slave Law, or any other law. The point is simply that there is no reason why any person cannot consistently: (1) hold the view that majority decisionmaking is the best of all forms of decisionmaking; (2) participate voluntarily in the decisionmaking process; and (3) believe that it is right for *anyone* to disobey majority decisions whenever the relevant moral circumstances obtain, e.g., whenever it would be worse to obey that law than to disobey it.

But this may be deemed too facile an answer; it also may be thought to miss the point. For it might be argued that there is a serious logical inconsistency of a different sort which must arise whenever a voluntary participant in a social decision-procedure claims that not all the decisions reached in accordance with that procedure need be obeyed. Take the case of majority rule. It is inconsistent for anyone voluntarily to participate in the decision process and yet at the same time to reserve the right to refuse to abide by the decision reached in any particular case. The problem is not an inability to universalize a principle of action. The problem is rather that of making any sense at all out of the notion of having a majority decide anything — of having a procedure by which to make group decisions. The problem is, in addition, that of making any sense at all out of the fact of voluntary participation in the decision procedure — in knowing what this participation can come to if it does not mean that every participant is bound by all of the decisions which are reached. What can their participation mean if it is not even an implicit promise to abide by all decisions reached? And even if the point is not a logical one, it is surely a practical one. What good could there possibly be to a scheme, an institutional means for making social decisions, which did not bind even the participants to anything?

The answer to this argument — or set of arguments — is wholly analogous to that which has been given earlier. But because of the importance and prevalence of the argument some repetition is in order.

One can simply assert that the notion of any social decision-making procedure is intelligible only if it entails that all participants always abide by all of the decisions which are made, no matter what those decisions are. Concomitantly, one can simply insist that any voluntary participant in the decision process must be consenting or promising to abide by all decisions which are reached. But what must be recognized is that one cannot give as a plausible reason for this assertion the fact that the notion of group decision making becomes *incoherent* if anything less in the way of adherence is required of all participants. And one cannot cite as a plausible reason for this assertion the fact that the notion of voluntary participation loses all meaning if anything less than a promise of absolute obedience is inferred.

It is essential to be clear about what is and is not at issue. It is true that the notion of a group decisionmaking procedure would be a meaningless notion if there were no respects in which a group decision was in any way binding upon each of the participants. Decisions which in no way bind anyone to do anything are simply not decisions. And it is also true that voluntary participation is an idle, if not a vicious, act if it does not commit each participant to something. If any voluntary participant properly can wholly and without more ignore the decisions which are reached, then something is surely amiss.

But to say all of this is not to concede the central point the argument seeks to make. Group decisionmaking can have a point just because it does preclude any participant from taking some actions which that person might have been justified in performing in the absence of the decision. And voluntary participation can still constitute a promise of sorts that one will not perform actions which, in the absence of voluntary participation, might have been justifiable. If the fact of participation in a set of liberal political institutions does constitute a promise of sorts, it can surely be a promise that the participant will not disobey a law just because obedience would be inconvenient or deleterious to him or her. And if this is the scope of the promise, then the fact of voluntary participation does make a difference. For in the absence of the participation in the decision to make this conduct illegal, inconvenience to the actor might well have been a good reason for acting in a certain way. Thus, participation can create new obligations to behave in certain ways without constituting a promise never to disobey the law under any circumstances. And if this is the case, adherence to a principle of justified disobedience is not inconsistent with voluntary participation in the decisionmaking process.

Indeed, a stronger point can be made. The notion of making laws through voluntary participation in democratic institutions is not even inconsistent with the insistence that disobedience is justified whenever the consequences of disobedience are on the whole more beneficial than those of obedience. This is so because a promise can be a *meaningful* promise even if an appeal to the consequences of performing the promise can count as a sufficient reason for not performing the promise.[21] And if this is the case for promises generally, it can be no less the case for the supposed promise or agreement to obey the law.

Finally, even if it were correct that voluntary participation implied a promise to obey, and even if it were the case that the promise precluded disobedience on the ground that the consequences would be better were this promise to be broken in this case, all of this would still not support the conclusion that one ought never to disobey the law. It would, instead, only demonstrate that disobeying the law must be prima facie wrong, that everyone has a prima facie obligation to obey the law. This is so just because it is sometimes right even to break one's own promises. And if this, too, is a characteristic of promises generally, it is, again, no less a characteristic of the promise to obey the law.

The notions of promise, consent, or voluntary participation do not, however, exhaust the possible sources of the obligation to obey the laws of a democracy. In particular, there is another set of arguments which remains to be considered. It is that which locates the rightness of obedience in the way in which any act of disobedience improperly distributes certain burdens and benefits among the citizenry. It has been suggested, for example, that any act of disobedience to the laws of the United States is "the ultimate negation of all neutral principles, to take the benefits accorded by the constitutional system, including the national market and common defense, while denying it allegiance when a special burden is imposed. That certainly is the antithesis of law."[22]

On the surface, at least, this claim seems overly simple; it appears to be the blanket assertion that the receipt of benefits of this character by any citizen through continued, voluntary presence necessarily implies that no act of disobedience could be justified. To disobey any law after having voluntarily received these benefits would be, it seems to suggest, so unjust that there could never be overriding considerations. This surely is both to claim too much for the benefits of personal and commercial security and to say too little for the character of all types of disobedience. For even if the receipt of benefits such as these did simply impose an obligation to obey the law, it is implausible to suppose that the obligation thereby imposed would be one that stringent.

But there is a more involved aspect of Professor Wechsler's thesis—particularly in his insistence that disobedience of the law, where benefits of this kind have been received, is the negation of all neutral principles. I am not at all certain that I understand precisely what this means, but there are at least two possible interpretations: (1) Unless everyone always obeyed the law no one would receive these obviously valuable benefits. (2) Since the benefits one receives depend upon the prevalence of conditions of uniform obedience, it follows that persons who willingly receive these benefits cannot justly claim them without themselves obeying. The first has already been sufficiently considered.[23] The second, while not unfamiliar, merits some further attention.

In somewhat expanded form, the argument is this. What makes it possible for any particular person to receive and enjoy the benefits of general, personal, and economic security is the fact that everyone else obeys the law. Now, if injustice is to be avoided, it is surely the case that any other person is equally entitled to these same benefits. But one will have this security only if everyone else obeys the law. Hence the receipt of benefits at others' expense requires repayment in kind. And this means universal obedience to the law.[24]

There are two features of this argument which are puzzling. First, it is far from clear that the benefits of security received by anyone necessarily depend upon absolute obedience on the part of everyone else. It just might be the case that an even greater quantum of security would have accrued from something less than total obedience. But even if I am wrong here, there is a more important point at issue. For reasons already discussed, it is undeniable that even in a democracy a price would be paid for universal obedience — the price that was paid by even partial adherence to the Fugitive Slave Law. If this is so, then the fact that a person received benefits from everyone else's obedience does not necessarily entail that it is always unjust to fail to reciprocate in kind. The benefit of general security is not the only thing of moral importance. A greater degree of flexibility on the part of others, a general course of obedience except where disobedience was justified, might have yielded a better, or more just, result. People may, in short, have done more or less than they should have. And if they did, the fact that anyone or everyone benefited to some degree in no way requires that injustice can only be avoided through like and reciprocal conduct. If it is better, all things considered, in at least some circumstances, to disobey a law than to obey it, there is nothing wrong or unjust in bringing this about through acts of *discriminate* disobedience.

If the argument based upon the receipt of certain benefits is therefore not persuasive, neither in all cases is the argument which is derived from the way in which any act of disobedience is thought to distribute burdens unfairly among the citizenry. The argument can be put very briefly: If there is one thing which any act of disobedience inevitably does, it is to increase the burdens which fall on all the law-abiding citizens. If someone disobeys the law even for what seems to be the best of reasons, that person inevitably makes it harder — in some quite concrete sense — on everyone else. Hence, at a minimum this is a good reason not to disobey the law, and perhaps a sufficient reason as well.

This argument is appealing because there is at least one kind of case it fits very well. It is the case of taxation. For suppose the following, only somewhat unreal, conditions: that the government is determined to raise a specified sum of money through taxation, and that, in the long, if not the short, run it will do so by adjusting the tax rate to whatever percentage is necessary to produce the desired governmental income. Under such circumstances it could plausibly be argued that one of the inevitable results of a successfully executed decision to evade the payment of one's taxes—a decision made, moreover, on ostensibly justifiable grounds—is that every other member of society will thereby be required to pay a greater tax than would otherwise have been the case. Thus in some reasonably direct and obvious fashion any act of disobedience—particularly if undetected—does add to the burdens of everyone else. And surely this is to make out a strong case of at least prima facie injustice.

Now, for reasons already elaborated, it would be improper to conclude that evasion of one's taxes could never be justified. But the argument is persuasive in its insistence that it does provide a good reason why evasion always must be justified and why it will perhaps seldom be justifiable. But even this feature of disobedience is not present in many cases. Tax evasion, as opposed to other kinds of potentially justified disobedience, is a special, far from typical case. And what is peculiar to it is precisely the fact that any act of disobedience to the tax laws arguably shifts or increases the burden upon others. Such is simply not true of most types of acts of disobedience because most laws do not prohibit or require actions which affect the distribution of burdens in any very direct, or comparable, fashion.

Thus, if we take once again the case of the violation of the Fugitive Slave Law, it is extremely difficult, if not impossible, to locate the analogue of the shifting of burdens involved in tax evasion. How did the violation of that law thereby increase the "costs" to or burdens upon anyone else? The only suggestion which seems at all plausible is that which was noted earlier in a somewhat different context. Someone might argue that it is the occurrence of illegal actions which increase the cost of maintaining a police force, a judiciary, and suitable correctional institutions. This cost is a burden which is borne by the citizenry as a whole. And hence, illegal acts increase their burdens—albeit very slightly. The difficulty here is threefold. First, if the act is performed in secret and if it remains undetected, then it is hard to see how there is any shift of economic burden at all.[25] Second, given the fact that police forces, courts, and prisons will always be necessary as long as unjustified acts of disobedience are a feature of social existence, it is very likely that the additional cost, if any, is insignificant.[26] And third, the added costs, if any, are in many cases assumed by the actor *qua* member of the citizenry. A person who engages in most forms of justified disobedience is not avoiding a burden, but at most adding something to everyone's— including his or her own—social financial obligations. Thus, in cases such as these, it is not at all evident that disobedience need even be prima facie unjust and hence unjustified.[27]

V

There is one final argument which requires brief elucidation and analysis. It is in certain respects a peculiarly instructive one both in its own right and in respect to my central thesis.

It may be true that on some particular occasions the consequences of disobeying a law will in fact be less deleterious on the whole than those of obeying it — even in a democracy. It may even be true that on some particular occasions disobeying a law would be just whereas obeying it would be unjust. Nevertheless, the reason why a person is never justified in disobeying a law — in a democracy — is simply this: The chances are so slight that a person will disobey only those laws in only those cases in which one is in fact justified in doing so, that the consequences will on the whole be less deleterious if no one ever disobeys any law. Furthermore, since anyone must concede the right to everyone to disobey the law when the circumstances so demand it, the situation is made still worse. For once we entrust this right to everyone we can be sure that many laws will be disobeyed in a multitude of cases in which there was no real justification for disobedience. Thus, given what we know of the possibilities of human error and the actualities of human frailty, and given the tendency of democratic societies to make illegal only those actions which would, even in the absence of a law, be unjustified, we can confidently conclude that the consequences will on the whole and in the long run be best if one never takes it upon oneself to "second-guess" the laws and to conclude that in a particular case disobedience is justified.[28]

The argument is, in part, not very different from those previously considered. And thus, what is to be said about it is not very different either. There is, as I have indicated, a weak sense in which the argument is quite persuasive and a strong sense in which it is not. For the argument makes, on one reading, too strong an empirical claim — the claim that the consequences will in the long run always in fact be better if no one in a democracy ever tries to decide when disobeying the law is justifiable. As it stands, there is no reason to believe that the claim is or must be true, that the consequences will always be better. Indeed, it is very hard to see why, despite the hypothesis, someone might still not be justified in some particular case in disobeying a law. Yet, viewed as a weaker claim, as a summary rule, it does embody a good deal that is worth remembering. It can, on this level, be understood to be a persuasive reminder of much that is relevant to disobedience: that in a democracy the chances of having to live under bad laws are reduced; that in a democracy there are often other means available by which to bring about changes in the law;

that in a democracy — as in life in general — a justified action may always be both inaptly and ineptly emulated; and that in a democracy — as in life in general — people often do make mistakes as to which of their own actions are truly justified. These are some of the lessons of human experience which are easy to forget and painful to relearn.

But there are other lessons, and they are worth remembering too. What is especially troubling about the claim that disobedience of the law is never justified, what is even disturbing about the claim that disobedience of the law is never justified in a democratic or decent society, is the facility with which its acceptance can lead to the neglect of primary moral issues. If no one was justified in disobeying the Supreme Court's decision in *Brown* v. *Board of Education,* this was so primarily because of what was and is morally objectionable about the system of racial segregation that the Brown case sought in some measure to undo. If there was much that was especially wrong in resistance to desegregation, it was not that persons were disobeying the law, but that they were seeking to preserve a system of oppressive, unjustifiable institutions — a system which, in fact, had been constructed in no small degree of laws which effectively had supported and maintained the system of oppression. Laws are two-edged social swords.

Disobeying the law in a reasonably decent society may be often — even usually — wrong; but this is so largely because the seriously illegal is there usually restricted to what is otherwise wrongful and because morally right conduct will still less often be illegal. If the laws were not of this sort, it would not be a reasonably decent society. But it is important to be aware of the fact that this has not always been the case, is not now always the case, and will never always be the case in any society, no matter how fair its procedures, how decent its ideals. And undue concentration upon what is wrong with disobeying the law rather than upon the rightness or wrongness of that which the law seeks to prevent or require can seriously weaken and misdirect that awareness.

NOTES

1. I have discussed some of the reasons why persons could have plausibly come to this view in the United States in respect to the Vietnam War in "The Relevance of Nuremberg," 1 *Phil. & Pub. Aff.* 22 (1971).

2. *See, e.g.,* Austin, *The Province of Jurisprudence Determined* (New York:

The Noonday Press, 1954 ed.), pp. 53-55; Hume, *A Treatise of Human Nature,* bk. III, §§ 9, 10; Locke, *The Second Treatise of Government,* chs. 18, 19.

3. A subject which has surely not received the philosophical attention it deserves is that of the nature of revolution. What, for instance, are the characteristics of a revolution? Must the procedures by which laws are made or the criteria of validity be altered? Or is it sufficient that the people who occupy certain crucial offices be removed in a manner inconsistent with existing rules? Must force or resistance accompany whatever changes or alterations are made? Whatever the answers may be to questions such as these, it is, I think, plain that particular laws may be disobeyed under a claim of justification without any of these features being present. One can argue that for one reason or another, any act of disobedience must necessarily lead to revolution or the overthrow of the government. But then this is an argument which must be demonstrated.

4. I discuss the views of two such theorists, Professor Lon Fuller and Professor Herbert Wechsler, in Parts II and IV of this essay.

5. *See, e.g.,* Bedau, "On Civil Disobedience," 58 *J. Phil.* 653 (1961); Dworkin, "Civil Disobedience," in Dworkin, *Taking Rights Seriously* (Cambridge, Mass: Harvard U. Press, 1977), p. 206; John Rawls, *A Theory of Justice* (Cambridge, Mass: Harvard U. Press, 1971), § 55.

6. Because I am concerned with the question of whether one is ever morally justified in acting illegally, I purposely make the actor's knowledge of the illegality of the action part of the description of the act. I am not concerned with the question of whether ignorance of the illegality of the action ought morally to be an excuse.

7. *New York Times,* Oct. 1, 1962, p. 22. It is probable that President Kennedy meant his remarks to be applicable only to the legal system which is a part of the set of political institutions of the United States. I discuss whether this qualification is sufficient in Part IV, *infra.*

8. The distinction can be put more generally in the following fashion. One person, A, might hold the view that any action in disobedience of the law is intrinsically bad. Some other person, B, might hold the view that no action is intrinsically bad unless it has the property, P, and that not all actions in disobedience of the law have that property. Now for A the fact of disobedience is always a relevant consideration, although it is not necessarily conclusive or sufficient, since an action in obedience to the law may under some other description be worse, or less justifiable than obedience. For B the fact of disobedience may always be initially relevant because of the existence of some well-established hypothesis which asserts that the occurrence of any action of disobedience is correlated highly with the occurrence of P. But if any particular case of disobedience does not turn out to have the property, P, then, upon reflection, it can be concluded by B that the fact that disobedience is involved is not a reason which weighs against the performance of the act in question. To understand B's position it is necessary to distinguish the relevance of considering the fact of disobedience from the relevance of the fact of disobedience. The former must always be relevant, the latter is not.

9. Hart, *The Concept of Law* (Oxford: At the Clarendon Press, 1961), pp. 27-48, contains one of the fullest and clearest analyses of the important distinguishing characteristics of different kinds of legal rules.

In this connection there is a stronger point than the one made to be noted. It is that there are many laws which, if they can be disobeyed at all, cannot be disobeyed in the way in which the typical criminal law can be disobeyed, for there are many laws that either impose or permit one to impose upon oneself any number of different legal obligations. And with many of these legal obligations, regardless of how created, it seems correct to say that one can breach or fail to perform them without thereby acting illegally or in disobedience of the law. One's obligation to obey the law may not, therefore, be coextensive with one's legal obligations. In the typical case of a breach of contract, for example, the failure to perform one's contractual obligations is clearly a breach of a legal obligation. Yet one can breach a contract and, hence, a legal obligation, without necessarily acting illegally. This last assertion may be open to question; arguments for its correctness would not here be germane. It is sufficient to recognize only that failing to honor or perform some types of legal obligations may be a quite different kind of activity from violating or disobeying a law or order which is backed up, in some very direct fashion, by a governmentally threatened sanction of a special sort.

10. It is worth emphasizing that I am not at all interested in the claim—which in many ways is an odd one to belabor—that there is a logical relationship between disobeying the law and acting illegally. *See, e.g.,* Carnes, "Why Should I Obey the Law?" 71 *Ethics* 14 (1960).

11. Professor Fuller appears to hold to some version of this view in his article, "Positivism and Fidelity to Law—A Reply to Professor Hart," 71 *Harv. L. Rev.* 630, 656 (1958), where, after characterizing the position of legal positivism as one which says that "On the one hand, we have an amoral datum called law, which has the peculiar quality of creating a moral duty to obey it. On the other hand, we have a moral duty to do what we think is right and decent." Professor Fuller goes on to criticize this bifurcation of law and morality on the grounds that "The 'dilemma' it states has the verbal formulation of a problem, but the problem it states makes no sense. It is like saying I have to choose between giving food to a starving man and being mimsey with the borogroves. I do not think it unfair to the positivistic philosophy to say that it never gives any coherent meaning to the moral obligation of fidelity to law."

Others who at least suggest adherence to such a position are: Baier, *The Moral Point of View* (Ithaca, N. Y.: Cornell U. Press, 1958), p. 134; Nowell-Smith, *Ethics* (London: Penguin Books, 1954), pp. 236–37; and Weldon, *The Vocabulary of Politics* (London: Penguin Books, 1953), pp. 57, 62, 66–67. And there are surely passages in Hobbes that could also be read in this way. *See, e.g.,* Hobbes, *Leviathan,* chs. XIII, XVIII. The claim that illegal entails immoral is closely related to, but surely distinguishable from, the position that Professor Fuller, among many others, may also hold, namely, that there are certain minimum "moral" requirements that must be met before any rule can be a law.

12. Especially, since the Fugitive Slave Law was held constitutional by unanimous decision of the United States Supreme Court in Ableman v. Booth, 21 How. 506 (1859).

13. Sir W. David Ross, for example, suggests that the obligation to obey the law is a prima facie obligation which is a compound of three more simple prima facie duties. Ross, *The Right and the Good* (Oxford: At the Clarendon Press, 1930), pp. 27–28.

14. For example, theories emphasizing either the strong or the weak sense of "prima facie" discussed above seem fully capable of handling the relevant cases. Perhaps a more attentive kind of conceptual analysis than I am inclined to pursue would provide grounds for favoring one theory over the other. I am uncertain. I am more confident that the resolution of this issue could not settle the questions I am most interested in examining.

While I do not call into question in this essay the possibility of believing there is a prima facie obligation to obey the law, I do not mean thereby to concede that there is one. I am uncertain about the force of the conceptual argument, and I do not consider directly the application of other arguments to this point. Others have, however, argued that there is no prima facie obligation to obey the law. A searching and very thoughtful defense of that thesis is presented by M. B. E. Smith in "Is There a Prima Facie Obligation to Obey the Law?" 82 *Yale L. J.* 950 (1973). A number of the arguments discussed there are similar to those I discuss, although the conclusion Smith derives is appreciably stronger than mine.

15. Socrates, for instance, supposes that were he to escape he might properly be asked: "[W]hat are you about? Are you going by an act of yours to overturn us — the laws and the whole state, as far as in you lies? Do you imagine that a state can subsist and not be overthrown, in which the decisions of law have no power, but are set aside and overthrown by individuals?" *Crito, 50b.* Analogous arguments can be found in Austin, *op. cit., supra* note 2, pp. 52-53; Hobbes, *Leviathan,* ch. XV; Hume, *A Treatise of Human Nature,* bk. III, pt. II, §§ 3, 6, 8, 9; Toulmin, *The Place of Reason in Ethics* (Cambridge: At the University Press, 1953), p. 151.

16. I discuss a very special and related version of this argument in Part V *infra.*

17. This is a particular illustration of the more general claim that for one reason or another utilitarianism cannot be a defensible or intelligible moral theory when construed as permitting one's moral obligation to do any particular action to be overridden by a direct appeal to the consequences of performing that particular action. For other statements of the claim *see, e.g.,* Nowell-Smith, *op. cit., supra* note 11; Rawls, "Two Concepts of Rules," 64 *Phil. Rev.* 3 (1955); Singer, *Generalization in Ethics* (New York: Alfred A. Knopf, 1961), pp. 61-138, 178-216; Toulmin, *op. cit., supra* note 15, at 144-65; Harrison, "Utilitarianism, Universalisation, and Our Duty To Be Just," 53 *Aristotelian Soc'y Proc.* 105 (1952-53).

I have criticized this restriction upon utilitarianism more fully in my book, *The Judicial Decision* (Stanford, Cal.: Stanford U. Press, 1961), pp. 118-37. *See, also,* Lyons, *Forms and Limits of Utilitarianism* (Oxford: Oxford U. Press, 1965); and Smith, *op. cit., supra* note 14.

18. Singer, *op. cit., supra* note 17, at 149-50.

19. Neither Singer nor I have adequately refuted A, if A is a confirmed ethical egoist who insists that she is prepared to generalize but only in the sense that X's nonpayment is justified if, and only if, the consequences of X's nonpayment would in X's case be more beneficial to A than those of payment. This is a problem which surely requires more careful attention than it typically receives. It will not do simply to insist that the egoist does not understand ordinary moral discourse. Instead, what must be demonstrated are the respects in which the egoist's position is an inherently unjust one. But to make this showing is beyond the scope of this essay.

20. Rawls's discussion of why civil disobedience might be justifiable, even in a nearly just society, depends upon this same point. Rawls, *op. cit., supra* note 5, §§ 55, 57, and 59.

21. Moral philosophers have often argued that one cannot appeal simply to the consequences of performing or not performing a particular promise as a reason for not performing that promise. And the reason they sometimes give is that the notion of having promised to do something would be *unintelligible* if the promisor could always, when the time came for performance, be excused if it were the case that the consequences of nonperformance were more beneficial than those of performance. This would make promising unintelligible, so the argument goes, because promis-

ing entails or means obligating oneself to do something. But if the appeal to consequences is what is to be determinative of one's obligations, then the promise becomes
a wholly superfluous, meaningless act. In his classic article, "Two Concepts of
Rules," Rawls, for instance, put the point this way: "Various defenses for not keeping one's promise are allowed, but among them there isn't the one that, on general
utilitarian grounds, the promisor (truly) thought his action best on the whole, even
though there may be the defense that the consequences of keeping one's promise
would have been extremely severe. While there are too many complexities here to
consider all the necessary details, one can see that the general defense isn't allowed
if one asks the following question: what would one say of someone who, when asked
why he broke his promise, replied simply that breaking it was best on the whole?
Assuming that his reply is sincere, and that his belief was reasonable (i.e., one need
not consider the possibility that he was mistaken), I think that one would question
whether or not he knows what it means to say 'I promise' (in the appropriate circumstances). It would be said of someone who used this excuse without further explanation that he didn't understand what defenses the practice, which defines a
promise, allows to him. If a child were to use this excuse one would correct him; for
it is part of the way one is taught the concept of a promise to be corrected if one uses
this excuse. The point of having the practice would be lost if the practice did allow
this excuse." Rawls, *supra* note 17, p. 17.

Now, I am not concerned to dispute Rawls's remark if it is to be taken as descriptive of our institution of promising. This may be a correct description of one
particular practice. But what is incorrect is the claim that seems also to be made
that promising would be literally a meaningless or pointless activity if the excuse
were permitted within the practice. I think I can show this to be a mistake through
the following two examples.

(1) A has promised B that he will mow B's lawn for B on Sunday. On Sunday, A
is feeling lazy and so he refuses to mow the lawn.

(2) A is sitting home on Sunday, feeling lazy, when B calls him up and asks him
to come over and mow B's lawn. A refuses to mow the lawn.

Ceteris paribus, it would be the case that A is wrong in refusing to mow B's lawn
in example (1) but not blameable for refusing to mow B's lawn in example (2). Why
is this so? Because A's promise to mow B's lawn creates an obligation which in the
absence of such a promise is nonexistent. If this is so, then permitting the general
utilitarian defense does not make a promise a meaningless gesture. This is so because there are many situations in which, in the absence of having promised to do
so, we are not, for example, obligated to inconvenience ourselves simply for another's convenience. Personal inconvenience then might be one excuse which must
be inconsistent with the practice of promising, even if the general appeal to consequences is not. Thus, promising would and could still have a point even if the general appeal to consequences were a good defense. It would still be intelligible to
have promised to do something.

The passage quoted from Rawls is not, I think, central to his main argument,
which is that the consequences of a different, weaker practice might, on the whole,
be undesirable. That is a very different argument, however, from one which seeks
to establish the conceptual impossibility or incoherence of a different practice of
promising.

22. Wechsler, "Toward Neutral Principles of Constitutional Law," 73 *Harv. L.
Rev.* 1, 35 (1959).

23. In Part III, *supra*.

24. For a somewhat related characterization of the source of the obligation to obey the law, see Hart, "Are There Any Natural Rights?" 64 *Phil. Rev.* 175, 185 (1955): "A third very important source of special rights and obligations which we recognize in many spheres of life is what may be termed mutuality of restrictions. . . . In its bare schematic outline it is this: when a number of persons conduct any joint enterprise according to rules and thus restrict their liberty, those who have submitted to these restrictions when required have a right to a similar submission from those who have benefited by their submission. The rules may provide that officials should have authority to enforce obedience and make further rules, and this will create a structure of legal rights and duties, but the moral obligation to obey the rules in such circumstances is due to the cooperating members of the society, and they have the correlative moral right to obedience. In social situations of this sort (of which political society is the most complex example) the obligation to obey the rules is something distinct from whatever other moral obligations there may be for obedience in terms of good consequences (e.g., the prevention of suffering); the obligation is due to the co-operating members of the society as such and not because they are human beings on whom it would be wrong to inflict suffering."

I would point out only two things. First, as Hart himself asserts — in a passage not quoted — the existence of this right in no way implies that one is never justified in disobeying the law. The right which any participating member has in others' obedience can justifiably be infringed in appropriate circumstances. Second, and here perhaps Professor Hart disagrees for reasons already elaborated, there is no reason that I can see why an appeal to the consequences of disobeying a particular law cannot be a sufficient justification for infringing upon that right. It is surely conceivable, at least, that this is all the submission to rules which anyone ought to have given, and hence all the submission which anyone is entitled to expect from others.

25. This, then, is one reason why, despite the common assumption about the greater justifiability of civil disobedience, civil disobedience might be *unjustifiable* in situations in which other kinds of disobedience might be justifiable.

26. Given a legal system in which laws are in general good and, therefore, given a society in which the possibility of justified disobedience is rare, the special or added cost of what will be an occasional act of justified disobedience is diminished still further. This, too, is a reason why it is a mistake always to think of civil disobedience as the form of disobedience which is justifiable, if any form of disobedience is. For there is a paradox, of sorts, that confronts the proponent of civil disobedience. Civil disobedience is an activity that is most plausibly undertaken only in a society with certain values, ideals, and the like — what might be called a reasonably just or humane society. However, in such a society the publicity of the act of disobedience may be enough to make the otherwise justifiable act of disobedience unjustifiable. Thus there will be, perhaps, a relatively narrow range of cases and social settings within which civil disobedience will be justifiable. Both within societies that are less humane and within societies that are more just, other forms of disobedience may turn out to be the more frequently justifiable forms of disobedience.

27. Arguments concerning the distribution of benefits and burdens also figure prominently in discussions of the retributivist case for punishment. I examine these in "Punishment," *infra.*, pp. 142–146.

28. Fuller analyses and assessments of this argument in other contexts are given in Rawls, *op. cit., supra* note 17, and in Wasserstrom, *op. cit., supra* note 17, pp. 118–71.

Punishment

I

Punishment, whatever else may be said of it, involves the intentional infliction of pain or suffering upon human beings by other human beings. For this reason punishment is a problem that must be confronted by all human beings concerned to be moral. To do something that intentionally increases human pain or suffering requires justification in a way in which many other things that we do to or with other persons do not. It is a special problem because the pain or suffering (what I shall hereafter refer to as a "deprivation") is intentionally imposed.

There are three main approaches, or responses, to the problem of punishment. The first approach advocates the abolition of punishment as a distinctive mode of response and the replacement in its stead of something variously called a system of treatment, reform, or rehabilitation. According to this view, the problem of punishment is solved by seeing that punishment is not justifiable and that something other than punishment is.[1] The second approach thinks that a system of punishment is justifiable, and wholly so on consequentialist grounds. The deprivation imposed is justifiable because of the worse consequences that would be present in its absence.[2] The third approach agrees with the second in its insistence that a system of punishment is justifiable, but it insists that backward-looking, or retributivist, considerations constitute the essential justification of punishment. Each of these ways of responding to the problem has its attractions, yet none is free of serious, if not fatal, weaknesses. An examination of them provides many insights about the law and philosophy while at the same time leaving our thinking on this subject unsettled and uncertain. At the end, while we know a good deal more than when we started, the problem of the justifiability of punishment remains, at least for me, unresolved.

Many recent philosophical discussions of punishment, in an attempt to bring order and understanding to these competing solutions to the problem of punishment, proceed in the following way. First, they begin by offering a description, if not an analysis, of the features of punishment. And second, many of those that are consequentialist[3] offer what they take to be a way out of the apparent conflict between retributive and consequentialist theories. The reconciliation, they claim, is attainable once it is realized that there are two different questions, or issues, that may be being addressed. One question is concerned with whether a particular case of punishment is justifiable. The other question is concerned with whether the practice or institution of punishment is itself justifiable. Retributivism, it is claimed, is most plausibly construed as dealing with the former question; consequentialist justifications of punishment, it is claimed, are most plausibly construed as dealing with the latter question. None of this seems to me to be unproblematic. I see problems internal to each of these proposals, and neither seems to solve the problem of providing a wholly satisfactory account that either adequately describes or justifies punishment.

I begin with an examination of the accounts of what punishment is. Then I consider the case for replacing punishment with rehabilitation. Next I consider the consequentialist justifications for punishment. And, finally, I examine the retributivist position. In each case I try in particular to bring out both what is plausible and what is troublesome about the theory under consideration.

II

There is no question but that it is instructive, if not essential, to begin by giving an account of what punishment is. The most important reason for doing so is that there are any number of things that may be done to persons that involve a deprivation and that are not instances of punishment at all. When they are done to persons, we are clear that we are not punishing them, and we correctly regard it as very important that they and we both understand that they are not being punished. This is important in many nonlegal contexts, as, for example, when we impose a deprivation upon children even though we are clear that we are not punishing them, and the distinction is a systemically necessary one for a legal system to be able to make. For there are many things that a legal system does or authorizes that may be done to persons that involve deprivations and that are not punishments. This can be brought out by examination of examples such as the following:

(1) Suppose a person has an infectious disease and is confined against his or her will to a special wing of a hospital. Such a confinement is typically a deprivation; yet it is not, without more, a punishment. How do we know this? How would we explain to a person who did not already know as much about our society and its practices and beliefs as we do that we are not punishing the persons so confined?

(2) Suppose X has made a contract with Y and has promised to pay $1,000 on Saturday for Y's car. On Saturday, Y produces the car and X refuses to accept it or to pay for it. Sometime thereafter the legal system requires X to pay Y some money. To be required to pay money is, typically, a deprivation; yet X is not being punished for her breach of the contract. How do we know this? How would we in this case explain to a person who did not already know as much about our society and its practices and beliefs as we do that we are not punishing X when we make X part with some of her money after a breach of contract?

(3) Suppose C walks into a bank, draws a gun, and tells the people in the bank to put up their hands or they will be shot. One of the bank guards, D, reaches for his gun, and C shoots him, wounding him in the arm. D has certainly suffered a deprivation and yet D has not been punished by C. Once again, how would we know that this was not a case of punishment? How would we explain to the visitor to our society that even though a deprivation had been imposed on D by C, D had not been punished by C?

One typical, highly influential account of what punishment is, which appears to provide a way to make the necessary differentiations, is provided by H. L. A. Hart in his piece, "Prolegomenon to the Principles of Punishment." Hart says:

> I shall define the standard or central case of "punishment" in terms of five elements:
>
> (i) It must involve pain or other consequences normally considered unpleasant.
>
> (ii) It must be for an offence against legal rules.
>
> (iii) It must be of an actual or supposed offender for his offence.
>
> (iv) It must be intentionally administered by human beings other than the offender.
>
> (v) It must be imposed and administered by an authority constituted by a legal system against which the offence is committed.[4]

Applied to the three examples described above, Hart's analysis might produce an account something like this. The deprivations suffered by the individuals in the three examples were not punishments because the individuals were not guilty of any offenses. A deprivation is only a punishment if it is imposed or inflicted after one has been adjudged, determined, or at least thought to be guilty of an offense. That is what needs explaining when it is punishment that is being imposed, and once this is understood we are able to distinguish those deprivations that are punishments from those that are not.

This way of proceeding has serious problems. The difficulty with a definition such as Hart's is that it seems, on the surface at least, to be circular—and in a way that is serious because the circularity is so abrupt. The circularity occurs in part because the idea of punishment employed by this approach depends so heavily upon the concept of an offense, which concept is utilized in elements (ii), (iii), (iv), and (v) of Hart's account. It is the notion of an offense in these characterizations of punishment which carries the primary burden of differentiating punishment from these other deprivations.

Yet, if the idea of an offense is central to an understanding of the concept of punishment, then we have to be able to make sense of the notion of what it is for something to be an offense. There must be a way to distinguish those things that are offenses from those that are not. The difficulty is that the idea of an offense seems to depend upon the concept of punishment for its meaning rather than providing an independent means by which to understand what punishment is. The concept of punishment seems, in fact, to be prior to that of the concept of an offense.

Suppose we were to ask what it is for something to be an offense. Suppose someone unfamiliar with a particular legal system were to ask whether it is an offense in that legal system to breach one's contracts, be afflicted with an infectious disease, or reach for one's gun when ordered not to do so by a bank robber. How would one decide whether these, or other things, were or were not offenses? The most obvious way would be to try to determine whether, within that legal system, these kinds of things were crimes. So, one possible and natural response to the inquiry would be to assert that those things are offenses which are crimes.

But what, then, is a crime? How would one decide, either in one's own system or in another one whose workings one did not yet understand, which things were crimes and which were not? Again, one possible and natural response would be to say that crimes were those things that were dealt with via punishment rather than through other possible means of response. It is not a crime to breach one's contract in our legal system. How do we know? Because persons are not punished for breach of contract. And the same goes for being afflicted with an infectious disease, or trying to prevent a bank robbery. But the problem with this strategy is that the idea of punishment is directly employed to make sense out of the idea of crime. An offense is anything which a legal system deals with through the punishment of those who engage in the proscribed acts. The circularity is sufficiently direct that this way of proceeding is also unilluminating and unsatisfactory.

One way out of the circle would be to give an account of what an offense or crime was that did not depend so directly upon the idea of punishment; another would be to give an account of punishment which did not require the idea of an offense in order to distinguish those deprivations that are punishments from those that are not.

Consider the former possibility first. Suppose we were to characterize an offense not as a crime but rather as any violation of the law. Here we would have a noncircular account of punishment which depended only on understanding the idea of a violation of the law. But is that idea sufficiently clear, or sufficiently strong, to do the job required of it? What constitutes a violation of the law? Is it a violation of the law to breach one's legal obligation, e.g., by intentionally breaching a contract? Is it a violation of the law to have an infectious disease? Is it a violation of the law to operate one's car negligently thereby injuring someone? Is it a violation of the law to be in the country without a permit? If the answer to any of these questions is "Yes," then "violation" cannot be substituted for "offense" because being required to pay damages for breach of contract is not a punishment; nor is being confined to a hospital; nor is paying damages for negligence a punishment; nor is deportation (at least obviously). If the answer is that these things are not violations of the law, while robbery, rape, and murder are, then the question once again is that of how they are to be distinguished. What will not do is to say that things such as breach of contract or having an infectious disease are not violations because they do not involve the punishment of persons. For this response is circular because it, too, used the idea of punishment to explain the idea of a violation.

A more promising approach is to treat "crime" and "offense" as roughly synonymous and to attempt to give a characterization of the idea of crime that does not so directly or exclusively depend on the idea of punishment. One plausible candidate is the more generic idea of wrongdoing. One thing to be said in favor of building the idea of wrongdoing directly into the account of punishment or indirectly into it through the concept of crime is that it seems in some ways to belong there.

Someone might propose that the concept of crime is linked in important ways with the idea of wrongdoing, so that crimes, or offenses, could be distinguished from other things in virtue of their essential wrongfulness rather than their punishability. Those cases that we would identify as the core cases of criminality in a society, so this line of analysis might go, all involve behavior that is regarded as seriously wrong by the society wholly apart from the illegality of the behavior. Typically, it is behavior that, viewed just as conduct, is thought seriously harmful or dangerous. Typically, too, it is behavior that, viewed in terms of the actor's culpability, was seriously culpable, i.e., it involved either the intentional or knowing infliction of injury on another.[5] Thus, it might be claimed, the core idea of criminality does appear to involve this idea of moral wrongdoing—coupled, perhaps, with the added idea that it is wrongdoing of the sort that is appropriately publicly condemned or denounced.[6] And for this reason it does seem to be both less circular and more illuminating to construct an account of punishment which utilizes this idea of criminality (or serious wrongdoing in the nonlegal context) instead of one which takes the undefined notion of an offense as central.

But even this approach is not without its difficulties. One problem is that many activities can be and are crimes even though they do not involve something that can properly be regarded as seriously blameworthy behavior on the part of the actor. Thus, in our own society, it is a crime, for example, to possess various weapons, to use drugs of various sorts, and to engage in various consensual sexual behaviors. It could be claimed, of course, that these are all cases of believed blameworthiness in that the lawmakers believed (although perhaps mistakenly) these things to be morally wrong and, hence, for that reason appropriately made criminal. But such a defense would not be adequate because it is both conceptually and empirically possible to have behavior that is clearly and unmistakably understood and recognized as criminal, and that is thought by no one within the society to be either "intrinsically" or seriously immoral.[7]

Now, one way to deal with this problem is to show that there is a perfectly plausible sense in which the law can and should make behavior wrongful even though it is not "intrinsically" so. Thus, someone might claim that while it is not "intrinsically" wrong, or even dangerous, to drive on the left rather than the right side of the road, it is important to drive on only one side or the other, and it is, therefore, dangerous and wrong to drive on the "wrong" side of the road, whatever side that may be in any given society. This modification works very well for a number of cases but less well for others, e.g., the prohibition of drug use on paternalistic grounds.

Another way to deal with this problem is to make the wrongdoing what might be termed "second order" rather than "primary" wrongdoing. On this view what would be a necessary characteristic of any crime would be the fact either that the behavior itself was seriously wrong, or that the behavior was seriously wrong in virtue of its being an intentional (or otherwise culpable) violation of a law. One problem with this approach is that it reintroduces the circularity, previously discussed, latent in the idea of a violation of the law. That is to say, we would still require some independent account of the idea of a violation of the law that did not explicate that idea through recourse to the concept of punishment. And a second problem is that it would have to be explained why it is always immoral intentionally to disobey the law. I do not think that such an explanation can easily be produced.[8]

Thus, the difficulty is that not all wrongful acts (breaches of contract, for example) are crimes, and not all crimes involve things that are in any obvious way wrongful. Since this is the case, the connection between wrongfulness and crime cannot be directly used to explicate the idea of crime and, by it, the idea of punishment.

There is still the other way to try to deal with the problem of circularity. Perhaps the idea of wrongfulness can still be employed — not for its direct connection with the idea of crime, but rather for its more direct connection with the idea of punishment. Here the claim would be that the intentional imposition of a deprivation is a punishment only if the person has done something wrong. This is a promising approach, although further qualifications would surely be required. One qualification is that the person need not in fact have done something wrong; it would have to be sufficient that the person were believed to have done something wrong. Nor could the claim be that persons who were known to be innocent could not in some sense be punished. For any defensible analysis of the concept of punishment must be able to account for or explain such a possibility.[9] This can be done, I think, by explaining that such cases are intelligible because they trade upon the conceptual connection between punishment and wrongdoing to effect the deception that the person who is innocent and known to be such is believed to have done something wrong and that is why the deprivation imposed on that individual will be viewed by others as punishment. There is conceptual incompatability between punishment and the absence of *all* beliefs, appearances, pretenses, etc. of wrongdoing, but that is a different case. If everyone knew an individual to be innocent it would be conceptually odd, if not impossible, to describe what is done to the person as an instance of punishment, just as it would be for someone to say, in a case where deception is not involved, "I know you are innocent but I am now going to punish you." We could make sense out of it, if at all, only by focusing on the similarity between the kind of deprivation inflicted and the deprivation that is a typical punishment and which is inflicted only where wrongdoing of some sort is believed to have occurred.

This account of the connection between punishment and wrongdoing does provide a means by which to explain why the person afflicted with a disease is not being punished even when confined against his or her will. The reason is that there is no belief that the person has done anything wrong in being sick and, therefore, there is nothing to punish the person for.

It is important that this account be distinguished from two other positions with which it might be confused. In the first place, even if correct, the account in no respect provides an answer to the question of whether it is justifiable to confine the individual so afflicted. There are all sorts of deprivations that can be imposed upon individuals that are not punishments.[10] The fact that they are not says nothing about the defensibility of their imposition. When they are imposed, rather than voluntarily assumed, and when they are deprivations, they require justification.

In the second place, the claim that the sick person is not being punished because he or she is not believed to have done anything wrong is a different one from that which we would be making if we appealed to the *wrongness* of punishing someone for something that was not voluntary. It is certainly possible to believe that persons can do something wrong even though what they did (or what happened to them) was not voluntary. There can be moralities which make nonvoluntary contamination or pollution wrongful — that is certainly one way to understand the Deuteronomic strand of Old Testament morality and one way to understand the background morality of Oedipus. Within such a morality there would be no acceptance of this moral principle about the conditions of the justifiability of punishment. But within such a morality there would, nevertheless, be the idea that there was something wrongful in the picture, and that is how or why it could make conceptual sense to talk about the imposed deprivation as a punishment.[11] Thus, if this account is correct, one conceptual requirement for a deprivation being a punishment is that there be some wrongful thing in virtue of which the deprivation is imposed or inflicted. While it is not essential that the wrongfulness even be voluntary, many, perhaps most, moralities do think of wrongfulness as requiring more, e.g., an action that is describable as an instance of wrongdoing.

This same account also provides a way of understanding why the shooting of the bank guard by the bank robber is not an instance of punishment (and why most intentional killings, batteries, and the like are also not punishments). It is that there is no belief on the part of the inflictor of the deprivation—or on the part of anyone else—that the deprivation is being imposed because of some wrongdoing. And in the absence of such belief, there is no inclination to describe what occurs as an instance of punishment.

What has been said so far cannot, however, make clear why requiring someone who has breached a contract to pay damages is not a case of punishing the person. The problem here is that we may very well believe that it is wrong to breach a contract and yet we may also be clear that the deprivation imposed on the one who has breached the contract is not a punishment. How, then, can we explain how it is that this case is not a case of punishment either?

Perhaps the answer is that another thing that is conceptually required to make a deprivation a punishment is that it be imposed because it is a deprivation. That is to say, deprivations are punishments only if they are intended (by the person or the institution) to be imposed in virtue of, or because, they are deprivations. If so, the response of our legal system to breaches of contract can be distinguished as not being punishments on the ground that the intention behind, or the point of, the resulting deprivation is not that the deprivation occur. Rather, the point is that the person who did not breach the contract be compensated, or otherwise be not worse off, as a result of the breach. There is nothing about the idea of being compensated for a loss or injury that requires that anyone else, even the person causing the loss or injury, be deprived. If the situation of the person who breaches the contract is improved, rather than worsened, either by the breach or by the payment of compensation, there is no conceptual tension present. The focus of the idea of compensation is upon the position of the person to whom the compensation is owed. A deprivation imposed upon the person who owes it is not an essential feature of the case at all. If a third party provided the compensation, there can be no complaint that the person who breached the contract did not.

This feature of punishment—that a deprivation be incurred by the person punished—gives an additional reason by which to distinguish confining the person afflicted with a disease from a case of punishment. The point of the confinement is not to produce a deprivation but is instead either to prevent others from contracting the disease or to cure the person of the disease. If there were a way to achieve either or both of these results in a way that did not require a deprivation for the person so afflicted, that would clearly be the preferred mode of response. There is simply nothing intrinsic to the idea of treating or curing a disease which carries with it the idea of any deprivation being intended or necessarily imposed.

These two conceptual points about punishment can be combined in the following way. The imposition of a deprivation is not, given our moral ideas, an instance of punishment unless: (1) the deprivation is imposed because it is a deprivation; (2) there is the belief that the person upon whom the deprivation is imposed is guilty of wrongdoing (whatever the conditions of guilt for wrongdoing may be believed to be); and (3) the person upon whom the deprivation is being imposed is to understand that the deprivation is being imposed because (1) and (2) are present.

On this view we can give an account of a crime by saying that it is anything that the law deals with by punishment rather than any alternative method of response to the behavior that has occurred. And we can determine whether punishment is involved by seeing whether the conceptual conditions for something being a punishment have been satisfied. If they have been, then we are dealing with a crime rather than something else. Because of the conceptual connection between wrongdoing and punishment, we can understand why many crimes do deal with serious wrongdoing and why all crimes are linked in some fashion or other to the idea of wrongdoing. We can also see that where the law punishes a kind of behavior that is not wrongful at all there is a conceptual dimension to the complaint that the behavior should not be criminal; namely, that the belief about the wrongfulness of the behavior is mistaken, and the conditions for punishment in that sense do not in fact obtain.

If the foregoing account is even roughly right, it shows that many of the typical accounts of punishment are either too weak to distinguish punishment from other typical deprivations, or circular in an unilluminating fashion. It shows, too, that an aspect of the retributivist point of view is built into the concept of punishment itself, namely, the primacy of the backward-looking characteristic of wrongdoing—something wrongful must be believed to have occurred. What has not been shown so far is whether it is justifiable to punish anyone, and if so, on what grounds. It remains, that is, an open question whether there are any sound arguments, retributivist or otherwise, which justify ever punishing persons. It is these arguments which must, of course, be examined before we can decide whether it is ever right to punish persons and under what circumstances and in virtue of what reasons. Before looking at these arguments, however, it will be useful to examine the view that we ought to abandon punishment in favor of something else, typically called reform, rehabilitation, or treatment.

III

There is a view, held most prominently but by no means exclusively by persons in psychiatry, that we ought never punish persons who break the law and that we ought instead to do something much more like what we do when we treat someone who has a disease. According to this view, what we ought to do to all such persons is to do our best to bring it about that they can and will function in a satisfactory way within society. The functional equivalent to the treatment of a disease is the rehabilitation of an offender, and it is a rehabilitative system, not a punishment system, that we ought to have if we are to respond, even to criminals, in anything like a decent, morally defensible fashion.

Karl Menninger has put the proposal this way:

If we were to follow scientific methods, the convicted offender would be detained indefinitely pending a decision as to whether and how to reintroduce him successfully into society. All the skill and knowledge of modern behavior science would be used to examine his personality assets, his liabilities and potentialities, the environment from which he came, its effects upon him, and his effects upon it.

Having arrived at some diagnostic grasp of the offender's personality, those in charge can decide whether there is a chance that he can be redirected into a mutually satisfactory adaptation to the world. If so, the most suitable techniques in education, industrial training, group administration, and psychotherapy should be selectively applied. All this may be best done extramurally or intramurally. It may require maximum "security" or only minimum "security." If, in due time, perceptible change occurs, the process should be expedited by finding a suitable spot in society and industry for him, and getting him out of prison control and into civil status (with parole control) as quickly as possible.[12]

It is important at the outset to see that there are two very different arguments which might underlie the claim that the functional equivalent of a system of treatment is desirable and in fact always ought to be preferred to a system of punishment.

The first argument fixes upon the desirability of such a system over one of punishment in virtue of the fact that, because no offenders are responsible for their actions, no offenders are ever justifiably punished. The second argument is directed towards establishing that such a system is better than one of punishment even if some or all offenders are responsible for their actions. A good deal of the confusion present in discussions of the virtues of a system of treatment results from a failure to get clear about these two arguments and to keep the two separate. The first is superficially the more attractive and ultimately the less plausible of the two. Each, though, requires its own explication and analysis.

One way in which the first argument often gets stated is in terms of the sickness of offenders. It is, so the argument begins, surely wrong to punish someone for something that he or she could not help, for something for which he or she was not responsible. No one can help being sick. No one ought, therefore, ever be punished for being sick. As the Supreme Court has observed: "Even one day in prison would be cruel and unusual punishment for the 'crime' of having a common cold."[13] Now, it happens to be the case that everyone who commits a crime is sick. Hence, it is surely wrong to punish anyone who commits a crime. What is more, when a response is appropriate, the appropriate response to sickness is treatment. For this reason what we ought to do is to treat offenders, not punish them.

One difficulty with this argument is that the relevance of sickness to the rightness or wrongness of the punishment of offenders is anything but obvious. Indeed, it appears that the conclusion depends upon a non sequitur just because we seldom, if ever, seek to punish people for being sick. Instead we punish them for actions they perform. On the surface, at least, it would seem that even if someone is sick, and even if the person cannot help being sick, this in no way implies that none of his or her actions could have been other than what it was. Thus, if the argument against ever punishing the guilty criminal is to be at all persuasive, it must be shown that for one reason or another, the sickness which afflicts all criminals must affect their actions in such a way that they are thereby prevented ever from acting differently. Construed in this fashion, the argument is at least coherent and responsive. Unfortunately, there is now no reason to be persuaded by it.

It might be persuasive were there any reason to believe that all criminal acts were, for example, instances of compulsive behavior; if, that is, we thought it likely to be true that all criminals were in some obvious and distinguishable sense afflicted by or subjected to irresistible impulses which compelled them to break the law. For there are people who do seem to be subjected to irresistible impulses and who are thereby unable to keep themselves from, among other things, committing crimes. And it is surely troublesome if not clearly wrong to punish them for these actions. Thus, the kleptomaniac or the person who is truly already addicted to narcotics does seem to be suffering from something resembling a sickness and, moreover, to be suffering from something which makes it very difficult if not impossible for such a person to control the actions so compelled. Pity not blame seems appropriate, as does treatment rather than punishment.[14]

Now, the notion of compulsive behavior is not without difficulties of its own. How strong, for instance, does a compulsion have to be before it cannot be resisted? Would someone be a kleptomaniac only if such an individual would steal an object even though a policeman were known by the person to be present and observing every move? Is there anything more that is meant by compulsive behavior than the fact that it is behavior which is inexplicable or unaccountable in terms of the motives and purposes people generally have? More importantly, perhaps, why do we and why should we suppose that the apparently "motiveless" behavior must be the product of compulsions which are less resistible than those to which we all are at times subjected. As has been observed, ". . . it is by no means self-evident that [a wealthy] person's yearnings for valueless [items] are inevitably stronger or more nearly irresistible than the poor man's hunger for a square meal or for a pack of cigarettes."[15]

But while there are problems such as these, the more basic one is simply that there is no reason to believe that all criminal acts are instances of compulsive behavior. Even if there are persons who are victims of irresistible impulses, and even if we ought always to treat and never to punish such persons, it surely does not follow that everyone who commits a crime is doing a compulsive act. And because this is so, it cannot be claimed that all criminals ought to be exempted from punishment — treated instead — because they have a sickness of this sort.

It might be argued, though, that while compulsive behavior accounts only for some criminal acts, there are other sicknesses which account for the remainder. At this juncture the most ready candidate to absorb the remaining cases is that of insanity. The law, for example, has always been willing to concede that a person ought never be punished if the person was so sick or so constituted that he or she did not know the nature or quality of the act, or if this were known, that the person did not know that the act was wrong. And more recently, attempts have been made, sometimes successfully, to expand this exemption to include any person whose criminal action was substantially the product of mental defect or disease.[16]

Once again, though, the crucial point is not the formulation of the most appropriate test for insanity, but the fact that it is far from evident, even under the most "liberal" test imaginable, that it would be true that everyone who commits a crime would be found to be sick and would be found to have been afflicted with a sickness which in some sense rendered the action in question unavoidable. Given all of our present knowledge, there is simply every reason to suppose that some of the people who do commit crimes are neither subject to irresistible impulses, incapable of knowing what they are doing, nor suffering from some other definite mental disease. And, if this is so, then it is a mistake to suppose that the treatment of criminals is on this ground always to be preferred to their punishment.

There is, though, one final version of the claim that every criminal action is excusable on grounds of the sickness of the actor. And this version does succeed in bringing all the remaining instances of criminality, not otherwise excusable, within the category of sickness. It does so only by making the defining characteristic or symptom of mental illness the commission of an illegal act. All criminals, so this argument goes, who are not insane or subject to irresistible impulses are sociopaths — people afflicted with that mental illness which manifests itself exclusively through the commission of antisocial acts. This sickness, like any other sickness, should be treated rather than punished.

Once this stage of the discussion is reached, it is important to be aware of what has happened. In particular, there is no longer the evidentiary claim that all criminal acts are caused by some sickness. Instead there is the bare assertion that this must be so — an assertion, moreover, of a somewhat deceptive character. The illness which afflicts these criminals *is simply* the criminal behavior itself. The disease which is the reason for not punishing the action is identical with the action itself. At this point any attempt to substantiate or disprove the existence of a relationship between sickness and crime is ruled out of order. The presence of mental illnesses of these kinds cannot, therefore, be reasons for not punishing, or for anything else.

Thus, even if it is true that we ought never to punish and that we ought always to treat someone whose criminal action was un-

avoidable because the product of some mental or physical disease —
even if we concede all this — it has yet to be demonstrated, without
begging the question, that all persons who commit crimes are afflicted with some disease or sickness of this kind. And, therefore, if it
is always wrong to punish people, or if it is always preferable to treat
them, then an argument of a different sort must be forthcoming.

In general form that different argument is this: The legal system ought to abandon its attempts to assess responsibility and punish
offenders and it ought instead to focus solely on the question of how
most appropriately the legal system can deal with, i.e., rehabilitate if
possible, the person presently before the court — not, however, because everyone is sick, but because no good comes from punishing
even those who are responsible.

One such proponent of this view is Lady Barbara Wootton.[17]
Her position is an ostensibly simple one. What she calls for is the
"elimination" of responsibility. The state of mind, or *mens rea*, of
the actor at the time he or she committed the act in question is no
longer to be determinative — in the way it now is — of how he or she
shall be dealt with by society. Rather, she asserts, when someone has
been accused of violating the law we ought to have a social mechanism that will ask and answer two distinct questions: Did the accused
in fact do the act in question? If he or she did, given all that we know
about this person (including his or her state of mind), what is the appropriate form of social response to him or her?

Lady Wootton's proposal is for a system of social control that is
thoroughly forward-looking, and in this sense, rehabilitative in perspective. With the elimination of responsibility comes the elimination of the need by the legal system to distinguish any longer between
wickedness and disease. And with the eradication of this distinction
comes the substitution of a forward-looking, treatment system for
the backward-looking, punitive system of criminal law.

The mental state or condition of the offender will continue to
be important but in a different way. "Such conditions . . . become
relevant, not to the question of determining the measure of culpability but to the choice of the treatment most likely to be effective in dis-
couraging him from offending again. . . ."[18]

> . . . one of the most important consequences must be to ob-
> scure the present rigid distinction between the penal and the
> medical institution. . . . For purposes of convenience offend-
> ers for whom medical treatment is indicated will doubtless tend
> to be allocated to one building, and those for whom medicine
> has nothing to offer to another; but *the formal distinction be-*

tween prison and hospital will become blurred, and, one may reasonably expect, eventually obliterated altogether. Both will be simply "places of safety" in which offenders receive the treatment which experience suggests is most likely to evoke the desired response.[19]

Thus, on this view even if a person was responsible when he or she acted and blameworthy for having so acted, we still ought to behave toward him or her in roughly the same way that we behave toward someone who is sick — we ought, in other words, to do something very much like treating him or her. Why? Because this just makes more sense than punishment. The fact that he or she was responsible is simply not very relevant. It is wrong of course to punish people who are sick; but even with those who are well, the more humane and civilized approach is one that concerns itself solely with the question of how best to effect the most rapid and complete rehabilitation or "cure" of the offender. The argument is not that no one is responsible or blameworthy; instead, it is that these descriptions are simply irrelevant to what, on moral grounds, ought to be the only significant considerations, namely, what mode of behavior toward the offender is most apt to maximize the likelihood that he or she will not in the future commit those obnoxious or dangerous acts that are proscribed by the law. The only goal ought to be rehabilitation (in this extended sense of "rehabilitation"), the only issue how to bring about the rehabilitation of the offender.

The moral good sense of this approach can be perceived most clearly, so the argument goes on, when we contrast this thoroughly forward-looking point of view with punishment. For if there is one thing which serves to differentiate any form of punishment from that of treatment, it is that punishment necessarily permits the possibility and even the desirability that punishment will be imposed upon an offender even though he or she is fully "cured" — even though there is no significant likelihood that he or she will behave improperly in the future. And, in every such case in which a person is punished — in every case in which the infliction of the punishment will help the offender not at all (and may in fact harm him or her immeasurably) — the act of punishment is, on moral grounds, seriously offensive. Even if it were true that some of the people who commit crimes are responsible and blameworthy, and even if it were the case that we had meaningful techniques at our disposal for distinguishing those who are responsible from those who are not — still, every time we inflict a punishment on someone who will not be benefited by it, we commit a seriously immoral act. This claim, or something like it, lies, I think, at the base of the case which can be made against the punishment even of the guilty. For it is true that any system of punishment does require that some people will be made to suffer even though the suffering will help them not at all. It is this which the analogue to a system of treatment, a rehabilitative system such as Lady Wootton's, expressly prevents, and it is in virtue of this that such a system might be thought preferable.[20]

There are, I think, both practical and theoretical objections to a proposal such as this. The practical objections concern, first, the possibility that certain "effective" treatments may themselves be morally objectionable, and, second, the possibility that this way of viewing offenders may create a world in which we all become indifferent to the characteristics that distinguish those who are responsible from those who are not. The ease, for example, with which someone like Menninger tends to see the criminal not as an adult but as a "grown-up child"[21] says something about the ease with which a kind of paternalistic manipulativeness could readily pervade a system composed of "places of safety."[22]

These are, though, contingent rather than necessary worries. A system organized in accordance with this rehabilitative ideal could have a view that certain therapies were impermissible on moral grounds, just as it could also treat all of the persons involved with all of the respect they deserved as persons. Indeed, it is important when comparing and contrasting proposals for rehabilitative systems with punishment to make certain that the comparisons are of things that are comparable. There are abuses present in most if not all institutional therapeutic systems in existence today, but there are also abuses present in most if not all institutional penal systems in existence today. And the practical likelihood of the different abuses is certainly worth taking seriously in trying to evaluate the alternatives. What is not appropriate, however, is to contrast either an ideal of the sort proposed by Wootton or Menninger with an existing penal one, or an ideal, just penal system with an existing therapeutic one.[23]

These matters to one side, one of the chief theoretical objections to a proposal of the sort just described is that it ignores the whole question of general deterrence. Were we to have a system such as that envisioned by Lady Wootton or Menninger, we would ask one and only one question of each person who violated the law: What is the best, most efficacious thing to do to this individual to diminish substantially the likelihood that he or she will misbehave in this, or similar fashion, again? If there is nothing at all that need be done in order for us to be quite confident that he or she will not misbehave again (perhaps because the person is extremely contrite, or because we are convinced it was an impulsive, or otherwise unlikely-to-be-repeated act), then the logic of this system requires that the individual be released forthwith. For in this system it is the future conduct of the actor, and it alone, that is the only relevant consideration. There is simply no room within this way of thinking to take into account the achievement of general deterrence. H. L. A. Hart has put the matter this way in explaining why the *reform* (when any might be called for) of the prisoner cannot be the general justifying aim of a system of punishment.

> The objection to assigning to Reform this place in punishment is not merely that punishment entails suffering and Reform does not; but that Reform is essentially a remedial step for which ex hypothesi there is an opportunity only at the point where the criminal law has failed in its primary task of securing society from the evil which breach of the law involves. Society is divisile at any moment into two classes (i) those who have actually broken a given law and (ii) those who have not yet broken it but may. *To take Reform as the dominant objective would be to forego the hope of influencing the second—and in relation to the more serious offences—numerically much greater class. We should thus subordinate the prevention of first offences to the prevention of recidivism.*[24]

A system of punishment will on this view find its justification in the fact that the announcement of penalties and their infliction upon those who break the laws induces others to obey the laws. The question why punish anyone at all *is* answered by Hart. We punish because we thereby deter potential offenders from becoming actual offenders. For Hart, the case for punishment as a general social practice or institution rests on the prevention of crime; it is not to be found either in the inherent appropriateness of punishing offenders or in the contingently "corrective" or rehabilitative powers of fines or imprisonments on some criminals.

Yet, despite appearances, the appeal to general deterrence is not as different as might be supposed from the appeal to a rehabilitative ideal. In both cases, the justification for doing something (or nothing) to the offender rests upon the good consequences that will ensue. General deterrence just as much as rehabilitation views what should be done to offenders as a question of *social control*. It is a way of inducing those who can control their behavior to regulate it in such a way that it will conform to the dictates of the law. The disagreement with those who focus upon rehabilitation is only over the question of whose behavioral modification justifies the imposition of deprivations upon the criminals. Proponents of general deterrence say it is the modification of the behavior of the noncriminals that matters; proponents of rehabilitation say it is the modification of the behavior of the criminals that is decisive. Thus, a view such as Hart's is less a justification of punishment than of a system of threats of punishment. For if the rest of society could be convinced that offenders would be made to undergo deprivations that persons would not wish to undergo we would accomplish all that the deterrent theory would have us achieve through our somewhat more visible applications of these deprivations to offenders. This is so because it is the belief that punishment will follow the commission of an offense that deters potential offenders. The actual punishment of persons is on this view necessary in order to keep the threat of punishment credible.

To put matters this way is to bring out the fact that the appeal to general deterrence, just as much as the appeal to rehabilitation, appears to justify a wholly forward-looking system of social control. And, it has been argued, all such appeals fail to capture both the essence of and the moral point behind anything that is in fact a system of punishment. What is missing, it is claimed, is captured by the retributive nature of the idea that punishment is in a conceptual sense, and also in a fundamentally moral sense, backward looking—that it is a deprivation that is intentionally imposed and properly so in the way that it is because of what was done in the past by the individual punished.

Proponents of a theory of general deterrence have sought to take account of an objection such as this and to show that it is readily assimilable into the structure of their theory. In fact, as was indicated at the outset, one very common kind of philosophical response is to claim that an adequate theory of punishment, which is nonetheless founded upon general deterrence, can be readily constructed. It is this response, and the problems generated by it, that must now be examined.

IV

Philosophers who wish to defend a consequentialist theory of punishment typically do so by claiming that their approach is not in conflict with anything that can plausibly be defended in retributivism. The conflict disappears, they argue, once it is seen that there are two very different issues addressed by a theory of punishment:

one issue relates to the justification of a system of punishment; the other to the justification of the punishment of particular individuals within that system. S. I. Benn puts the matter this way. Utilitarianism, he says, has

> . . . the merit, as an approach to the justification of punishment that it provides a clear procedure for determining whether the institution is acceptable in general terms. This the retributivist approach cannot do because it denies the relevance of weighing advantages and disadvantages, which is what we ultimately must do in moral criticism of rules and institutions. Consequently, a retributivist justification of punishment as an institution usually turns out to be a denial of the necessity for justification, a veiled reference to the beneficial results of punishment (a utilitarianism in disguise), or an appeal to religious authority. When it is a question of justifying a particular case of punishment, however, the retributivist is in a far stronger position. There would be no point in having a general rule if on every occasion that it had to be applied one had to consider whether the advantages in this particular case warranted acting in accordance with it. Moreover, the point of punishment as deterrent would be quite lost were there no general expectation, based on the general operation of the rule, that guilty men would be punished. Assuming, then, that a penal system can be justified in utilitarian terms, any offense is at least prima facie an occasion for a penalty. Equally, without an offense there is no question of penalty. The retributivist contention that punishment is justified if, and only if, it is deserved is really applicable, therefore, to the justification of particular instances of punishment, the institution as such being taken for granted.[25]

A fundamental problem with this way of proceeding is that it does not get to the heart of the retributivist position. On a view such as Benn's, virtually all of the interesting and important questions concerning whether it is right to punish people, and if so why, are the utilitarian questions that are to be answered on consequentialist grounds. Retributivism is reduced to a special instance of the general case for having a system follow and apply its own rules whatever they may happen to be. This is a general view of doubtful plausibility,[26] but even if it were plausible as a defense of rule-applying behavior, it misses most, if not all, of the retributivist's point. What the retributivist can show fairly persuasively I believe, is that any general justification of this form fails to meet a number of key issues in a convincing or illuminating fashion.

   To begin with, it does not explain why we should attach the
importance that we do to the state of mind or culpability of the offender. In "Legal Responsibility and Excuses," for instance, H. L. A.
Hart argues that the principle that is involved is ". . . that it is unfair
and unjust to punish those who have not 'voluntarily' broken the
law. . . ." and that "[w]hat we need to escape confusion here is a distinction between two sets of questions. The first is a general question
about the moral value of the laws: Will enforcing them produce
more good than evil? If it does, then it is morally permissible to enforce them by punishing those who have broken them, unless in any
particular case there is some 'excuse.'"[27] The last sentence is the crucial one. Why is it morally permissible to punish persons just as long
as there is not some excusing condition present in the case of the otherwise guilty person? In "Legal Responsibility and Excuses," Hart of-
fers a theory to explain why it would be *worse* if persons were punished even when the excusing conditions were present. But this is different from providing a reason why it *is* appropriate to punish in the
presence of guilt and the absence of any of the excusing conditions.
The retributivist can claim that that is the crucial question for any
theory of punishment, and that the answer has got to have a good
deal more to do with such things as the wrongdoing of the actor and
the deservedness of the punishment than this standard consequentialist account can allow. The deterrence of others cannot be an adequate answer because that would make the punishment of the guilty
(in the absence of excusing conditions) unjustifiable whenever it was
the case that no increase in deterrence would result from the punishment of this individual or a class of individuals engaged in a specifi-
able type of behavior. At the very least, a justification of punishment
founded upon general deterrence surely requires that only a certain
minimum number and type of even guilty offenders be punished;
namely, the number and kind required to produce the desired level
of deterrence. If punishing only a third or a half of the guilty would
produce as much deterrence as is obtained by punishing all of the
guilty, a theory of punishment founded upon general deterrence
provides no obvious reason for the punishment of a greater number.
   In addition, the argument from general deterrence leaves unanswered the question of on what grounds it is just, or right, to punish the guilty when the relevant excusing conditions do not apply. To
know that a special injustice would obtain if those who were guilty
but excusable were punished, is not thereby to know that no injustice
would obtain if those who were guilty but not excusable were punished. And there is some reason to think that it is unjust to punish the

guilty, if the reason for punishing them is the deterrence of others. To punish in order to deter others is in an important respect to use the persons punished as a means by which to benefit others. The fact that it would be worse to use them in this way if they were not guilty does not by itself explain the rightness of so using them when they are.

There is still a different point that can be made. What is missing is a very satisfactory explanation of why it is so important to punish only the guilty. An account such as Benn's or Hart's, a retributivist could argue, does not succeed very well in capturing the peculiar force of the wrongfully punished person's complaint that a special, serious injustice was done to him or her because he or she was not guilty of the crime for which the person was convicted. If the overall system was fair, if the person was not intentionally convicted falsely, and if the consequences were on the whole good in terms of general deterrence, it is hard to see why the complaint should be thought such a serious one. But it is. Any consequentialist account that can be constructed does not seem able to account easily for the acknowledged gravity of that wrong and the acknowledged severity of the complaint.

Finally, the limitations of a theory of general deterrence can be brought out by identifying some important features that need explaining which justifications founded on the consequences of either general or special deterrence cannot readily or easily explain, namely, that there are cases in which punishment seems appropriate and in which appeals to deterrence appear to be thoroughly beside the point.

Consider the following thought-experiment. Suppose that somehow Hitler had been found alive and well in Argentina, say, five years after the end of World War II. The Nazi apparatus had been fully dismantled, the East and West German governments were fully viable, and the Nazi ideology was now quite unpopular. Isn't it clear, it might be urged, that if Hitler had been found it would have been right, perhaps even important, to punish him? Yet surely the case even for the permissibility of punishing him could not have rested very plausibly on the ground that punishment was appropriate or required in order to convince future Hitlers that they would be punished were they to do what he had done. More to the point, even if punishment in order to achieve deterrence made some sense, would we not also want to say that any appeal to the consequences just does not get to the heart of what would be involved in the rightness of punishing persons such as Hitler?

Now, of course, it might be added that if this is regarded as a marginal case for punishment, then it can simply be rejected as a confusing borderline case. But if it is seen as a central or clear case, then acceptance of general deterrence and the rejection of retributivism as a general justification for punishment is less easy.

It does seem to me that a retributivist would be right in calling attention to the fact that there are cases such as these and that they are central rather than marginal cases just in the sense that they are clear cases of potentially appropriate punishment. If anyone ought to be punished for his or her wrongdoing—one might be tempted to say—it was persons such as the Nazi leaders. And if that is so, then any adequate theory of punishment must provide a convincing justification for punishment in instances like these. Since justifications focused upon general deterrence cannot convincingly do so, this at least counts as a mark against them both.

All of this can be related back to the discussion of the concept of punishment in Part II. If the idea of punishment is linked conceptually with the idea of wrongdoing, then it is not implausible to suggest that punishment is also linked in a fundamental way with the idea of blameworthiness. And the relationship between blame and punishment is both more important and more intimate than consequentialist accounts appear to allow. While it would doubtless be too strong a view to propose that punishment *is* simply a harsher form of blame, it is not at all implausible to observe that the standard case of punishment is reserved for those cases in which at least blame is appropriate and in which mere blame is insufficient. Insufficient, however, not in the sense that blaming would not deter while punishment would, but rather insufficient in the sense that blaming would not do justice to the seriousness of the wrong. Thus, if punishment in many cases is reasonably viewed as a more extreme kind of blame, and if blame cannot be justified on consequentialist grounds, then this, too, casts doubt upon the justification of punishment by any straightforward appeal to the consequences.

At the very least, it is difficult to develop a convincing consequentialist rationale for blaming. We can and do blame others silently, to ourselves. We can and do decide that those long since dead are properly to blame for things they did while alive; or that someone long considered blameworthy is, in fact, not blameworthy at all. These activities are cases of blaming. They play important roles in the lives of many persons. We can, of course, if pressed, construct a consequentialist account that takes these activities into account and justifies them on consequentialist grounds. But the arguments do not ring true. The theory can always be saved, but at a price. We do not always, or even typically, blame in order to deter or to reform—or even publicly to denounce.

Any adequate theory of blame would, I think, have to acknowledge this, and either account for all the important cases or urge that all of the nonconforming cases be extinguished from the repertoire of acceptable human behaviors. Hence, given the intimacy of the connection between wrongdoing and blame and wrongdoing and punishment, consequentialist defenses of punishment are rendered suspect on this ground as well.

For all of these reasons, therefore, consequentialist justifications of punishment do not seem adequate. They seem to miss the point of the idea of punishment itself, and they do not seem to justify punishing persons in at least some of the cases where punishment, if it is ever to be justified, seems most defensible. That is why retributivist theories of punishment are more attractive and plausible than is often supposed. If there are any theories of punishment that are unequivocally such, it is retributivist ones. If there are any theories of punishment that will locate the justifiability of punishment in the fact of wrongdoing already having occurred it is retributivist ones. Hence, it is they that should receive a good deal more attention than the passage from Benn suggests.

V

As has been suggested in the preceding section, there are two related but distinguishable questions that any fully adequate theory of punishment should address and answer. The first is that of why it is so important to punish *only* the guilty; the second is that of why it is right, i.e., fully justifiable, to punish *all* of the guilty. Theories concerned with the justifiability of punishment can, therefore, be either weak or strong. Weak ones establish some or all of the conditions under which punishment is not justifiable. They address only the first question. Strong ones provide arguments that seek to establish the justifiability of the punishment of each and every one of the guilty. They address the second question. Hart's account, in "Legal Responsibility and Excuses," of why it is wrong to punish when the excusing conditions are present is one kind of weak theory.[28] Another kind of weak theory seeks to give an account of the limitations on the things that can justifiably be done to persons by other persons—in the guise of either treatment or punishment. In their most modest form they can be construed as seeking to establish the conditions that must be satisfied before the intentional infliction of a deprivation, be it as a part of a punishment or a treatment, could be justifiable. Herbert Morris's critique of certain possible therapeutic systems is an example of this sort of weak theory.[29]

Still another theory, sometimes thought of as retributivist, is hard to classify because it depends upon a justification that is "forward looking" but rather different from the typical consequentialist defense of punishment. It is that punishment can function as a social mechanism by which an offender can achieve expiation for his or her wrongdoing. As such, punishment can play an essential and humanizing role in the maintenance of society. Submission to punishment can be a means by which an offender retains his or her membership in society despite the serious transgression. So we can then speak, within such a context, of punishment as involving the "paying" of one's "debt" to society, and, more importantly, we can also speak of an offender's claim to renewed acceptance in the society once his or her punishment has terminated and the "debt"to society has been paid by the offender.

The reason why this, too, is a weak theory is that it is an argument only for the rightness of punishing those who desire expiation, or perhaps for those who desire to live in a system in which expiation for wrongdoing is attainable. It is not an adequate justification for punishing those who desire neither expiation nor a system in which achieving expiation through such a mechanism is possible.

Accounts such as these are important and illuminating. As has been indicated, however, they leave unanswered the second question which seems to be the more fundamental moral one: What is it about the past wrongful action that thereby justifies the punishment of the actor and that makes it right to punish each and every guilty person? Unless that question can be answered, some if not many cases of punishment remain in important respects incompletely defended and to that degree unjustified. Genuinely persuasive and complete theories of punishment, all of which will have a retributivist aspect, must be strong enough to provide such an answer.

The simplest way, I think, to justify doing something to the wrongdoer because of what he or she has done is in terms not of punishment but, instead, in terms of the idea of *exclusion* as an appropriate response to an unwillingness to comply with defensible, generally accepted rules. It is a feature of virtually all cooperative activities that stand any chance of succeeding that there be a minimal kind of compliance with the rules that define and regulate the pursuit and practice of the activity in question. Games are one kind of cooperative activity; living in civil society is perhaps another. In both, the interdependence of the participants is made both possible and reasonable by a degree of common acceptance of and compliance with the relevant constitutive and regulatory rules. A game simply cannot be played if one or more of the players refuses to accept and to follow the basic rules adhered to by the other players. When such a situation occurs it is a reasonable response for those who desire to play the game to exclude those who clearly will not follow the rules. Of course, many games have rules which anticipate violations and which provide for their occurrence within the game. Striking the body of a player who is shooting a basketball is provided for by the rules of basketball, and there is no requirement that prospective players be committed to an intention not to foul. But a failure to accept the rule that the person fouled is entitled to two shots is different. Full acceptance of that rule is essential; and a refusal to adhere to that requirement seems in a quite direct way to justify a refusal to permit continued participation in the game.

A picture such as this might provide a rationale for a justifiable response to certain kinds of wrongdoing. On this view, banishment and exile are the paradigmatically appropriate responses to individuals who indicate an unwillingness to observe the core rules of the criminal law — adherence to which is required if life in civil society is to be either possible or decent. On this view, imprisonment for the violation of these rules could be seen not as punishment for past wrongdoing but rather as the closest approximation to banishment that is now possible.

Exclusion, while a deprivation, is not, on this account, a punishment. It need not be quite the kind of deprivation a punishment must be. One is deprived of the opportunity to continue participating but there is so far no requirement that one thereby be worse off than the rest. The point of exclusion, on this account, is to prevent those who have elected not to adhere to the basic rules from interfering unduly with the desires of the rest to engage in interdependent behavior which depends upon a willingness to adhere. Similarly, the relevance of past behavior for punishment is different from what it is for exclusion. As has been suggested, the link between past behavior and punishment is an extremely strong one — conceptual at least in part. Past wrongdoing is the reason for punishment — if anything is. That is both a truth and the source of the continuing puzzle for theories of punishment. Under this account of the idea of exclusion, past behavior is merely evidence of an election or likelihood to refuse to abide by the rules. What would be required at a minimum to make exclusion justifiable is a well-founded belief in the continuing unwillingness to comply. Past behavior which consists in the disregard of the core rules of the criminal law may be powerful evidence of the existence of a continuation of the conduct. But it is only evidence and can never be more than that. Whatever the past behavior, if the evidence is now convincing that there will be a conscientious determination to comply, then exclusion on this approach makes no conceptual or moral sense. That is one of the attractive features, as well as a limitation upon, this alternative way of viewing things. It does provide a defensible rationale for doing some of the things we do in respect to serious crime without regard for the wishes of the criminal and with regard for his or her past action. But it is not a theory of punishment; it does not justify responding to the offender solely in virtue of the fact of past wrongdoing; and it does not justify doing anything to the offender unless the relevant conditions for exclusion are found to be present. Exclusion or banishment could, of course, be a punishment. But for reasons already discussed additional conditions would have to be satisfied before that was the case.

Are there, then, any plausible arguments for a theory strong enough to justify *punishing* all offenders? As has been indicated, such a theory must be retributive in certain respects if it is to be unambiguously a theory of punishment. And it must also be a theory of a certain degree of strength and character. It must justify the punishment of the guilty rather than the innocent. It must justify the actual punishment of persons rather than the appearance of punishment. And it must justify the punishment of all of those who are guilty.

There are several arguments that can be given for a theory of punishment of the requisite strength and character. The problem, however, is that none of them is wholly satisfactory.

One argument can be put like this. Many persons, e.g. Hart, acknowledge it is unjust to punish those who are in fact innocent. Indeed, as has been suggested, all would recognize the claim of an innocent person (no matter how fair the system within and through which he or she was found guilty and punished) that a particular injustice of an identifiable sort had occurred. But if we can understand so readily and clearly that it is unjust to punish the innocent, that must be because it is also the case that it is just to punish the guilty. To understand that the innocent do not deserve punishment is also necessarily to understand that the guilty do deserve it. That justice requires the punishment of the guilty is but a different aspect of the widely accepted idea that justice forbids the punishment of the innocent.

This argument does not work. Even if it were unproblematic to move from "It is unjust to punish the innocent," to "It is not unjust to punish the guilty," and even if the connection between the two propositions were one of entailment, there is an important difference in meaning between "It is not unjust to punish the guilty" and "It is just to punish the guilty." And there is even more important difference in meaning between "It is just to punish the guilty" and "Justice requires the punishment of the guilty." There is a special injustice in punishing the innocent such that *that* injustice is not present when the guilty are punished. It is true, therefore, that in that special sense or respect it is not unjust to punish the guilty. Furthermore, it may even be the case that if anyone is to be punished, justice thereby requires that it be the guilty, rather than the innocent. But none of this gets any strong version of retributivism where it wants to go: to the claim that justice itself requires, and hence justifies, that there be the punishment of the guilty. If we are to be convinced of that truth about justice and punishment, then other arguments must be forthcoming.

The two that seem to be the most promising are advanced by Herbert Morris in "Persons and Punishment." The first argument involves the fairness of imposing those burdens that the criminal law imposes on us all. The second concerns the unfairness of letting the criminal keep the benefits he or she has unfairly appropriated through violating the law.

The first argument goes like this:

> It is only reasonable that those who voluntarily comply with the rules be provided some assurance that they will not be assuming burdens which others are unprepared to assume. Their disposition to comply voluntarily will diminish as they learn that others are with impunity renouncing burdens they are assuming.[30]

There are, I take it, two related points here. One is that the system will not work well, if it works at all, unless the guilty are punished; not because the threat needs to be made credible to those who have not yet broken the law but who otherwise might, but because those who have not broken the law will have no reason to continue to be law abiding (indeed, it would be extremely imprudent for them to be law abiding) unless they can count on reasonably successful efforts being made to keep down the amount of dangerous crime.[31]

The argument has considerable appeal and power. It can be restated even more explicitly to make the point that the criminal law requires that there be punishment connected to violations of the criminal law. Punishments are necessary because, if they were absent, persons who would otherwise be willing, indeed anxious, to comply with the criminal law would lack the minimum guarantees or

assurances of general compliance which make their compliance prudent as well as moral. That is to say, they would through their compliance be making themselves more vulnerable to the wrongful
actions of others than is rationally prudent. They would, on this account, like to comply with the criminal law because in the core cases
of criminality at least, to fail to comply would, without more, be to
behave immorally. But the moral life would be an unduly risky and
dangerous one to live unless there were a genuine likelihood that others will also adhere to its basic demands, and, over and above this,
many things that it is desirable and appropriate for persons to be
able to do in living their lives would also become unreasonably risky
ventures unless the compliance by others could, in general, be
counted upon. One way to look at things, therefore, is to recast the
argument from general deterrence as an argument for the *criminal
law* — and, as such, for the background conditions that make social
life of any decent sort possible. Another way to view matters is to see
the criminal laws as among the kinds of laws that rational persons
would choose to have as constituent elements of the legal system of
any reasonably just society, and for the same sorts of considerations
enumerated above they would necessarily choose to have criminal
laws with punishments attached.

The problem is not so much one of whether this is a good or
convincing argument as it is one of determining how far the argument goes or what truths we ought now be convinced of. It is a good
argument for why some system of criminal law would be a part of any
conception of the good society that is not a hopelessly utopian and,
thereby, irrelevant one. The question is rather what the argument
produces in the way of a complete justification of the punishment of
the guilty. If it is construed as a restated version of the argument
from general deterrence it is an argument for the punishment of at
least *some* of the guilty; namely, those whose punishment is necessary in order to make these background conditions a reality. As has
been seen, however, this by itself does not justify the punishment of
all of the guilty. Can a stronger justification be derived?

One way to try to produce one is to argue that the connection
between criminal laws and punishment is a conceptual one, that to
have criminal laws entails that all violations be punished. Here it
might be claimed that the idea of being required to do or abstain
from doing something means that one will be punished if one refuses
or fails to adhere to the requirement.[32] The problem with this approach, I think, is that the idea of a requirement is not that strong.
We can understand the idea of something being required, and in
that sense being different from a request or, more generally, what is

optional, without the idea of a punishment being attached to the doing of what is not optional. Juries, for example, are regularly instructed that they are required to apply the law as given by the judge. This is a readily understandable instruction even though there is no punishment that is connected either in theory or practice to a jury's failure to do what is required. And as Hart has observed, correctly I believe, ". . . we can distinguish clearly the rule prohibiting certain behavior from the provision for penalties to be exacted if the rule is broken, and suppose the first to exist without the latter. We can, in a sense, subtract the sanction and still leave an intelligible standard of behavior which it was designed to maintain."[33]

Another way to try to produce a stronger justification is to make the argument a moral one. Hart, for example, suggests that something like a principle of fairness as equal treatment may be at issue. In discussing the scale of punishments and the question of proportionality, Hart observes that "It is indeed important that the law should not in its scale of punishments gratuitously flout any well-marked common moral distinctions. But this is because the claim of justice that 'like cases should be treated alike' should always be heard; and where the law appears to depart from common estimates of relative wickedness it should make clear what moral aims require this."[34] Perhaps the argument can be made more general. Any decent society properly will have a system of criminal law and for that reason will justifiably punish some offenders. But if persons in that society are to be treated fairly, then there is no defensible basis upon which to distinguish those who will be punished from those, similarly situated violators of the criminal law, who will not. Justice as equality requires, therefore, that since some will rightly be punished, all should be. The difficulty with this argument is that, when pushed in this direction it becomes perverse. For punishment is a deprivation, the imposition of which requires special justification. The move from the justifiability of punishing some to the justifiability of punishing all out of a consideration of fairness to those some who are justifiably punished seems neither weighty nor attractive. If it could be shown that the deprivations otherwise imposed on some would be less were the deprivations to be imposed on all, that would be a further, more convincing point. But in its absence, the argument does not very adequately give a reason for increasing the amount of human suffering beyond what is necessary to provide the background assurances deprivations must produce.

Still a third argument might be constructed. In imagining what a decent society would be like, all rational persons would, as has been seen, opt for the existence of a system of criminal law in which there would be punishment. If so, the argument might continue, there are none who can reasonably complain when they are punished for their offenses. Therefore, no offenders can complain when punishment is meted out to each and every one of them. The system is precisely the one that each would have acknowledged to be a right and important constituent of the decent society. Once again, it is not clear how deeply or strongly the argument cuts. In its weaker form it is an argument for why it is not wrong to punish those who are guilty. It removes from the guilty one a powerful complaint that might otherwise be available to them, but that is by no means identical to providing a reason why it is right and desirable to punish all of them. To achieve the requisite degree of strength, it must be the argument that rational persons conducting this thought experiment would see the necessary appropriateness of punishing all offenders and would, therefore, be committed to the rightness of doing so. The difficulty here is that the background assurances that were reasonably sought simply do not appear to require this. It is, at the very least, far from obvious that rational persons reflecting in this way could or would correctly conclude that nothing less than the invariable punishment of all offenses was what they, themselves, should elect. And without that stronger, less plausible stipulation, the punishment of all offenders cannot be justified either on the ground that it was, in this special sense, chosen by them, or on the ground that it is otherwise required as a precondition for the existence of a decent, defensible social existence.

There is a different retributivist argument, given by Morris, that deserves serious consideration. It is this. One way to understand the criminal law is to see it as a system of prohibitions which directs us all not to act in those various ways in which it is wrong to act, although we are all inclined to some extent to do so. To act in accordance with the criminal law is, therefore, to take on a kind of burden — the burden that is connected with voluntarily restraining ourselves from doing many things that we would like to do. And this burden is only fairly assumed by anyone if it is equally assumed by everyone. Or, to put it another way, it is not fair that the criminal in committing the crime has thrown off the burden assumed by the rest. Punishment is fair — is required by justice — because it is the way to most nearly replace the missing burden where it properly belongs.

Morris puts it this way:

> . . . [I]t is just to punish those who have violated the rules and caused the unfair distribution of benefits and burdens. A person who violates the rules has something others have — the bene-

fits of the system — but by renouncing what others have assumed, the burdens of self-restraint, he has acquired an unfair advantage. Matters are not even until this advantage is in some way erased. Another way of putting it is that he owes something to others, for he has something that does not rightfully belong to him. Justice — that is, punishing such individuals — restores the equilibrium of benefits and burdens by taking from the individual what he owes, that is, exacting the debt.[35]

Justice, on this account, requires that the guilty be punished because of two interrelated facts: burdens have been unfairly assumed vis-à-vis the criminal by the law-abiding citizens and benefits have been unfairly appropriated by the criminal vis-à-vis the law-abiding citizens. The wrongdoer has obtained a benefit to which he or she is not entitled by not restraining himself or herself from acting on inclination and desire in the way in which the rest of us did. Thus, in punishing the offender we take away that benefit and thereby restore the social equilibrium which existed before the offense.

There are, I believe, at least two problems with this way of thinking about the justifiability of punishment. In the first place, it is not always plausible to think of criminal and law-abiding behavior in terms of benefits and burdens. Sometimes it is, but sometimes it is not. The structure of the argument seems to fit reasonably well cases like that of tax evasion. Paying taxes is a burden. No one is naturally inclined or disposed to pay them. If everyone else does pay their taxes and I do not, I do benefit unfairly — and in two ways. I get to keep more of my income than the rest, and I also get the "public" benefits that are bought by the tax monies, e.g., the security provided by an army or a fire department. In addition, the taxpayers are unfairly burdened — also in two ways. They bear a burden that they ought reasonably be required to bear only if everyone bears it. And the burden is, perhaps, greater than it otherwise would have been because of my evasion.

There are, I think, problems with this way of analyzing the injustice of tax evasion.[36] But even if there are none, one more central question is whether most cases of serious criminality are fundamentally analogous. And there appear to be some important respects in which they are not. Consider, for example, rape instead of tax evasion. If someone who is inclined to rape a woman fails to restrain that inclination and commits a rape, it is hard to see how he has been unfairly benefited in respect to *all* of the other members of society. For suppose, as seems reasonably likely, they lack the inclination to rape anyone — irrespective of what the law does or does not prohibit.[37] Because they are not, therefore, burdened at all by the criminalization of rape, it is difficult to understand in what respect they have been unfairly burdened; nor is it easy to see the manner in which the rapist has unfairly benefited himself, *as against those who abstain from rape*. Of course rape is wrong. Of course rape is a case of the rapist treating the victim very wrongly; rape violates the rights of the person raped and is, therefore, a case of injustice. But rape, torture, murder—many of the worst things one person can possibly do to another—do not neatly or obviously fit the model of the misallocation of benefits and burdens described by Morris as constituting the background justification for the punishment of the guilty. What is more, given the argument thus far, it is only a background for a justification for the punishment of the guilty. That is so because the claimed unfairness in the distribution of benefits and burdens brought about by the crime itself only goes to show what may be the injustice produced by committing the crime. The further part of Morris' argument, which has not yet been examined, is also necessary before there is a reason to think that the punishment of the criminal is just. Both of these issues, then, require additional analysis.

There are at least two ways to try to produce a better fit between this view of the criminal law and a system of benefits and burdens. The first is to make explicit and defend a view of human nature that would make the claim of burden more plausible. That is to say, if it is the case that all humans are strongly and naturally inclined to do most if not all of the things that the criminal law properly forbids and if it is the case that they do work long and hard to restrain themselves from doing those things they are all inclined to do, then the criminal has thrown aside the burden that the rest of the citizens continue to bear. This is certainly a possible theory of human nature, but not obviously a correct one.[38] Hence an argument such as the above is at best incomplete in the absence of a vindication of the theory of human nature upon which it depends. What is surely instructive is the respect in which a consideration of an argument such as Morris's does reveal the degree to which some if not all theories of punishment and crime do depend in quite fundamental ways upon theories of human nature that are seldom if ever made explicit or overtly defended.[39]

The second way to try to make these cases fit better would be to retreat to a kind of second-order set of benefits and burdens. It is not, on this view, the inclination to do what a particular law prohibits that is involved. Instead, it is the inclination in each individual to do some of the things prohibited by the criminal law that underlies the analysis in terms of benefits and burdens. I restrain myself from doing those wrong things I am inclined to do and it is only fair that you restrain yourself from doing those wrong things you are inclined to do. You benefit from my law abidingness and I benefit from yours. A theory of human nature still underlies the argument, but it is a somewhat more benign or optimistic one.

But even if the underlying theory of human nature were correct, this approach would assimilate the additional cases only by paying a high price. For much of the force of the original claim is dissipated once this retreat is made. What began as a powerful appeal to a direct and obvious sense in which committing a particular crime burdened unfairly those who did not commit that crime and benefited unfairly those who did has been altered to become a far more abstract, more controversial appeal to the general benefits and burdens of law abidingness.[40]

The second general objection concerns the relevance of the analysis (even if it is correct in terms of benefits and burdens) to punishment. For it remains to be seen how it is that *punishing* the wrongdoer constitutes a taking of the wrongfully appropriated benefit away from him or her. Where the benefit is a tangible good still in existence, e.g., the payroll from the bank robbery, we do, of course, take it away from the bank robber and return it to the bank. But that is not even punishment, that is restitution. That seems to restore the social equilibrium in respect to the thing wrongfully appropriated. And where the wrong caused by the crime is of a different type, so that restitution is not possible or adequate, what seems most appropriately called for is compensation to the victim by the wrongdoer. Thus, compensation or restitution to the victim by the wrongdoer, not his or her punishment, appears to be the natural and direct way to restore the balance in respect to wrongful appropriation of something that belonged to the victim.

Perhaps, though, the argument is that punishment can be seen as preventing the wrongdoer from enjoying the fruits of his or her wrongdoing. Perhaps in some sense, punishment is appropriately inflicted to restore the equilibrium when, for example, we cannot find the stolen payroll and we know it has not yet been spent or enjoyed by the robber. But in many, if not most, cases the "removal" of the benefit through punishment will at best be metaphorical and indirect. How, for instance, does punishment for rape take the unfairly appropriated benefit away from the rapist? How does it even keep him from enjoying the benefits of his wrongdoing, since the direct benefit has already been appropriated? To speak of the taking away of a benefit as punishment for rape does not seem to illuminate very fully the way in which the premise of the argument is true. Nor is it easy to see exactly how, even if the wrongfully appropriated benefit can be taken away by punishment, the social equilibrium is thereby restored. Perhaps the point is that there is less disequilibrium if something burdensome is done to prevent the full enjoyment of a wrongfully seized benefit than if nothing burdensome is done to the wrongdoer to counterbalance the satisfaction. But still, why should this kind of greater equilibrium, which retains its metaphorical features, be the sort required by justice? Punishment, even punishment for obvious and serious wrongdoing, also produces a kind of greater disequilibrium. Where there was previously the unhappiness, pain, suffering, or deprivation caused by the wrongdoing, there is now, after the punishment, the additional deprivation that is the punishment. To view punishment as restoring the social equilibrium and to regard as required by justice the creation of this particular kind of equilibrium — one which necessarily depends upon the intentional production of additional human deprivation — does not in the end appear to explain in a wholly satisfactory way why the punishment of wrongdoers is a justifiable practice. It does not seem to be much more illuminating than to speak of punishment for rape, for example, as deserved because of the seriousness of the wrong. It is to return, perhaps, to the fairly plausible intuition with which retributivism begins — that serious crime, seriously culpable behavior, deserves to be punished — but it is not yet to give a generally applicable set of reasons for thinking that intuition defensible. Thus, while strong retributivist theories are the kinds of theories that a justification of punishment requires, such theories do not appear to contain a set of moral arguments sufficiently sound, unambiguous, and persuasive upon which to rest the general justifiability of punishment. For this reason, whether it is right to punish persons and, if so, for what reasons, are, I think, still open questions both within philosophic thought and the society at large.

NOTES

1. Rehabilitation, reform, and treatment are clearly different in that it is not necessarily a part of any system of reform, treatment, or rehabilitation that there be the intentional infliction of a deprivation. Whether a deprivation should be imposed is wholly contingent; it depends upon the likelihood of a deprivation (as op-

posed, say, to a reward, to vocational education, or to psychotherapy) changing the future behavior of the person involved in the desired way.

2. As I shall argue, there are problems with regarding such a system unequivocally as a system of punishment.

3. Such theories are typically referred to as utilitarian theories of punishment. Because utilitarianism is in part a particular historical theory with features that are not essential to a general discussion of punishment, I prefer to use the more neutral term "consequentialist" to describe the class of theories of which utilitarianism is, perhaps, the most prominent member.

4. H. L. A. Hart, "Prolegomenon to the Principles of Punishment," 60 *Proc. Aristotelian Soc.* 1 (new series, 1959), reprinted in Hart, *Punishment and Responsibility* (Oxford: Oxford U. Press, 1968), p. 1, pp. 4-5.

Hart acknowledges that his account is similar to ones provided by other philosophers such as Kurt Baier, "Is Punishment Retributive?" 16 *Analysis* 25 (1955); Anthony Flew, "The Justification of Punishment," 29 *Philosophy* 291 (1954) and S. I. Benn, "An Approach to the Problems of Punishment" 33 *Philosophy* 325 (1958).

In his account Hart goes on to relegate to the position of "substandard" or "secondary" cases those which involve:

"(a) Punishments for breaches of legal rules imposed or administered otherwise than by officials (decentralized sanctions).

"(b) Punishments for breaches of nonlegal rules or orders (punishments in a family or school).

"(c) Vicarious or collective punishment of some members of a social group for actions done by others without the former's authorization, encouragement, control, or permission.

"(d) Punishment of persons (otherwise than under (c) who neither are in fact nor supposed to be offenders." Hart, *ibid.*, p. 5.

I am puzzled by the decision to mark off the standard case in this way. I see no strong reason to believe that the case of legal punishment is any more the paradigm of punishment than is, for example, the case of parental punishment. There are, of course, nonstandard cases, and they are worth distinguishing. They are of at least two sorts. On the one hand there are those which are only metaphorically describable as punishment — as, for instance, when we talk of one team punishing another. On the other hand there are those which are less clear cases of punishment because they lack one or more of the features of the standard or typical case of punishment — as, for instance, when persons who know that another is innocent inflict a deprivation on the innocent person in order to get others to believe that the guilty person has been apprehended and is being punished. This example, which is typically offered as a decisive defect of utilitarianism, I discuss further, *infra*, pp. 118-119.

Cases such as these to one side, I see no reason to focus upon the law rather than the school, the family, or a voluntary association as the standard or central setting for punishment. This suggests, perhaps, that the standard case does suppose the existence of a set or network of institutional arrangements (so that all cases of one friend punishing another friend are nonstandard cases), but that seems to me to be the correct feature to focus upon, not the existence of a legal system. Although I do not believe anything of great importance turns on this point, the linking of the concept of punishment with the law seems to me mistaken and at times to obscure rather than illuminate what is at issue.

5. This would only be the case in societies where wrongdoing, or at least blameworthiness, is intimately connected with something like intentional behavior of

some sort. Such a connection is not, however, essential either to the idea of moral wrongdoing or to the idea of moral blameworthiness. I discuss this point further, *infra*, pp. 119-120.

6. Hart's discussion of criminality (as opposed to his discussion of punishment) does seem at times to come close to this point. *See, e.g.,* H. L. A. Hart, *The Morality of the Criminal Law* (Jerusalem: Magnes Press, Hebrew University, 1964), p. 28; and H. L. A. Hart, *The Concept of Law* (Oxford: At the Clarendon Press, 1961), p. 165. I have discussed this issue at greater length in my article, "H. L. A. Hart and the Doctrines of *Mens Rea* and Criminal Responsibility," 35 *U. Chi. L. Rev.* 92 (1967).

Joel Feinberg also emphasizes the public, denunciatory aspect of punishment in "The Expressive Function of Punishment" in Feinberg, *Doing and Deserving* (Princeton: Princeton U. Press, 1970), p. 95.

7. Strict liability offenses also create a problem for this account. Even if, as I have suggested elsewhere ["Strict Liability and the Criminal Law," 12 *Stanford L. Rev.* 731, (1960)] such offenses are not as "strict" as is often supposed, it would be implausible to construe many of them as in any way dependent upon prior beliefs about the blameworthiness of the behavior in question.

8. *See,* "The Obligation to Obey the Law," *supra.*

9. In this respect, the view I am here considering is different from that advanced by Quinton in "On Punishment," 14 *Analysis* 133 (1954). In that piece Quinton considers the common criticism of utilitarianism that it could, in certain circumstances, justify, if not require, the punishment of an individual known to be innocent by the persons imposing the punishment, *i.e.,* when some greater harm would be prevented by doing so. Quinton's solution is a conceptual one. The concept of punishment, he argues, entails that the person punished be guilty.

"It is not, as some retributivists think, that we *may* not punish the innocent and *ought* only to punish the guilty, but that we *cannot* punish the innocent and *must* only punish the guilty. Of course, the suffering or harm in which punishment consists can be and is inflicted on innocent people but this is not punishment, it is judicial error or terrorism or, in Bradley's characteristically repellant phrase, 'social surgery.' The infliction of suffering on a person is only properly described as punishment if that person is guilty." (p. 137)

Thus, according to Quinton, the correct answer for the utilitarian to give to this objection is that the imagined circumstances cannot obtain. The innocent cannot be punished.

There are at least two things wrong with this line of argument. First, there is surely a sense in which even persons known to be innocent can be punished. The objection to utilitarianism is intelligible and understandable. Any analysis of the concept of punishment must be able to explain how this is so. Second, the moral point to the objection cannot be conceptually dissolved. The utilitarian still has to be able to defend the theory against the charge that the theory permits, if it does not require, that an individual can be treated or used in the way the example imagines in order to prevent a greater evil. Part of the force of the example is the wrongness of using the person known to be innocent by punishing him or her in order to prevent a greater evil. This feature of the case, too, must be dealt with and cannot be avoided on conceptual grounds.

10. Although the point seems obvious, it is often ignored—particularly in the writings of psychologists. B. F. Skinner, for example, consistently treats the concepts of punishment, aversive stimuli, the withdrawal of a positive reinforcement,

and the presentation of a negative reinforcement as indistinguishable. *See, e.g.*, Skinner, *Science and Human Behavior* (New York: Macmillan Co., 1953), pp. 182–93. This illuminates nothing and confuses much that it is important to keep clear.

11. One way to think about such moralities is to view them as being unconcerned with questions of culpability and as being concerned only with the presence of a certain kind of wrongness. It is sufficient that the contamination or pollution has occurred, and it is irrelevant what role the person's conduct or intentions played in becoming contaminated.

12. Menninger, "Therapy Not Punishment," reprinted in Murphy (ed.), *Punishment and Rehabilitation* (Belmont, California: Wadsworth Publishing Co., 1973), p. 136.

13. Robinson v. California, 370 U.S. 660 (1962).

14. The Supreme Court has worried about this problem in, for example, the case of chronic alcoholism, in Powell v. Texas, 392 U.S. 514 (1968). The discussion in this and related cases is neither very clear nor very illuminating.

15. Barbara Wootton, *Social Science and Social Pathology* (London: G. Allen & Unwin, 1959), p. 235.

16. *See, e.g.*, Durham v. United States, 214 F. 2d 862 (D.C. Cir., 1954); United States v. Brawner, 471 F. 2d 969 (D.C. Cir., 1972); and Model Penal Code § 4.01.

17. Barbara Wootton, *Crime and the Criminal Law* (London: Stevens, 1963).

18. *Ibid.*, p. 77.

19. *Ibid.*, pp. 79–80 (emphasis added).

20. There are some additional, more practical arguments that might be offered in support of such a proposal.

To begin with, by making irrelevant the question of whether the actor was responsible when he or she acted, the operation of the criminal law could be greatly simplified. More specifically, by "eliminating" the issue of responsibility we thereby necessarily eliminate the requirement that the law continue to attempt to make those terribly difficult judgments of legal responsibility which our system of punishment requires to be made. And, as a practical matter, at least, this is no small consideration. For surely there is no area in which the techniques of legal adjudication have functioned less satisfactorily than in that of determining the actor's legal responsibility as of the time he violated the law. The attempts to formulate and articulate satisfactory and meaningful criteria of responsibility; the struggles to develop and then isolate specialists who can meaningfully and impartially relate these criteria to the relevant medical concepts and evidence; and the difficulties encountered in requiring the traditional legal fact-finding mechanism—the jury—ultimately to resolve these issues—all of these bear impressive witness, it could plausibly be claimed, for the case for ceasing to make the effort.

In addition, it is no doubt fair to say that most people do not like to punish others. They may, indeed, have no objection to the punishment of others; but the actual task of inflicting and overseeing the infliction of an organized set of punishments is distasteful to most. It is all too easy, therefore, and all too typical, for society to entrust the administration of punishments to those who, if they do not actually enjoy it, at least do not find it unpleasant. Just as there is no necessary reason for punishments ever to be needlessly severe, so there is no necessary reason for those who are charged with the duty of punishing to be brutal or unkind. Nonetheless, it is simply a fact that it is difficult, if not impossible, to attract sensitive, kindly or compassionate persons to assume this charge. No such analogous problem, it might be argued, attends the call for treatment.

21. "What might deter the reader from conduct which his neighbors would not like does not necessarily deter the grown-up child of vastly different background. . . . .
"It is not the successful criminal upon whom we inflict our antiquated penal system. It is the unsuccessful criminal, the criminal who really doesn't know how to commit crimes and who gets caught. . . . The clumsy, the desperate, the obscure, the friendless, the defective, the diseased — these men who commit crimes that do not come off — are bad actors, indeed. But they are not the professional criminals, many of whom occupy high places." Menninger, *op. cit., supra* note 12, pp. 134–35.

22. These are discussed persuasively and in detail by Morris in his important article, "Persons and Punishment," 52 *The Monist* 475 (1968), pp. 476–90.

23. I think that Morris at times indulges in an improper comparison of the two. *Ibid.*

24. H. L. A. Hart, *The Concept of Law, op. cit. supra* note 6, p. 181 (emphasis added).

25. Stanley I. Benn, "Punishment," *The Encyclopedia of Philosophy* (New York: Macmillan Co., 1967), vol. 7, pp. 31–32.

26. I discuss aspects of this issue in "Preferential Treatment," *supra,* pp. 72–75, and in "The Obligation to Obey the Law," *supra,* pp. 91–104.

27. H. L. A. Hart, "Legal Responsibility and Excuses," in *Punishment and Responsibility, op. cit., supra* note 4, p. 39.

28. *Ibid.*

29. Morris, *op. cit., supra* note 22.

30. *Ibid.,* p. 477.

31. The former is what I take Hart's main argument from general deterrence to be, *op. cit., supra* note 24, but perhaps he means the latter to apply, too. There is certainly a sense in which the latter argument can plausibly be viewed as consequentialist rather than retributive. Like the one concerning the redemptive features of a punishment system, it is an important one seldom discussed as falling within the usual catalogue of utilitarian justifications.

32. An argument of this sort is presented and developed with appreciable subtlety and power by Fingarette in "Punishment and Suffering," 50 *Proc. Am. Phil. A.* 499 (1977).

33. Hart, *op. cit., supra* note 24, p. 34.

34. Hart, "Punishment and the Elimination of Responsibility," in *Punishment and Responsibility, op, cit., supra* note 4, pp. 171–72.

35. Morris, *op. cit., supra* note 22, p. 478.

36. I have discussed the issue and the arguments in more detail in "The Obligation to Obey the Law," *supra,* pp. 103–104.

37. Some, perhaps many, men may not be so inclined; few, perhaps no, women would be inclined to rape a man (assuming rape were to be defined in a sex-neutral fashion). Furthermore, since what are being discussed are the arguments for the justice of punishment in a decent, or reasonably just, society, it is reasonable to suppose that fewer individuals would be so inclined in that society. This point is discussed in somewhat more detail *infra,* pp. 144–145.

38. Such a theory of human nature can be found, perhaps, in, for instance, Freud, *Civilization and Its Discontents* (New York: J. Cape J. H. Smith, 1930).

39. There is, though, a special problem of the sort alluded to in note 37, *supra.* The relevant theory of human nature must be the theory that would accurately describe human beings as they would still be inclined to behave in the reasonably just society. For that is the kind of society in which arguments for the justice of punish-

ment most plausibly have application and weight. If the society is in fact unjust in serious and systemic respects, then the conditions which are the necessary preconditions of these arguments do not obtain. This issue is more fully and quite convincingly examined by Murphy in "Marxism and Retributivism," 2 Phil. & Pub. Aff. 217 (1973). Thus, what is needed is both a plausible theory of human nature, of the ways persons would be disposed to behave within a reasonably just (or at least not seriously unjust) society, and a plausible description of the basic institutional structure of such a society. The two issues are surely interrelated and a part of any larger, more comprehensive theory of the just society. *See, e.g.*, Rawls, *A Theory of Justice* (Cambridge, Mass.: Harvard U. Press, 1971).

40. *See*, "The Obligation to Obey the Law," *supra*.

Conduct and Responsibility in War

I

A common way to think about normative issues of war is to concentrate upon the question of how persons ought to behave in time of war. For the question of what is permissible and impermissible in war seems both answerable and important in a way in which other moral questions about war are not. Persons who approach war this way are, therefore, inclined to focus their attention upon the laws of war — upon, that is, the rules that deal with matters such as the use of poison gas and the treatment of prisoners of war — and to view the fundamental moral issue as one of the degree to which there has been compliance with the laws of war. Implicit in this way of thinking of things is the idea that if war is fought in accordance with the laws of war then behavior in time of war is, on the whole, morally unproblematic. Concomitantly, if in war persons engage in acts that violate the laws of war, that is morally wrong, and such persons, typically soldiers, are properly held accountable for misbehavior of a most serious sort.

This way of thinking about things was certainly common in the United States during the Vietnam War. Many commentators upon, and even many critics of, the war tended to direct their attention to the question of whether the United States forces were violating any of the laws of war in the way they were fighting. If they were, that was an identifiable wrong and one that needed correction; if they were not, there were no significant *moral* issues to discuss. Similarly, many persons thought it ludicrous to consider whether the military and civilian leaders should be held accountable or thought culpable for any aspect of the Vietnam War, but they had no comparable incredulity when considering the behavior of soldiers in combat.

There is much about this general point of view that is puzzling, unsatisfactory, and even paradoxical. In what follows I consider several of the most troublesome features and consequences of this concentration upon how war should be fought and upon the centrality of the laws of war as the focus of inquiry.

In respect to the substantive laws of war, I first elucidate one common conception of them and then seek to delineate the ways in which this system of rules is seriously flawed, if it is taken to be one that captures important, defensible criteria by which to distinguish the right and wrong ways to engage in war. In respect to the classes of individuals who might be held responsible for behavior in time of war, I examine some of the key features which seem to diminish, if not excuse, the culpability of soldiers for the commission of what are ostensibly violations of the laws of war, and I explore some problems concerning the accountability of military and civilian leaders. In this latter case, I concentrate primarily upon one common argument for the nonculpability of the military and civilian leaders of the United States in respect to Vietnam and try to show why that argument is neither sound nor persuasive.

II

There are two general, quite distinct arguments for this notion of the primacy of the laws of war. One is that the laws of war are important and deserving of genuine respect and rigorous enforcement because they reflect, embody, and give effect to fundamental moral distinctions and considerations. The other is that, considered simply as laws and conventions, they merit this dominant role because general adherence to them has important, desirable effects. The former of these arguments emphasizes the contents of the laws of war and the connection they have with more basic moral considerations. The latter argument emphasizes the beneficial consequences that flow from their presence and acceptance.

The arguments are clearly not mutually exclusive; indeed, they are related to each other in several important respects. Nonetheless, it is useful to distinguish sharply between them for purposes of analysis and to examine the strengths and weaknesses of each in turn.

Before doing so, however, it is necessary to explicate more fully the conception of the laws of war with which I shall be concerned. I believe it to be the case that this account constitutes an accurate description of the existing laws of war and the dominant conception of a war crime.[1] I am not, however, interested in insisting that it is the only possible explication of the nature and character of the laws of war. Indeed, it is part of the burden of my argument that, were there a different conception, the adherence to the laws of war would then be a genuinely more important matter. It is sufficient for my purposes to claim, as I am prepared to, that the conception I discuss is the one that many if not most lawyers, commentators, military tribunals, and courts have had in mind when they have talked about the laws of war and the responsibility of individuals for the commission of war crimes.

The conception I want to describe and assess is that of a system of rules, principles, and the like, which contains the following general features. There are, to begin with, a number of formal agreements, conventions, and treaties among countries that prescribe how countries (chiefly through their armies) are to behave in time of war. And there are, as well, generally accepted "common law" rules and practices which also regulate behavior in warfare. Together they comprise the substantive laws of war. For the most part, the laws of war deal with two sorts of things: how classes of persons are to be treated in war, e.g., prisoners of war, and what sorts of weapons and methods of attack are impermissible, e.g., the use of poison gas. Some of the laws of war—particularly those embodied in formal documents—are narrow in scope and specific in formulation. Thus, Article 4 of the Annex to the Hague Convention on Land Warfare, 1907, provides in part that all the personal belongings of prisoners of war, "except arms, horses, and military papers," remain their property. Others are a good deal more general and vague. For example, Article 23(e) of the same Annex to the Hague Convention prohibits resort to ". . . arms, projectiles, or material calculated to cause unnecessary suffering." Similarly, Article 3 of the Geneva Conventions on the Law of War, 1949, provides in part that "Persons taking no active part in the hostilities . . . shall in all circumstances be treated humanely. . . ." And at Nuremberg, crimes of war were defined as follows:

> . . . violations of the laws or customs of war. Such violations shall include but not be limited to, murder, ill-treatment or deportation to slave-labour or for any other purpose of civilian population of or in occupied territory, murder or ill-treatment of prisoners of war or persons on the seas, killing of hostages, plunder of public property, wanton destruction of cities, towns or villages, or devastation not justified by military necessity.[2]

One very important question that arises in respect to the laws of war is the extent to which the laws of war are to be understood as prohibiting only acts of violence, suffering, and killing that are not connected in either a direct or important way with the waging of war. For if that is all that they are designed to prohibit, then there will inevitably be much remaining conduct that is allowed and yet is, on moral ground, difficult if not impossible to defend.

There is reason to think that this is a plausible way, on the whole, to understand them. As one commentator has put it, the laws of war have as their objective that ". . . the ravages of war should be mitigated as far as possible by prohibiting needless cruelties, and other acts that spread death and destruction and are not reasonably related to the conduct of hostilities."[3]

This is reflected in the language of many of the laws themselves. But it is demonstrated as well by the way even relatively unambiguous and absolute prohibitions are to be interpreted. The former characteristic is illustrated by that part of the Nuremberg definition of crimes of war which prohibits the ". . . *wanton* destruction of cities, towns or villages" (emphasis added), and which thereby appears to allow the destruction of cities, towns, or villages whenever the destruction is not wanton, i.e., whenever the destruction is connected with a defensible military objective. The latter characteristic is illustrated by the following commentary upon Article 23(c) of the Annex to the Hague Convention quoted above. That article prohibits the resort to arms calculated to cause unnecessary suffering. But "unnecessary suffering" means suffering that is not reasonably related to any military advantage to be derived from its infliction. "The legality of hand grenades, flame-throwers, napalm, and incendiary bombs in contemporary warfare is a vivid reminder that suffering caused by weapons with sufficiently large destructive potentialities is not 'unnecessary' in the meaning of this rule."[4]

It is also essential to determine the role and range of application of the doctrine of "military necessity" within this conception. That doctrine is written explicitly into a number of the laws of war as providing a specific exception to their applicability. Thus, for example, in the Nuremberg definition of crimes of war, the otherwise unspecified "devastation" prohibited in the final phrase is that which is ". . . not justified by military necessity."

The doctrine of military necessity appears, moreover, to be more firmly centrally embedded in this conception of the laws of war than illustrations of the preceding type would suggest. The doctrine does not merely create an explicit exception, i.e., as in "devastation not justified by military necessity." Instead, it functions at least to some degree as a general justification for the violation of some, if not

all, of even the specific prohibitions which constitute a portion of the
laws of war. Thus, according to one exposition of the laws of war, the
flat prohibition against the killing of enemy combatants who have
surrendered is to be understood to permit the killing of such persons
where that is required by "military necessity." There may well be
times in any war when it is permissible to kill combatants who have
laid down their arms and tried to surrender.

> Small detachments on special missions, or accidentally cut off
> from their main force, may take prisoners under such circum-
> stances that men cannot be spared to guard them or take them
> to the rear, and that to take them along would greatly endanger
> the success of the mission or the safety of the unit. The prisoners
> will be killed by operation of the principle of military necessity,
> and no military or other court has been called upon, so far as I
> am aware, to declare such killings a war crime.[5]

An assertion such as this is ambiguous. Taylor may not mean
that the laws of war permit an exception in this kind of case. He may
mean only that the laws are uncertain here and that he knows of no
court decision which has yet authoritatively declared behavior of this
sort either a violation of the laws of war or a permissible exception.
Even if the weaker interpretation is adopted, even if what is meant is
that it is an open question whether the doctrine of military necessity
applies here, this is enough to show the potential general applicability of the doctrine within this conception.

Another case in which the doctrine of military necessity made
ostensibly impermissible conduct permissible concerned the London
Naval Treaty of 1930. That treaty required that no ship sink a merchant vessel "without having first placed passengers, crew and ship's
papers in a place of safety." The provisions of this treaty were regularly violated in the Second World War. Nonetheless, these violations were not deemed violations of the laws of war and were not
punished at Nuremberg. This is so, says Taylor, for two reasons.
First, the doctrine of military necessity makes the treaty unworkable.
If submarines are to be effective instrumentalities of war, they cannot surface before they attack merchant ships, nor can they stand
around waiting to pick up survivors. So the answer is not that it is
wrong to use submarines. Rather it is that in the interest of military
necessity the prohibitions of the treaty cease to be prohibitions. And
second, even if considerations of military necessity were not decisive
here, violations of the London treaty would still not have been war
crimes because the treaty was violated by both sides during the Sec-

ond World War. And the applicability of a putative war crime, says Taylor (at least in the absence of a genuine international tribunal), is limited by the extent to which the enforcing party also failed to comply with the relevant law of war.[6]

> . . . [A]s long as enforcement of the laws of war is left to the belligerents themselves, whether during the course of hostilities or by the victors at the conclusion, the scope of their application must be limited by the extent to which they have been observed by the enforcing party. To punish the foe — especially the vanquished foe — for conduct in which the enforcing nation has engaged, would be so grossly inequitable as to discredit the laws of themselves.[7]

Once again there is an ambiguity here. Taylor may mean that it is procedurally unfair to punish the loser but not the victor for the same act. Or he may mean that there is a principle within this conception of the system of the laws of war which legitimizes a previously proscribed practice once the practice becomes a widespread and efficient way to engage in war.

For my purposes, the most significant aspect of the laws of war concerns the question of the permissibility of aerial warfare. Once more I take Telford Taylor's analysis to be illustrative of the conception I am trying to delineate. The bombing of cities was, he observes, not punished at Nuremberg and is not a war crime. This was so for two reasons. Since it was engaged in by the Allies — and on a much more intensive level than by the Germans or the Japanese — it would have been improper to punish the Germans and the Japanese for what we also did. But more importantly, the bombing of cities is generally permissible because bombing is an important instrument of war.[8]

The general test for the impermissibility of bombing is, says Taylor, clear enough. Bombing is a war crime if and only if there is no proportionate relationship between the military objective sought to be achieved by the bombings and the degree of destruction caused by it.

Two potentially relevant considerations are explicitly ruled out: the fact that bombs are the sorts of weapons that cannot discriminate between combatants and noncombatants and the fact that bombing is an inherently inaccurate undertaking. These are not relevant to the question of whether bombing is a war crime because bombs are such important weapons of war.

The foregoing constitutes, then, a brief sketch of the collection of specific prohibitions, accepted conventions, and general excusing and justifying conditions which comprise that conception of the laws of war with which I am concerned. I want now to discuss more fully both the arguments for taking a system such as this seriously and the ways in which this system of substantive rules and principles is flawed in genuinely fundamental ways.

III

As was indicated at the outset, one argument for the importance and value of this conception of the laws of war is that the collection of rules and principles contained therein do reflect, embody, and give effect to the fundamental moral distinctions and considerations that ought to obtain even in time of war. If they do, then they can be understood to impose the sorts of limitations upon behavior that ought to be adhered to and that make it appropriate to assess, condemn, and punish activity which is in violation of them. The question is whether and to what extent they can fairly be viewed as possessing this character. There are, as I have suggested, reasons for thinking they cannot be so viewed. This can be brought out in the following way.

Consider the different grounds upon which one might criticize any particular set of rules, principles, and the like, which constituted the substance of a system of criminal laws.

First, we might criticize such a system on the ground that it was *overinclusive,* that it contained, for instance, particular substantive rules that ought not be present because the proscribed behaviors were not those that it was wrong for persons to engage in. So, a system of criminal law might be criticized because it punished the use of marijuana even though there was nothing otherwise wrong with using marijuana.

Second, we might criticize a system of criminal law because it was *incomplete.* Here the complaint would be that, while it proscribes a number of things that ought to be proscribed and regards them with the appropriate degree of seriousness, it fails to proscribe other things that ought, *ceteris paribus,* to be included within the set of prohibitory rules. So, on this ground a system of criminal law might be criticized because it failed to make criminal the commission of acts of deliberate racial discrimination, or because it failed to make criminal nonconsensual intercourse between a husband and wife.

Third, both of these types of situations can be compared with a system of criminal law that made criminal only various thefts. Such a code would be incomplete in a different way from the code that just omitted to prohibit racial discrimination. It would be systematically incomplete in the sense that it omitted to forbid many of the most wrongful types of behavior, behavior that any minimally defensible criminal code ought to and would prohibit. It would, I think, be appropriate to describe such a code as a morally incoherent one and to regard this incoherence, by itself, as a very serious defect. The code would be incoherent in that it could not be rendered intelligible either in terms of the moral principles that ought to underlie any criminal code or even in terms of the moral principles that justified making theft illegal. One could not, we might say, make moral sense out of a scheme that regarded as most seriously wrong (and hence a fit subject for the criminal law) a variety of harmful acts against property, but which permitted, and treated as legitimate in this sense, all acts of violence against persons. It would be proper to regard such a code as odious, it should be noted, even though one thought that thefts were, on the whole, among the sorts of things that should be prohibited by the criminal law.

It is this last kind of criticism that I believe can be made of the conception of the system of the laws of war set out above. For reasons I shall endeavor to make clear shortly, the system possesses, I think, the kind of incompleteness and incoherence analogous to that which would be present in a system of criminal law that punished only theft.

Someone might, however, think that the laws of war are not in this sense systematically incomplete and incoherent but are instead reasonably complete and coherent for the phenomenon of war. The claim would then be that the difference between, say, the system of the laws of war and a domestic criminal code is that the laws of war just set a lower standard for behavior than that set by the typical criminal code. Even in war, so the argument would go, morality has some place; there are some things that on moral grounds ought not to be permitted even in time of war.[9] Admittedly, the argument might continue, the place to draw the line between what is permissible and impermissible is different, is "lower," in time of war than in time of peace, but the guiding moral principles and criteria remain the same. The laws of war can quite plausibly be seen as coherently reflecting, even if imperfectly, this lower but still intelligible morality of war. Thus, the argument might conclude, the laws of war are not like a criminal code that only punishes theft. Rather, they are like a criminal code that only punishes intentional homicides, rapes, and serious assaults and thefts, and allows many less serious types of wrongful conduct to occur unregulated by the criminal law.

What I want to challenge is the claim that the system of the laws of war as I have sketched it can be plausibly understood as reflecting or embodying in any coherent fashion a lower but still intelligible conception of wrongful and nonwrongful behavior in time of war.

Consider first the less permissive, and hence more attractive, conception of the laws of war, the conception that does not always permit military necessity to be an exception or an excuse. It still cannot be plausibly claimed, I think, that this scheme of what is permissible and impermissible reflects simply a lowering of our basic moral expectations or standards. The primary reason is reflected in the failure to regard as impermissible almost all cases of the resort to aerial warfare and the use of weapons of mass destruction. And this is such a serious defect because it virtually eliminates the distinction between combatants and noncombatants. The distinction is one of central moral importance because it reflects a concern for at least two basic moral considerations that ought to have as much force in war as elsewhere, namely, the degree of choice that persons had in getting into the position in which they now find themselves, and the likelihood that they are or are about to be in a position to inflict harm on anyone else — especially the opponents in war.

To be sure, the distinction between combatants and noncombatants is a relatively crude one. Some noncombatants are able in reasonably direct ways to inflict harm on others, e.g., workers in a munitions factory. And some noncombatants may very well have knowingly and freely put themselves in such a position. Concomitantly, many combatants may have been able to exercise very little choice in respect to the assumption of the role of a combatant, e.g., soldiers who are drafted into an army under circumstances where the penalties for refusing to accept induction are very severe, and difficulties such as these would make it plausible to argue that the laws of war cannot reasonably be expected to capture perfectly these distinctions. For this reason, it would, I think, be plausible to argue that it is unreasonable to expect anyone or any weapon to be able to distinguish the conscripts from the volunteers in the opponent's army. It would, perhaps, even be plausible to argue (although less convincingly, I think) that civilians who are engaged in activities that are directly connected with the prosecution of the war can reasonably be expected to understand that they will be subject to attack. If the laws of war even preserved a distinction between soldiers, munitions workers, and the like on the one hand, and children, the aged, and the infirm on the other, one might maintain that the laws of war did succeed in retaining — at a low level and in an imprecise way — these distinctions of fundamental moral importance. But the laws of war that relate to aerial warfare and the use of weapons of mass destruction do not endeavor to preserve a distinction of even this crudity. What is perhaps ruled out (although by no means certainly so after Dresden and Hiroshima) is the deliberate bombing of wholly civilian populations for the sole purpose of destroying those populations. What is clearly permissible is the knowing destruction of civilian populations — women, children, and the like — provided only that a military objective is sought to be achieved by the bombing mission.

I do not think that a plausible justification can be found for continuing to regard this kind of behavior as permissible. I do not see any rational ground by which to distinguish in a fundamental and convincing way the knowing destruction of noncombatants with bombs dropped from a B-52 from shooting them at close range with a machine gun. If the latter is wrong because it does violence to the distinction between combatants and noncombatants, then the former is too. I find especially unpersuasive two grounds for differentiation which are sometimes advanced.

The first of these is that a bomb is the kind of weapon that cannot discriminate between combatants and noncombatants whereas a machine gun, when properly aimed, can. This is doubtless true; what is hard to understand is the conclusion that weapons that cannot distinguish combatants from noncombatants are therefore permissibly used in circumstances in which it is known that noncombatants of the most clearly identifiable type will be killed. If the distinction between combatants and noncombatants is one of real significance even in time of war and if a concern for the distinction is what is thought to make defensible the existing laws of war, then the view taken of the permissibility of aerial warfare where noncombatant populations are known or believed to be present seems indefensible. A convincing adherence to the moral importance of the distinction would appear to make it more plausible to require that the use of such weapons be prohibited — at least in those cases where the relevant distinctions between combatants and noncombatants can in no reasonable way be made.

Nor is it convincing at this point to appeal to a version of the doctrine of military necessity to justify the permissibility of aerial warfare. In this context, this way of thinking gets reflected in the view that bombs and other weapons of mass destruction are properly not proscribed because these weapons play too central a role in the prosecution of modern warfare. If this is a sufficient reason for regarding the use of these weapons as permissible, then the primary constraints on behavior in time of war are clearly not moral ones but rather ones of military efficiency.

A similar analysis can be made of those laws of war that deal primarily with combatants. Here, though, there is a bit more that can be said on behalf of the defensibility of some of the relevant laws of war. The strongest case is that for the special, relatively unequivocal prohibitions against the mistreatment of prisoners of war and the infliction of damage upon hospitals and medical personnel. Someone might object that these make no sense, that there is no difference between attacking a wounded soldier in a hospital and attacking an unwounded soldier with a weapon against which he is defenseless, e.g., strafing or bombing infantrymen armed with rifles. Similarly, it might be objected that there is no coherent principle that distinguishes the wrongness of killing (generally) prisoners of war and the permissibility of killing enemy soldiers who are asleep.

Such an objection would be too strong, for there does seem to be a morally relevant distinction between these two kinds of cases. It is the distinction between those who have obviously been rendered incapable of fighting back (the wounded and the prisoners of war) and those who only may be incapable of fighting back.

Nonetheless, it would be wrong to make too much of this point. In the first place, for the reasons suggested earlier, distinctions among combatants are morally less significant than the distinction between combatants and noncombatants. And in the second place, the principle justifying this distinction among combatants is a rather crude and not wholly attractive one. In particular, it does not very convincingly, I think, establish the obvious appropriateness of using deadly force against combatants who pose no direct threat and who are defenseless against the force used.[10]

Be that as it may, this is the strongest case for these particular laws of war. There are others for which no comparable rationale can be urged. Thus, it cannot be argued successfully that the laws of war concerning combatants can be generally understood to be a reflection or embodiment of a lower but coherent set of standards relating to how combatants ought to behave toward one another. More specifically, it cannot be maintained, as persons sometimes seek to maintain, that the laws of war relating to which weapons are permissible and which are impermissible possess a similar coherence. Someone might argue, for example, that there are some ways of killing a person that are worse, more inhumane and savage, than other ways. War both permits and requires that combatants kill one another in a variety of circumstances in which, in any other context, it would be impermissible to do so. Nonetheless, so the argument might continue, the laws of war do record and give effect to this perception that some techniques of killing are so abhorrent that they ought not be employed even in war.

Once again, my response is not a direct challenge to the claim that it may be possible to distinguish on some such ground among methods of killing. Indeed, were such a distinction to be preserved by the laws of war, important alterations in the conception of how wars should be fought would almost surely have to take place. What I am concerned to deny is that the laws of war that deal with weapons can be plausibly viewed as reflecting distinctions of genuine moral significance. Since it is permissible to kill an enemy combatant with an antipersonnel bomb, a nuclear weapon, or even a flamethrower, it cannot very plausibly be maintained that it is a war crime to kill a combatant with poison gas because it is morally worse to use poison gas than to invoke the former methods of human destruction.[11]

It must be observed that so far I have been concerned with that morally more attractive view of the laws of war which does not permit a general exception to all of the laws on grounds of military necessity. Once such a general exception is permitted, whatever plausibility and coherence there is to this conception of the laws of war is diminished still further. That this is so can be shown in the following fashion.

To begin with, it is important to notice that the doctrine of "military necessity" is employed in an ambiguous and misleading fashion. "Necessity" leads us naturally to think of various sorts of extreme circumstances which excuse, if they do not justify, otherwise impermissible behavior. Thus, the exception to the rule about taking prisoners is, perhaps a case where necessitarian language does fit: if the prisoners are taken by the patrol deep in enemy territory the captors will themselves almost surely be captured or killed. They cannot, in such circumstances, be held to the rule against killing prisoners because it is "necessary" that the prisoners be killed, if they, the captors, are to avoid being killed.

Now, one may not be convinced that necessitarian language is appropriately invoked even in this case. But what should nonetheless be apparent is the inappropriateness of describing the doctrine that justifies aerial warfare, submarine warfare, or the use of flamethrowers as one of military *necessity*. As has already been suggested, necessity has nothing whatsoever to do with the legitimacy of the aerial bombardment of cities or the use of other weapons of mass destruction. To talk of military necessity in respect to such practices is to surround the practice with an aura of justification that is in no way deserved. The appeal to the doctrine of military necessity is in fact in cases such as these an appeal to a doctrine of military utility. The laws of war really prohibit (with only a few minor exceptions) some wrongful practices that also lack significant military value. The laws of war permit and treat as legitimate almost any practice, provided only that there is an important military advantage to be secured.

The more that *this* doctrine of military necessity permeates the conception of the laws of war, the less intelligible and attractive is the claim that the laws of war are a coherent, complete, or admirable code of behavior — even for the jungle of warfare. Given the pervasiveness of this doctrine of military utility, the laws of war are reducible in large measure to the principle that in war it is still wrong to kill (or maim or torture) another person for no reason at all, or for reasons wholly unrelated to the outcome of the war. But the laws of war also tell us what it is permissible and legitimate to do in time of war. Here the governing principle is that it is legitimate, appropriate, and, in the case of soldiers in combat, sometimes obligatory to do almost anything to anybody, provided only that what is done is reasonably related to an important military objective. It is, in short, to permit almost all possible moral claims to be overridden by considerations of military utility. Whatever else one may wish to claim for the preservation of such a system of the laws of war, one cannot, therefore, claim that they deserve either preservation or respect because of the connection these laws maintain with most of the fundamental demands of morality.

Finally it should be noted, too, that the case is hardly improved by the condition that a practice which is otherwise prohibited ceases to be so if the practice was engaged in by both sides. As I indicated earlier, this may not be the way to interpret the argument for not punishing the Germans for, say, engaging in unrestricted submarine warfare. But if part of the idea of a war crime is, as some of the literature surely suggests it is, that an offense ceases to be an offense once the practice becomes uniform, then this, too, must count against the possibility of making the case for the attractiveness of this conception of the laws of war rest on moral grounds.

There is, however, another way to approach the laws of war and to argue for their worth and significance. This route emphasizes the benefits of having and enforcing the existing laws of war with all of their imperfections and is relatively unconcerned with the "intrinsic" morality of the rules. The arguments in support of this view go something like this.

Despite some real fuzziness about the edges (or even closer to the center) many of the laws of war are reasonably precise. A number of the laws of war are written down and embodied in rather specific conventions and agreements. It is relatively easy, therefore, to tell, at least in a good many cases, what is a war crime and what is not. It is certainly simpler to decide, for example, what constitutes a war crime than it is to determine whether a crime against peace or humanity has been committed. And the fact that the laws of war are more readily ascertainable has certain important consequences of its own.

To begin with, there is the intellectual confidence that comes from dealing with rules that are written down and that are reasonably specific and precise. More to the point, it is this feature which makes it quite fair to hold persons responsible for violations of the laws of war but less so for other behavior in respect to war. The laws of war can be ascertained in advance by the individuals concerned, they can be applied impartially by an appropriate tribunal, and they can be independently "verified" by disinterested observers. They are, in sum, more like typical criminal laws than any of the other rules or principles that relate to war.

A second argument for the primacy of the laws of war also concerns their enforceability. It goes like this.

It is certainly not wholly unrealistic to imagine the laws of war being enforced, even while a war is going on. More importantly it is not wholly unrealistic to imagine the laws of war being enforced by a country against members of its own armed forces, as well as against members of the opposing army. Such has indeed been the case in the United States as well as in other countries. Once again, the contrast with crimes against peace is striking. It is quite unlikely that the perpetrators of crimes against peace, who will be the leaders of the enemy, will ever be caught until the war is over. It is surely unlikely, therefore, that the existence of rules making the waging of aggressive war a crime will ever deter leaders from embarking on aggressive war. If they win, they have nothing to fear. If they lose, they expect to die whether they are guilty or not.

The case is more bleak still where the perpetrators of crimes against peace are the leaders of one's own country. While one can in theory imagine the courts of a country holding the leaders of the country liable for waging aggressive war, this is a theoretical but not a practical possibility. While a war is going on the one thing that national institutions are most unlikely to do is to subject the conduct of the leaders of the nation to cool, critical scrutiny. The leaders of a country are hardly likely to be deterred by the prospect that the courts of their own country will convict them of having committed crimes against peace.[12]

The situation in respect to crimes defined by the laws of war is markedly different in both cases. Soldiers fighting on the opposing side do run a real risk of being caught while the war is on. If they know that they may be captured and if they also know that they may be punished for any war crimes they have committed, this can have a significant effect on the way they behave toward their opponents. Similarly, the knowledge that they may be punished by their own side for misbehavior toward the enemy can influence the way soldiers in the army go about fighting the war. Hence there is a genuine prospect that the members of both armies will behave differently just because there are laws of war than they would have were there no such laws.

What all of this shows is that the laws of war will influence the behavior of persons in time of war. In addition there are additional arguments, connected with those that have just been presented, to show that the behavior will be affected in ways that are both desirable and important.

The first such argument is that, despite all of their imperfections, the laws of war do represent the consensus that does at present exist about how persons ought to behave in time of war. The fact that the laws of war are embodied in conventions and treaties, most of which have been explicitly ratified by almost all the countries of the world, means that we are dealing with conduct about whose character there can be relatively little genuine disagreement. To be sure, the conventions may not go as far or be as precise as we might like. The laws of war may be unambitious in scope and even incoherent in the sense described earlier. Nonetheless, they do constitute those rules and standards about which there is universal agreement concerning what may not be done, even in time of war. And the fact that all nations have consented to these laws and agreed upon them gives them an authority that is almost wholly lacking anywhere else in the area of morality and war.

Closely related to, but distinguishable from, the above is the claim that past experience provides independent evidence of the importance and efficacy of having laws of war. They have worked to save human life. If we look at wars that have been fought, we see that the laws of war have had this effect. Perhaps this was because the participants were deterred by the threat of punishment. Perhaps this was because the laws of war embody standards of behavior that men, even in time of war, thought worth respecting. Perhaps this was because countries recognized a crude kind of self-interest in adhering to the conventions as a means of securing adherence by the other side. It does not matter very much why the laws of war were respected to the degree that they were—and they were respected to some extent even in the total wars of the twentieth century. What matters is that they were respected. Telford Taylor has put the matter this way:

> Violated or ignored as they often are, enough of the rules are observed enough of the time so that mankind is very much better off with them than without them. The rules for the treatment of civilian populations in occupied countries are not as susceptible to technological change as rules regarding the use of weapons in combat. If it were not regarded as wrong to bomb military hospitals, they would be bombed all of the time instead of some of the time.
>
> It is only necessary to consider the rules on taking prisoners in the setting of the Second World War to realize the enormous saving of life for which they have been responsible. Millions of French, British, German and Italian soldiers captured in Western Europe and Africa were treated in general compliance with the Hague and Geneva requirements, and returned home at the end of the war. German and Russian prisoners taken in the eastern front did not fare nearly so well and died in captivity by the millions, but many survived. Today there is surely much to criticize about the handling of prisoners on both sides of the Vietnam war, but at least many of them are alive, and that is because the belligerents are reluctant to flout the laws of war too openly.[13]

The final argument for the preservation of the laws of war concerns the effect of the laws—or their absence—upon the moral sensibilities of individuals. Were we to do away with the laws of war, were we to concede that in time of war anything and everything is permissible, the effect upon the capacity of persons generally to respond in accordance with the dictates of morality would be diminished rather than enhanced. This, too, is one of Telford Taylor's main theses. "All in all," he argues, "this has been a pretty bloody century and people do not seem to shock very easily, as much of the popular reaction to the report of Son My made depressingly plain. The kind of world in which all efforts to mitigate the horrors of war are abandoned would hardly be a world sensitive to the consequences [of total war]."[14]

The consequences for military sensibilities are at least as important, Taylor continues, as are the consequences for civilian sensibilities. The existence of the laws of war and the insistence upon their importance prevent combatants from becoming completely dehumanized and wholly vicious as a result of their participation in war. The laws of war, Taylor asserts, are

> . . . necessary to diminish the corrosive effect of mortal combat on the participants. War does not confer a license to kill for personal reasons — to gratify perverse impulses, or to put out of the way anyone who appears obnoxious, or to whose welfare the soldier is indifferent. War is not a license at all, but an obligation to kill for reasons of state; it does not countenance the infliction of suffering for its own sake or for revenge.
>
> Unless troops are trained and required to draw the distinction between military and nonmilitary killings, and to retain such respect for the value of life that unnecessary death and destruction will continue to repel them, they may lose the sense for that distinction for the rest of their lives. The consequence would be that many returning soldiers would be potential murderers.[15]

There is something to arguments like these, but not as much as is often claimed.

It is, to begin with, far less obvious than the argument would have it that the laws of war possess the kind of specificity we typically require of an ordinary criminal law. In particular, the pervasive character of the doctrine of military "necessity" comes close to leaving as unambiguously criminal only senseless or gratuitous acts of violence against the enemy.

Similarly, the fact that countries have been able to agree upon certain conventions does not seem to be a matter of particular significance. At the very least, it is certainly a mistake to infer from this fact of agreement that we have somehow succeeded in identifying those types of behavior that really matter the most. Indeed it is at least as likely as not that agreement was forthcoming just because the behaviors thereby regulated were not of great moment. And it is surely far more likely than not that agreement was forthcoming just because it was perceived that adherence to these laws would not affect very much the way wars got fought.

Considerations such as these to one side, there are substantial criticisms that can be made against the assertion that only beneficial consequences of various sorts flow from respecting and enforcing the laws of war. Take first the claim that adherence to the laws of war teaches important moral lessons (or prevents soldiers from becoming totally corrupt). Just what sort of things about killing do the laws of war teach soldiers (in theory, let alone in practice); will someone who has mastered the distinctions established by the laws of war thereby be less a potential murderer? It is difficult to see that getting straight about the laws of war will permit someone to learn important moral lessons and to maintain a decent respect for the value of human life. It is difficult to be at all confident that soldiers who have mastered the distinctions established by the laws of war will be for that reason turned away from the path of murder. This is so just because the laws of war possess the kind of incompleteness and incoherence described earlier. We can, of course, teach soldiers to obey the laws of war, whatever their content may happen to be. But we must not confuse that truth with the question of whether we will have, through that exercise, taught them to understand what it is to behave in morally responsible ways.[16]

The issue is made more doubtful, still, because the laws of war inescapably permit as well as prohibit; they make some conduct criminal and other conduct legitimate. The evidence is hardly all in, either from the twentieth century in general or Vietnam in particular. It will probably never be in. But it surely appears to be at least as likely as not that the laws of war — if they have taught anything at all — have taught soldiers and civilians alike that it is permissible and lawful to kill and maim and destroy, provided only that it will help to win the war. And, if so, this constitutes morally retrograde rather than progressive movement.

But this still leaves unanswered what may appear to be the most important argument of all, the argument put forward by Telford Taylor and others that the laws of war are important and deserving of respect because they work. Is it not sufficient that even somewhat irrational, incoherent, and incomplete rules have the consequences of saving lives? Even if it is permissible to kill women and children whenever military necessity requires it, is it not important to save the lives of those women and children whose deaths are not necessitated by military considerations?

The argument is both sound and deceptive. Of course it is better to save some lives rather than none at all. If adhering to the laws of war as we now have them will save the lives of persons (and especially the lives of noncombatants) in time of war, that is a good reason (but not a decisive one) for maintaining these laws of war and a demand for compliance with them.

But to concede this is not to put an end to the matter at hand. For reasons I have tried to indicate, there are costs as well as gains from concentrating our attention upon the laws of war and their enforcement. There is, to put it simply, a risk to human life that is quite substantial. The risk is that we inevitably and necessarily legitimate behavior that is morally indefensible, and that should be viewed as clearly criminal. The cost — and it is a cost in human life — is, for example, that the more sanitized war in Vietnam that would have resulted from a scrupulous adherence to the laws of war would have increased still further our tolerance for and acceptance of the horror, the slaughter, and the brutality that is the essence of twentieth century war.[17] There is something genuinely odious about a code of behavior that says: If there is a conflict between the attainment of an important military objective and one or more of the prohibitions of the laws of war, it is the prohibitions that quite properly are to give way. And there is something dangerous about a point of view that accepts such a system and directs us to concentrate our energies and our respect upon its enforcement. The corrosive effect of living in a world in which we embrace such a code and insist upon its value seems to me appreciably more dangerous than the effect of a refusal to accord a position of primacy to the sometimes bizarre, often morally incoherent, laws of war.

The answer is not, of course, to throw out the laws of war with a view toward inculcating in us all the belief that in war anything goes. But neither is it an acceptable answer to take as given the nature of modern war and modern weapons and to conform the laws of war as best one can to *their* requirements. This, it seems to me, is the fatal flaw in the conception of the laws of war with which I have been concerned. The beginning of a morally defensible position is surely to be found in a different conception of the laws of war, a conception sufficiently ambitious that it refuses to regard as immutable the character of contemporary warfare and weaponry, and that requires instead that war itself be viewed as appropriately conducted, if at all, only in a way that conforms to the minimum demands of morality.

IV

The case that many persons think is the easiest case in which to justify judgments of culpability and decisions of punishment is that of the soldier in combat who violates the laws of war. I think it is a far less easy case than is typically supposed. For one thing, if persons are to be held to answer for their behavior in time of war, it is surely important that they be held to answer under a scheme of substantive law that is not fundamentally unfair. This requires that they should not be held liable for actions that are indistinguishable in the significant, relevant respects from actions that are not proscribed. Thus, if it is correct that the bombing of cities cannot be distinguished in a convincing way from other ways of killing civilians, it is hard to justify the punishment of persons who do the latter while persons who do the former go unpunished (and even sometimes receive medals). For another thing, it is important that there be defensible *mens rea* requirements that a soldier be shown to have satisfied before liability for behavior can properly be thought to attach.[18] The dominant conception of the laws of war makes it very difficult, as I shall try to show, to formulate and apply a defensible set of *mens rea* requirements to the typical combat soldier.

One prominent issue, typically present in any situation of combat, is that of the problem of superior orders. An army is, by definition, a rigidly hierarchical structure in which activities are undertaken as a result of commands and orders proceeding in a uniform direction from the top to the bottom. As a result, the person who finally executes the action that directly constitutes a putative violation of the laws of war is usually the combat soldier who receives, but does not himself give, military orders and commands. The question, therefore, is whether individuals in that place in the hierarchy can claim that they are excused from whatever liability might otherwise exist because what they did was done pursuant to orders from above.

The existing laws of war, to the extent to which they address principles of individual responsibility, illustrate some of the difficulties in resolving this issue. The issue was addressed in a quite confusing way at Nuremberg.[19]

The Charter of the International Military Tribunal was the document prepared in 1945 by France, Great Britain, Russia, and the United States that stated the principles that were to be employed by the Tribunal in the war crimes trials that were to be held. The Charter took what might be characterized as a very hard line in respect to the problem of superior orders.

> The fact that the defendant acted pursuant to order of his government or of a superior shall not free him from responsibility, but may be considered in mitigation of punishment if the Tribunal determined that justice so required.[20]

The Tribunal, when it came to apply the provisions of the Charter to the particular cases before it and to state its reasons for its decisions in its written Judgment, modified (without indicating it was doing so) the position of the Charter by only accepting in part the Charter's rejection of the plea of superior orders as a complete defense or excuse. The Tribunal did this by introducing some sort of a defense of duress—but what sort is not clear. What the Tribunal said was this:

> It was . . . submitted on behalf of most of these defendants that in doing what they did they were acting under the orders of Hitler, and therefore cannot be held responsible for the acts committed by them in carrying out these orders. . . .
>
> The provisions of . . . Article [Eight] are in conformity with the law of all nations. That a soldier was ordered to kill or torture in violation of the international law of war has never been recognized as a defense to such acts of brutality, though, as the Charter here provides, the order may be urged in mitigation of the punishment. The true test, which is found in varying degrees in the criminal law of most nations, is not the existence of the order, but whether moral choice was in fact possible.[21]

It is difficult, I think, to imagine a more obscure way of characterizing the nature of the defense that the Tribunal was prepared to allow, but what is clear is that the Tribunal accepted superior orders as an excuse (provided "moral choice" was not possible) whereas in the Charter they were at best a mitigating circumstance.

A problem exists because the idea of *moral choice* and its absence is not a clear one. One notion which probably underlies the Tribunal's concern and which makes good sense is this. The mere fact that an actor had been ordered to do something does not by itself excuse the actor from responsibility for his actions. This is as it should be because, at a minimum, we must know something about both the stipulated consequences for disobedience and the likely consequences of disobedience before we can decide whether someone who acts in obedience to orders should be excused for his obedience. This is what the talk about the existence of "moral choice" comes to. Suppose, for instance, that there is a general standing order that soldiers are to kill rather than capture all enemy prisoners. At the very least, we would not want to excuse completely a soldier who complied with that order and who shot all his prisoners until we knew a good deal more about such things as the announced penalty for disobeying that order, the probable penalty for disobedience, the typical soldier's reasonable beliefs about the penalty, and this soldier's belief as to what the penalty was. If, for example, the announced, probable, and understood penalty for disobedience was summary execution the case would be a very different one from that where the penalty was demotion in rank. Where the penalty for disobedience is very great, and believed to be such, then one rationale for permitting the defense — for saying moral choice was not possible — is that of excuse; in such circumstances a person will be very strongly inclined, almost inevitably inclined, to act so as to avoid the very severe penalty. In such circumstances, there is at least some pull in the direction of regarding the action in compliance with the order as one that the actor could not help but perform.

A somewhat different rationale would not focus upon the causal difficulty of choosing to disobey in such circumstances so much as upon the poignancy of the dilemma in which the actor finds himself. It is not that he cannot help but seek to avoid the penalty; it is rather that human beings, when caught in such circumstances, ought not be blamed for opting so as to save their lives even at the cost of causing the deaths of others. Persons, on this view, are not to be blamed, even when they act wrongly, for failing to behave heroically, or with a high degree of altruism by bringing consequences of such a severely detrimental character upon themselves.

In either case, the defense of superior orders would be a defense provided the accused could show that the choice involved either had this forced quality to it or was an unduly hard one to require individuals to make in a certain way.

But to say that a soldier in combat is only excused from liability where the consequences of disobedience were perceived by him to be very severe does not, I think, do full justice to the plight of the ordinary combat soldier. For what this account leaves out is the context within which he will surely have been trained and within which he will find himself once in combat. His training will consist very largely in a process designed to inculcate within him habits of obedience to command. And this is, I think, an inevitable part of military training because an army functions successfully only if habitual, unquestioning obedience is as a rule forthcoming on the part of the ordinary soldier. Thus, even if a portion (and it will often be a very small portion) of basic training is devoted to a discussion of the laws of war, even if a soldier is instructed that he ought not obey any order that is manifestly prohibited by the laws of war, the dominant thrust of his training will have consisted of efforts directed toward transforming him into a person who will obey without question and without hesitation. Thus, it may not be sufficient to excuse him when moral choice was not present; he ought, perhaps, to be excused whenever he does what he is told to do because this is what he will have been trained and even conditioned to do.

But, suppose that a soldier's training is not this monolithic in respect to obedience to orders. Suppose instead that a genuine and serious attempt is made to inculcate only habits of limited obedience. Suppose soldiers are earnestly encouraged to believe that while obedience to orders is important it is not all that is important; and suppose in particular, that soldiers are convincingly taught that an order that is clearly or obviously illegal, one that requires the soldier to do what it is clearly wrong to do, ought not to be obeyed. Even if there were such a system of training there is still a powerful argument that obedience to orders ought to be a defense in many cases. The argument turns upon the character of the existing laws of war and, concomitantly, upon the soldier's capacity to assess what is and is not a violation of the laws of war. There are two related characteristics of the system of the laws of war that are of particular significance. In the first place, although war crimes are typically thought to be the most clearly defined of the three sorts of activities in respect to war for which persons may be held responsible, they, themselves, are often extremely vague and imprecise. Thus, to revert once again to Article 23(e) of the Annex to the Hague Convention of 1907, which prohibits the use of weapons calculated to cause unnecessary suffering, it seems to me to place an ordinary soldier in an extremely difficult position to require him to decide when he is using a weapon calculated to cause unnecessary suffering. In a more systematic way, moreover, the doctrine of military necessity (conceived of as even a partial, general justifying condition) makes it virtually impossible for the soldier to determine from his limited perspective whether an ostensible war crime in fact comes under this exemption. It is, in short, often a fiction that the soldier in the field is in any position to ascertain to which situations the laws of war apply and to which they do not.

In the second place, the problem of knowledge is compounded by the fact that the laws of war are not a rational, coherent scheme of rules and principles. Were there an intelligible rationale to the laws of war, recourse to this rationale might assist the soldier in his attempt to determine which of his actions were war crimes and which were not. For the reasons already indicated, it does not appear that such a rationale can be derived from the existing laws. As a result, unless the soldier happens to get ordered to do one of those few, unambiguously proscribed acts, like firing a projectile filled with glass, there is no readily applicable general principle to which he can ap-

peal for guidance. As the laws of war are presently constituted, he
cannot, for instance, appeal in any simple, straightforward way to
the idea that either the intentional or knowing killing of noncombatants is necessarily a prohibited act — as it is not, for instance, when
the army of which he is a part shells or bombs occupied, urban areas.

So far I have discussed primarily the problem of the soldier
who is ordered to do an action that may be a war crime. I have tried
to explain why, in such cases, there are serious problems of duress
and knowledge that ought to be dealt with before criminal liability is
fairly imposed. But still, it might be urged, all of this leaves unaffected cases of the gratuitous commission of war crimes — cases where
there were no direct superior orders and where soldiers on their own
behaved in ways that were clearly proscribed by the laws of war, and
known by them to be such. My Lai, arguably, was one such case; no
one ordered the soldiers involved to line up the unarmed women,
children, and elderly people and machinegun them. The laws of war
do make it plain that such behavior is forbidden. What is to be said
about this kind of case?

I think there is no question but that there is genuine culpability
in such cases. However, the culpability even here is diminished, perhaps, by a variety of factors typically present. At the very least we
can, I believe, understand why the ordinary soldier sometimes regards this sort of behavior as reasonable and appropriate, even
though it is not.

To begin with, all that I have said about the uncertainty and
irrationality of the laws of war applies regardless of whether the soldiers in question did what they did because they were ordered to do it
or for some other reason. What is more, the typical combat situation
is hardly conducive to a reflective consideration of the application of
the laws of war to particular situations.

In addition, contemporary ideas about warfare have certain
consequences of their own. In combat it is certainly more plausible
than it would be in any other context to regard everyone who is not
clearly on your side as your enemy. Because so many things are permissible in war that are not permissible elsewhere, and because even
more things are practiced which would never be practiced elsewhere,
it certainly makes it reasonable to be extremely suspicious of anyone
who is not unquestionably your friend or who is not utterly and completely helpless. If the threat to your life as a foot soldier can so easily
and permissibly come from so many sources against which you are
defenseless (e.g., airplanes), apparent cruelty and wanton barbarism
often turn out to be nothing more than moderately pursued self-

defense. Such is one consequence, one might say, of the logic of contemporary war.

Closely related to what has just been said is the fact that modern war can be extraordinarily corruptive of the capacity to behave morally. If the distinctions between what is obligatory, what is permissible, and what is prohibited appear to rest on no intelligible grounds or persuasive principles, if one is encouraged in war to neglect as morally uninteresting many of those distinctions which in any other context are of utmost moral importance, and if one has no reasonable assurance (as one cannot in time of war) that others will behave with a careful regard for the moral point of view, then it is not surprising if persons lose interest in and concern for even the minimum demands of morality. They are somewhat excusable, even when they do terrible things, because war has, in some important ways, the very strong tendency to make a kind of psychopathic view of matters appear reasonable. Thus, I find quite unconvincing the claim, mentioned earlier, that the laws of war are important and valuable because they ". . . diminish the corrosive effect of mortal combat on the participants."[22] The distinction between military and nonmilitary killings, in which the former are justifiable and the latter not, is neither a clear nor morally very central one. The laws of war do not embody and reflect in a coherent way fundamental moral distinctions or truths. As a result, the distinctions soldiers grasp in conforming their behavior to the laws of war will not by themselves do very much to keep the soldiers moral during war or to return the soldiers to civil society with a well-grounded sense for the requirements of the moral life.

Once again, the dominant conception of the laws of war and its view of how modern war limits the nature and applicability of these laws have a good deal to do with this state of affairs, because it is the laws of war that define what is and is not permissible for soldiers to do in time of war. If there were a different, more rigorous conception of the nature of war crimes, if the laws of war corresponded more convincingly and fully with fundamental moral principles, it would surely be easier and more appropriate than it is at present to expect or require behavior consistent with them on the part of combatants. But that, as I have suggested, would require a substantial reexamination of the context within which the laws of war are formulated. It would require that many of the most familiar and effective ways by which wars are fought today be abandoned because of their unjustifiable effect upon noncombatants. It would require at a minimum that the conception of the very nature of modern warfare be altered drastically in the direction of a more limited kind of combat fought largely if not exclusively between armies.

V

When we turn to the leaders — both civilian and military — we come to those persons to whom many principles of responsibility most obviously and plausibly apply, and to whom culpability most fairly and appropriately appears to attach. For these are the persons who are least subject to formal military discipline, they have substantially more discretion in respect to their own behavior; they are the ones who give orders and formulate battle plans and objectives; they are in a position more accurately to assess the consequences of their action; they are removed from combat and can, therefore, reflect and deliberate. To the degree to which various *mens rea* requirements ought to depend upon the presence of just these conditions, these requirements are satisfied here in a way in which they are seldom satisfied in the case of combat soldiers.

This truth is, of course, reflected in the principles and the practices of Nuremberg. It was the leaders — both civilian and military — whose culpability seemed easiest to establish and most difficult to deny. In terms of what was done at Nuremberg, as well as what was said, it was leaders and not ordinary soldiers who were held primarily responsible for the commission of crimes against peace and crimes against humanity.

I do not, however, mean to suggest that there are no problems with the standards and principles of responsibility that were applied at Nuremberg to the various leaders. To take just one example, the already described vague and elastic properties of the substantive laws of war create some of the same difficulties for leaders that they do for all other persons. And there are, as I shall indicate later, major issues that center upon any particular leader's knowledge of and causal connection with the actual commission of war crimes by others under his supervision, direction, or control. Nonetheless, the problems of culpability in respect to leaders often are too greatly exaggerated. What is more, other issues of a puzzling, more extraneous sort are often introduced. That is certainly one of the things that happened when the question was raised of the culpability of the military and civilian leaders of the United States for the conduct of the war in Vietnam.

I am not referring to the argument that it would have been impractical, nationally divisive, or generally unwise to try to hold the leaders of the United States criminally responsible for their respective roles in the Vietnam War. Nor am I referring to the practical difficulty of getting the formal, legal institutions of a country to take seriously the question of the culpability of high-ranking members of the civilian and military establishment. Instead, I am referring to the rather widely held view that they did not at all satisfy the conditions of either legal or moral culpability. At least, that is the way the topic was sometimes discussed — when it was even taken seriously enough to be discussed at all.

One rather common argument for the view that there were no genuine issues of culpability in respect to the leaders — although it was far more often held implicitly rather than stated explicitly — was that there is a special *mens rea* requirement that must be satisfied before leaders (but not combat soldiers) can properly be thought culpable or held accountable. One version of this argument was presented by Townsend Hoopes in an article entitled, "The Nuremberg Suggestion." It states both the claim I wish to examine and the general sense of incredulity that greeted proposals by opponents of the Vietnam War that the Nuremberg framework applied in a straightforward way to American leaders.

> The tragic story of Vietnam is not, in truth, a tale of malevolent men bent upon conquest for personal gain or imperial glory. It is the story of an entire generation of leaders (and an entire generation of followers) so conditioned by the tensions of the Cold War years that they were unable to perceive in 1965 (and later) that the communist adversary was no longer a monolith, but rather a fragmented ideology and apparat. . . .
> Lyndon Johnson, though disturbingly volatile, was not in his worst moments an evil man in the Hitlerian sense. And his principal advisers were, almost uniformly, those considered when they took office to be among the ablest, the best, the most humane and liberal men that could be found for public trust. No one doubted their honest, high-minded pursuit of the best interests of their country, and indeed of the whole noncommunist world, as they perceived those interests. Moreover, the war they waged was conducted entirely within the framework of the Constitution, with the express or tacit consent of a majority of the Congress and the country until at least the autumn of 1967, and without any press censorship. . . .
> . . . [S]hould we . . . establish a war crimes tribunal . . . and try President Nixon and Dr. Kissinger as "war criminals?" The absurd questions answer themselves.

> . . . [A]bove all [we must avoid] the destructive and childish pleasure of branding as deliberate criminals duly elected and appointed leaders who, whatever their human failings, are struggling in good conscience to uphold the Constitution and to serve the broad national interests according to their lights.[23]

Several features of the argument are puzzling; the one I wish to concentrate upon is the insistence that there was something about the state of mind of the leaders of the United States which made it obvious that their conduct in respect to Vietnam was not culpable.

We might, I think, be tempted to reject the argument out of hand on the ground that it confuses two notions that the criminal law tries very hard to keep straight, namely, motive and intention. That is to say, one way to regard what Hoopes has to say is to see it as depending upon the claim that a person whose motives are good is not properly held legally, and perhaps even morally, culpable for his or her acts. On this view, it is wrong to characterize or regard as criminal the behavior of leaders whose motives in waging war were not evil ones and who sought to pursue the national interest as they understood it. The good motives make all of the difference; Hitler was different: his motives in waging war were malevolent because he sought personal gain and imperial glory. He was evil. Those who were punished at Nuremberg were properly punished there for the doing of those proscribed acts which they did with despicable motives for acting.

Now it is plain, I think, that in any simple form this is not an accurate account of the way in which the criminal law views the relevance of one's motives for acting, nor is it such an obviously attractive view for the criminal law to take of things. We might, for example, think that a person who robs a poor widow of her life savings in order to have a wild week in Monaco is worse than a person who robs the same widow in order to give the money to the cancer fund. We might even think it appropriate that the punishment of the two persons should be different. But we would reject, I take it, the claim that a person ought not be held liable at all merely because his motive in robbing the widow was, in the abstract, a commendable one. And the same is true in more overtly political contexts. A black militant who selflessly risked her life in order to help other black militants escape from prison would be deemed fully culpable by the criminal law even if she sincerely believed (even reasonably so) that they had been unjustly convicted and confined there. What would be said in the law is that we are not interested primarily in the motive or in the purpose in acting. What we want to know is whether the actor intended to do the act in question; whether he intended to take another's money by force, whether she intended to aid in an escape from jail. If so, then the crimes were committed. Similarly, for Nuremberg to be applicable, it would be sufficient within this set of culpability requirements for the leaders to have intended (in this sense) to have done those actions that are in fact prohibited by Article Six of the Charter; it would not be of central importance to inquire into their motives for acting.

But this is not, perhaps, to put an end to the matter. Someone might reply that the distinction between intention and motive is not always a clear one. Nor, someone might add, is it obvious that motive ought to be as irrelevant to issues of serious culpability as the criminal law appears at times to make it. Moreover, it might still be claimed, there does seem to be something to be said for the original argument that the American leaders were different from the leaders of the Nazi regime in ways that are of moral, if not legal, significance.

Thus, there is, I think, a somewhat more sophisticated defense that might be made of Hoopes's position, although it, too, ultimately does not succeed. To begin with, it might be argued that at least some of the crimes established at Nuremberg did mean to include motive (in the sense I have been using it) as a part of the definition of the offense. Thus, it could be maintained that the waging of aggressive war means not simply the initiation of war (whatever the motive or purpose) but rather the initiation of war provided there is a certain objective or end in view, namely, to achieve personal gain or the imperial accession of territory. Even more to the point, given the way the laws of war encompass the notion of military necessity, the separation of motive and intention seems less easy than appeared at first; perhaps the idea of military necessity implies something about the view of things taken by the actor. Up to a point, suggestions such as these seem to me plausible and I want to consider them further. However, it is also important to observe that there is nothing about the Nuremberg principles and the judgment of the Tribunal that supports in an unqualified way an interpretation of this sort. While it may be true that the German motives for doing some of the things that were done were especially despicable, it is certainly a mistake to identify the Nuremberg rationale for culpability with a condemnation of wrongful behavior only if it was accompanied by motives such as theirs.

Still, as I have said, there may be something to this point of view. Perhaps the truth to be extracted is that culpability is and ought to be limited to those actions that the actor knows to be wrong.

This is not quite the same as insisting upon the presence of a malevolent motive. Rather it is to emphasize that serious liability ought not
attach unless the actor had a certain conception of what he was doing
—unless he knew or should have known that what he was doing was
wrong.[24] And this is a principle that we do—at least to some degree—
embrace in the operation of our own municipal legal system.

However, it is ambiguous to put it this way, too. The principle
that the actor must know that what he is doing is wrong can be the
principle that the actor must know that what he is doing is legally
wrong—that it is forbidden by the legal system. Or, it can be the very
different principle that the actor must know that what he is doing is
morally wrong—that he is doing what one who is concerned to be
moral ought surely not do.

In our own legal system it is certainly sufficient, although not
necessary, if the actor knows, or ought to know,[25] that what he or she
is doing is legally wrong. It is regarded as wholly appropriate to impose criminal liability upon an actor who intended to do an action
that he knew to be proscribed by the law, and in such a case the actor
is not absolved of liability by his belief that it was morally right, or
not morally wrong, to do the action.[26]

It is also surely the case that the conception with which the Nuremberg Tribunal worked was one in which intending to do an illegal act was sufficient to justify liability, irrespective of the knowledge
on the actor's part that the action was illegal. For the Tribunal was
concerned to establish that the actions of the accused were violations
of international law and in some cases known to be such by them.
The Tribunal took appreciable pains to demonstrate the preexisting
illegality of the acts denominated as crimes against peace and crimes
of war. It did so, arguably, because it deemed it wholly sufficient to
justify the imposition of criminal liability that these acts were in fact
illegal. To be sure, the Tribunal may also have been concerned to establish that the defendants either knew or should have known of the
illegality of their acts. It may even have been confident that the defendants were fully aware of the gross immorality of their conduct.
But none of this was made an essential condition for liability. The
point is that the Tribunal was quite unconcerned to establish the way
things might have looked from within the defendant's point of view.
It did not see as central the views of the accused about either the illegality or immorality of their actions.

It is possible to fall back to still another position: that in respect
to the kinds of crimes dealt with at Nuremberg, persons ought only
to be held accountable if they knew or ought to have known that they

were violating the relevant laws and had bad motives for doing so. At this stage it is not clear how one ought to reply. This is not the requirement that was applied at Nuremberg. It is, indeed, quite possible that some of the leaders convicted at Nuremberg did not have bad motives at all, for example, Speer. Perhaps the claim is that if this is so, such persons ought not to have been punished. This would certainly not be a question that could easily or briefly be answered. What is plain is that the case for such a new, more stringent *mens rea* requirement has yet to be made out. Until it is, it is hard to see why the motives of United States leaders ought to have been taken to be a decisively relevant aspect of the question of their culpability for war crimes in Vietnam.

If we reject the idea that bad motives are an essential requirement for responsibility, we are left with the question of what is the appropriate test for the responsibility of leaders. Anyone thinking about this topic is led sooner or later to the Yamashita case.[27] For it does deal with the two significant factors of knowledge and causality.

General Yamashita was the Commanding General of the Japanese Army in the Philippine Islands during the latter part of the Second World War. He was brought to trial before a United States military commission in 1945 on the charge that, while commander, he violated the laws of war by failing to discharge his duty to control the soldiers under his command, thereby permitting them to commit acts in violation of the laws of war against both civilians and prisoners of war. He was convicted by the commission and sentenced to death. The case found its way to the United States Supreme Court for final review. One central issue was that of for what acts and omissions General Yamashita had in fact been found culpable.

A majority of the Court, speaking through Chief Justice Stone, upheld the conviction and sentence on the theory that the standard applied to General Yamashita was an appropriate one and one specified by the laws of war. That standard made a commander culpable for failing to take measures within his control to prevent violations of the laws of war by his subordinates. The majority declined to reexamine the factual determination made by the commission that there had been measures within his control that General Yamashita had failed to take.

Justices Murphy and Rutledge dissented and joined in each other's opinions. The opinion of Justice Murphy focused upon the degree to which there was insufficient evidence in the record to establish that there was anything General Yamashita could have done that he failed to do to prevent his troops from committing the atrocities they committed. In his view, General Yamashita was held to a standard of virtual strict liability under which he was held liable for having been the commander of troops who engaged in widespread violations of the laws of war. As Justice Murphy saw it, there was no charge or proof that General Yamashita had committed, ordered, or condoned any violations of the laws of war by his troops. Nor was there any evidence that he was negligent in failing to do more than he did, or that he could have done anything more. The commission, he argued, founded its conviction wholly upon the assumption that the violations must have resulted from General Yamashita's inefficiency, and hence negligence, as a commander.

As the discussions of the Yamashita case engendered by the Vietnam War brought out, there are two rather different ways in which the case can be thought relevant. One approach is to concentrate upon the situation in which General Yamashita found himself, to focus upon the apparent harshness of holding him responsible for the behavior of his troops in the circumstances of that case. The other approach is to emphasize the criteria for culpability elaborated in the majority opinion without worrying about whether those criteria were in fact fairly applied to General Yamashita.

There is something to be said for the former, quite draconian approach, but not, I think, a great deal. If it is the case that General Yamashita was unaware of the brutalities committed by his troops, was not even responsible for having encouraged them to behave as they did, and was in no position to have prevented them from so behaving, then it is tempting, surely, to conclude that he was unjustly held criminally liable for their conduct. As a result, we might also be led to conclude that it would have been equally unjust to hold American leaders responsible if they were in a similar position in respect to the commission of war crimes in Vietnam.

However, it is not quite as easy as that. For we can surely find intelligible the claim that it would have been inappropriate in the context of Vietnam to engage in a scrupulous reexamination of the fairness of the treatment by the United States of the German and Japanese leaders after the Second World War. The point is not that precedents ought or must be mindlessly applied without regard to the fairness of the rule. Rather, the point is that, having ourselves applied rules and principles to others in a certain way, the institutions of the United States were then in a poor position to determine that those same rules and principles were really unfair and therefore not to be applied to United States leaders.

One can, I think, acknowledge the force of this argument without being wholly convinced by it. If General Yamashita was treated as badly as he appears to have been, that might have been a good reason for trying to make certain that no one else ever was treated in a similar fashion in the future — even those from the country responsible for his mistreatment.

But to reject this application of the Yamashita case is not to dismiss the problem with which the case dealt. For there is still the question of the appropriate test for the culpability of leaders for war crimes committed by forces in the field.

It is reasonably clear that under any plausible theory it would have been appropriate to hold the military and civilian leaders of the United States responsible for those acts which they ordered United States and South Vietnamese troops to perform and which they knew to be violations of the laws of war. Thus, the live issues concern, rather, their culpability in less clear cases. The chief issues were and are these: (1) Is it sufficient if the leaders simply adopted or knowingly permitted the adoption of policies and objectives the realization of which were likely to lead to the commission of war crimes? Under this test, if an emphasis upon "body counts" led to the killing rather than the capture of enemy soldiers who wished to surrender, then the leaders who knowingly encouraged or permitted this emphasis would have been properly held liable for the ensuing war crimes. (2) Is it necessary, as an addition to (1), that the leaders should have known that such a policy was likely to have such consequences? That is to say, is it necessary to ask whether the leaders should have known that an emphasis upon body counts would have this effect? Or, (3) is the test more stringent, still? Must there have been an inquiry into the actual state of mind of the leaders to see whether they in fact knew that such a policy was likely to have such consequences?

Similar questions can be asked about policies or programs, the implementation of which may in fact have constituted the commission of war crimes. Thus, if the use of antipersonnel bombs is a war crime, is it sufficient that the leaders directed or knew of the use of this weapon? Or is it necessary to establish that they ought to have known that the use of such a weapon was a war crime? Or is it necessary to establish that they in fact knew that the use of such a weapon was a war crime?

As I have indicated, actual knowledge in either of these kinds of cases has not usually been required, and was certainly not required in respect to the leaders prosecuted after the Second World War. On the other hand, strict liability is hardly a more attractive notion for war crimes than it is in our own legal system. The appropriate test in this regard appears, therefore, to be what the leaders ought to have known or foreseen about the policies and programs under their authorship, direction, or control. It is upon this question, and not the question of their motives, that attention ought to have focused far more intensely than it was during and after the Vietnam War.

But what remains troublesome, after all of this, is the idea that the crucial matter was whether the laws of war were violated. For they were taken to be the substantive principles which alone established what were the permissible and impermissible things to do in fighting that war. And, for reasons I have already tried to make clear, this seems a mistaken and dangerous way to have approached matters. Here, even more than in the context of domestic law, the danger was great that the illegal would be confused with the impermissible and the legal with the permissible. The requisite culpability states for leaders and for soldiers in the field can be determined by appeal to conventional, but still rather convincing, arguments. The fundamental problem is that the laws of war do not provide a coherent or defensible context within which to locate these further questions concerning the appropriate *mens rea* requirements for different classes of individuals when engaged in the conduct of war.

NOTES

1. For my purposes I treat all violations of the laws of war as war crimes and do not, therefore, make distinctions between violations of the laws of war and a broader notion of a war crime that in other contexts would be necessary. That broader notion would include all behavior *in respect to* war which might be regarded as criminal, *e.g.*, initiating a war in a situation in which that would be thought to be a crime against peace. *See,* for example, "The Question of War Crimes: A Statement of Perspective," in Richard Falk, Gabriel Kolko, and Robert J. Lifton (eds.), *Crimes of War* (New York: Random House, 1971), p. 33.

2. The Charter of the International Military Tribunal, Article Six (b).

3. Telford Taylor, *Nuremberg and Vietnam: An American Tragedy* (New York: Quadrangle, 1970), p. 20.

4. Georg Schwarzenberger, *The Legality of Nuclear Weapons* (London: Stevens & Sons, 1958), p. 44.

5. Taylor, *op. cit., supra* note 3, p. 36. A plausible objection to my assertion that I am accurately characterizing the existing laws of war would call attention to the following quotation from the U.S. Army field manual *The Law of Land Warfare,* chapter I, section I, 3:

"The law of war places limits on the exercise of a belligerent's power in the interests mentioned in paragraph 2 and requires that belligerents refrain from employing any kind or degree of violence which is not actually necessary for military purposes and that they conduct hostilities with regard for the principles of humanity and chivalry.

"The prohibitory effect of the law of war is not minimized by 'military necessity' which has been defined as that principle which justifies those measures not forbidden by international law which are indispensable for securing the complete submission of the enemy as soon as possible. Military necessity has generally been rejected as a defense for acts forbidden by the customary and conventional laws of war inasmuch as the latter have been developed and framed with consideration for the concept of military necessity."

I do not know exactly what this means. It seems to anticipate, on the one hand, that the laws of war and the doctrine of military necessity can conflict. It seems to suppose, on the other hand, that substantial conflicts will not arise either because the laws of war prohibit militarily unnecessary violence or because they were formulated with considerations of military necessity in mind. I do not think that the view expressed in the quotation is inconsistent with the conception I am delineating. But if it is, then some of my objections do apply with less directness to one actual system that gives the doctrine of military necessity a more restrictive role. I discuss systems of both sorts in what follows.

6. Taylor, *op. cit., supra* note 3, p. 39.

7. *Ibid.*

8. *Ibid.*, pp. 38, 39.

9. I have discussed and criticized the view that, when war is involved, morality has no place in "Three Arguments Concerning the Morality of War," 65 *J. Phil.* 578 (1968) and in "On the Morality of War: A Preliminary Inquiry" 21 *Stanford L. Rev.* 1627 (1969).

10. It is, for example, legitimate to bomb the barracks of soldiers who are not at the front lines, to ambush unsuspecting (and even unarmed) enemy soldiers, and to use all sorts of weapons against which the particular combatants may be helpless. At some stage, therefore, it just ceases to be very satisfactory to insist that this is unobjectionable because the combatants could defend themselves if they chose and because they chose to be combatants in the first place. Both claims about the combatants may be false and even known to be such.

11. Thomas Nagel attempts to provide a rationale for many of the laws of war, as well as to articulate a general, defensible view of permissible and impermissible behavior in time of war, in terms of the single principle: "that hostility or aggression should be directed at its true object. This means both that it should be directed at the person or persons who promote it and that it should aim more specifically at what is provocative about them." Nagel, "War and Massacre," 1 *Phil. & Pub. Aff.* 123, 135 (1972). I think the first part of the principle a good deal more central and defensible than the second. It corresponds to the centrality I attach to the distinction between combatants and noncombatants.

As Nagel concedes, even given this meaning, the principle does not account very well for much of what is and is not included within the laws of war.

12. This was surely the way most persons in positions of power and authority in the United States thought about the claims that the leaders of the United States should be held accountable under the Nuremberg Principles. I have discussed this

issue in more detail in "The Relevance of Nuremberg," 1 *Phil. & Pub. Aff.* 22 (1971), and I discuss one aspect of this general issue below in Part V, *infra.*

13. Taylor, *op. cit., supra* note 3, p. 40.

14. *Ibid.,* p. 39.

15. *Ibid.,* pp. 40-41.

16. This is so, for reasons discussed more fully in "The Obligation to Obey the Law," *supra.*

17. I have discussed different conceptions of the nature of war and the way issues of morality in respect to war may be affected by the conception employed in "On the Morality of War: A Preliminary Inquiry," *op. cit., supra* note 9.

18. This is a particular instance of the more general point that blameworthiness or culpability be linked not just with a wrongful act or wrongdoing, but with relevant mental states going to the actor's intentions, knowledge, purposes, and the like.

19. Although I tend to draw upon the proceedings at Nuremberg per se, I mean in some of my references to Nuremberg to include all of the war crimes trials that took place after the Second World War.

20. The Charter of the International Military Tribunal, Article Eight.

21. Judgment of the International Military Tribunal, Trial of the Major War Criminals I, pp. 223-24.

22. Taylor, *op. cit., supra* note 3, p. 40.

23. Hoopes, "The Nuremberg Suggestion," in Falk, Kolko, and Lifton, *op. cit., supra* note 1, pp. 235-37.

24. Aspects of this issue are discussed in "Punishment," *supra,* pp. 119-120.

25. There are clearly differences between the requirement that the actor *know* and the requirement that the actor *ought to know*. For the present I wish to ignore the differences, but I return to them at the very end.

26. It might, of course, have been the right thing to do, even if it was against the law. This is the question discussed in "The Obligation to Obey the Law," *supra.*

27. In re Yamashita, 327 U.S. 1 (1945).